THE MEN OF THE BIBLE

the Smart Guide to the Bible™ series

BE SMART · BE INSPIRED ™

Larry Miller

Larry Richards, General Editor

THOMAS NELSON
Since 1798

NASHVILLE DALLAS MEXICO CITY RIO DE JANEIRO BEIJING

Men of the Bible
The Smart Guide to the Bible™ series
© 2007 by GRQ, Inc.

Published in Nashville, Tennessee, by Thomas Nelson. Thomas Nelson is a trademark of Thomas Nelson, Inc.

Originally published by Starburst Publishers under the title *Men of the Bible: God's Word for the Biblically-Inept*. Now revised and updated.

Thomas Nelson, Inc. titles may be purchased in bulk for educational, business, fundraising, or sales promotional use. For information, please e-mail SpecialMarkets@ThomasNelson.com.

Scripture quotations are taken from the New King James Version® (NKJV), copyright 1982 by Thomas Nelson, Inc. Used by permission. All rights reserved.

General Editor: Larry Richards
Managing Editor: Lila Empson
Associate Editor: W. Mark Whitlock
Scripture Editor: Deborah Wiseman
Assistant Editor: Amy Clark
Design: Diane Whisner

ISBN 10: 1-4185-1000-9
ISBN 13: 978-1-4185-1000-8

Printed in the United States of America
07 08 09 10 RRD 9 8 7 6 5 4 3 2 1

Introduction

Welcome to *Men of the Bible—The Smart Guide to the Bible*™. This book is part of a series designed to bring God's encouraging and loving message to you in an easy-to-understand and relevant style. You are about to discover a new commentary that will change your outlook on the Bible forever.

To Gain Your Confidence

You will also gain confidence, as you skip the complicated stuff and zero in on the truth of God's Word. If you want clear information, *Men of the Bible—The Smart Guide to the Bible*™ is for you!

What Is the Bible?

The Bible is like no other book. Written over a span of fifteen hundred years, it is a collection of sixty-six books written by at least forty different authors but with one message to tell: God loves you and wants the best for you!

The Bible is divided into two main sections: an "Old" Testament and a "New" Testament. The Old Testament was written between 1400 BC ("Before Christ") and 400 BC. The New Testament was written in about sixty years, between AD (*Anno Domini*, which is Latin for "in the year of our Lord") 40 and AD 100. The Old Testament deals with the *old* covenant that God had with his chosen people (the Hebrews) before the birth of Jesus Christ, while the New Testament is about the *new* covenant—Jesus's birth, life, resurrection, and the spread of the early church by Jesus's followers.

Centuries later, experts divided the books of the Bible into chapters and verses. Thus, Genesis 12:3 refers to the twelfth chapter and the third verse in the book of Genesis. If you know the name of the book and its chapter and verse number, you can locate specific Bible verses, stories, and teachings.

Who Wrote the Bible?

At least forty different people wrote the Bible, but all of them believed they were writing the word of God. Some were educated; some were not. Some were mighty kings, and others were lowly shepherds. Moses, for example, was a prisoner and a slave before free-ing the Hebrews with God's help. He is credited with writing the first five books of the Old Testament: Genesis, Exodus, Leviticus, Numbers, and Deuteronomy. King David, on the other hand, was Israel's greatest king and wrote many worship songs and poems in the book of Psalms. Four of Jesus's disciples, all from different backgrounds, wrote what are known as the Gospels, which are titled by the names of those disciples: Matthew, Mark, Luke, and John.

The disciple John also wrote the book of Revelation under the guidance of its true author—the Holy Spirit, the third person of the Trinity. The word *trinity* is not found in the Bible, but we use the term to describe the three ways God reveals himself: God the Father; God the Son, Jesus Christ; and God the Holy Spirit. Think of the Trinity as three different expressions of God just as you express yourself in three different ways, actions, spoken words, and written words.

The Languages of the Bible

The first books of the Bible and most of the Old Testament were written in Hebrew. Parts of the books of Daniel and Ezra, however, were written in Aramaic, a related lan-guage spoken by most Near Eastern peoples from about 600 BC onward. The people of Jesus's day also spoke Aramaic in everyday situations but studied the Bible in their ancient tongue, Hebrew. About a hundred years before Christ, the Old Testament was translated into Greek, because most people throughout the Roman Empire spoke Greek.

The New Testament was written in the Greek spoken by ordinary people. This meant that the New Testament was easy for all people throughout the Roman Empire to under-stand so the message of Jesus spread quickly.

Because the Old and New Testament books were recognized as holy, first by Jews and then by Christians, they were copied accurately and carefully preserved.

Why Study the Bible?

Because . . . for over two thousand years, millions of people have improved their lives by following its wisdom. The Bible tells us repeatedly that when we study the Bible we will receive valuable blessings.

Because . . . many people believe that God communicates with us through the Bible. Within its pages God tells us he wants us to know him and to follow his guidelines for how to live. Romans 15:4 tells us, "Whatever things were written before were written for our learning, that we through the patience and comfort of the Scriptures might have hope" (NKJV).

Because . . . all of us want to respond to life's challenges in a godly way. Even though the Bible was written many years ago in a totally different place and culture than ours, the Bible offers answers to the troublesome situations and the difficult questions we all face today.

Why Learn About Men of the Bible?

The men of the Bible can show us how to live, what choices to make, and why. These men faced failure and success just as we experience them. No matter where we are in our lives, we can gain courage and wisdom from these men. They struggled through difficulties, yet most endured and built their faith. Moses led the Israelites from Egypt but struggled with fear and uncertainty. David led a kingdom but succumbed to temptation; he is remembered as "a man after [God's] own heart" (Acts 13:22 NKJV). We can learn to lead our families and lives with purpose and confidence by examining these examples in the Bible.

God had a purpose for each man in the Bible, from Caleb's faithful and courageous walk to Saul's utter collapse. God also has a purpose for each one of us. By studying the lives of the men of the Bible, we can know God, bring him into every area of our lives, and build our faith and character.

Many men failed and then rallied to success. Some men compromised and demonstrated their faithlessness. When we examine each life, principles for success are showcased and the consequences of disobedience are painfully driven home. (For a time line of the men of the Bible covered in this book, see Appendix A.)

How to Use *Men of the Bible—The Smart Guide to the Bible*™

As you read this book, keep in mind its main sections:

- Part One, "Men of the Old Testament" (chapters 1–12), discusses major men of the Old Testament—Adam, Abraham, Isaac, Jacob, Joseph, Moses, and David—as well as some others whose stories you will find enlightening.
- Part Two, "Men of the New Testament" (chapters 13–16), presents the stories of Jesus and of Paul, Peter, and other men who were influenced by Jesus.

Dates

Unlike any other book, the Bible was written over a span of fifteen hundred years! Because of this long period of time, biblical experts sometimes differ in the dates they give for various events. Thanks to archaeologists and their discoveries, however, the accuracy of these dates has improved. We can now accurately date many of the events in the Bible. See Appendix A for time lines that show when in history the men of the Bible lived.

A Word About Words

As you read *Men of the Bible—The Smart Guide to the Bible*™, you'll notice some interchangeable words: *Scripture, Scriptures, Word, Word of God, God's Word,* etc. All these terms mean the same thing and come under the broad heading of "the Bible."

In most cases the phrase "the Scriptures" in the New Testament refers to the Old Testament. Peter indicated that the early writings of the apostle Paul were quickly accepted in the early church as equal to "the rest of the Scriptures" (2 Peter 3:16 NKJV). Both Testaments consistently demonstrate the belief that is expressed in 2 Timothy 3:16: "All Scripture is given by inspiration of God" (NKJV).

One Final Tip

God gave us these stories of the men of the Bible so we could learn from them. With God's help, you can use what you learn from this book to improve and bless your life. Open your heart. Ask God to speak his Word to you.

About the Author

Larry Miller is a husband, father, author, speaker, and retired police lieutenant for the Huntington Beach Police Department in California. Larry was a policeman for thirty-one years and currently speaks to men's groups and writes books. His wife, Kathy Collard Miller, is an author and popular women's conference speaker. Together they speak at couples' events.

Larry has authored several books, including *God's Vitamin "C" for the Spirit,* and he and Kathy collaborated to write *What's in the Bible for Couples.*

Larry has spoken in several states and three foreign countries. When he's not writing at his desk or speaking before a group, you'll find him on the golf course.

About the General Editor

Dr. Larry Richards is a native of Michigan who now lives in Raleigh, North Carolina. He was converted while in the Navy in the 1950s. Larry has taught and written Sunday school curriculum for every age group, from nursery through adult. He has published more than two hundred books, and his books have been translated into some twenty-six languages. His wife, Sue, is also an author. They both enjoy teaching Bible studies as well as fishing and playing golf.

Understanding the Bible Is Easy with These Tools

To understand God's Word you need easy-to-use study tools right where you need them—at your fingertips. The Smart Guide to the Bible™ series puts valuable resources adjacent to the text to save you both time and effort.

Every page features handy sidebars filled with icons and helpful information: cross references for additional insights, definitions of key words and concepts, brief commentaries from experts on the topic, points to ponder, evidence of God at work, the big picture of how passages fit into the context of the entire Bible, practical tips for applying biblical truths to every area of your life, and plenty of maps, charts, and illustrations. A wrap-up of each passage, combined with study questions, concludes each chapter.

These helpful tools show you what to watch for. Look them over to become familiar with them, and then turn to Chapter 1 with complete confidence: You are about to increase your knowledge of God's Word!

Study Helps

The thought-bubble icon alerts you to commentary you might find particularly thought-provoking, challenging, or encouraging. You'll want to take a moment to reflect on it and consider the implications for your life.

Don't miss this point! The exclamation-point icon draws your attention to a key point in the text and emphasizes important biblical truths and facts.

death on the cross
Colossians 1:21–22

Many see Boaz as a type of Jesus Christ. To win back what we human beings lost through sin and spiritual death, Jesus had to become human (i.e., he had to become a true kinsman), and he had to be willing to pay the penalty for our sins. With his <u>death on the cross</u>, Jesus paid the penalty and won freedom and eternal life for us.

The additional Bible verses add scriptural support for the passage you just read and help you better understand the <u>underlined text</u>. (Think of it as an instant reference resource!)

How does what you just read apply to your life? The heart icon indicates that you're about to find out! These practical tips speak to your mind, heart, body, and soul, and offer clear guidelines for living a righteous and joy-filled life, establishing priorities, maintaining healthy relationships, persevering through challenges, and more.

This icon reveals how God is truly all-knowing and all-powerful. The hourglass icon points to a specific example of the prediction of an event or the fulfillment of a prediction. See how some of what God has said would come to pass already has!

What are some of the great things God has done? The traffic-sign icon shows you how God has used miracles, special acts, promises, and covenants throughout history to draw people to him.

Does the story or event you just read about appear elsewhere in the Gospels? The cross icon points you to those instances where the same story appears in other Gospel locations—further proof of the accuracy and truth of Jesus' life, death, and resurrection.

Since God created marriage, there's no better person to turn to for advice. The double-ring icon points out biblical insights and tips for strengthening your marriage.

The Bible is filled with wisdom about raising a godly family and enjoying your spiritual family in Christ. The family icon gives you ideas for building up your home and helping your family grow close and strong.

something significant had occurred, he wrote down the substance of what he saw. This is the practice John followed when he recorded Revelation on the **Isle of Patmos.**

What does that word really mean, especially as it relates to this passage? Important, misunderstood, or infrequently used words are set in **bold type** in your text so you can immediately glance at the margin for definitions. This valuable feature lets you better understand the meaning of the entire passage without having to stop to check other references.

the big picture

Joshua
Led by Joshua, the Israelites crossed the Jordan River and invaded Canaan (see Illustration #8). In a series of military campaigns the Israelites defeated several coalition armies raised by the inhabitants of Canaan. With organized resistance put down, Joshua divided the land among the twelve Israelite

How does what you read fit in with the greater biblical story? The highlighted big picture summarizes the passage under discussion.

what others say

David Breese
Nothing is clearer in the Word of God than the fact that God wants us to understand himself and his working in the lives of men.[5]

It can be helpful to know what others say on the topic, and the highlighted quotation introduces another voice in the discussion. This resource enables you to read other opinions and perspectives.

Maps, charts, and illustrations pictorially represent ancient artifacts and show where and how stories and events took place. They enable you to better understand important empires, learn your way around villages and temples, see where major battles occurred, and follow the journeys of God's people. You'll find these graphics let you do more than study God's Word—they let you *experience* it.

Chapters at a Glance

Part Two: Men of the New Testament

Part One:
Men of the Old Testament

Chapter 1: Adam–Man of Dust and Destiny

Chapter Highlights:
- Creation of Man
- Creation of Woman
- The Fall
- Blaming Others
- Consequences of the Fall

Let's Get Started

Imagine waking up and being the only person alive. Of course, for Adam, it didn't seem strange at all because he didn't know anything different. For us, the idea of being utterly alone on the planet is incomprehensible. God saw right away that it wasn't good for Adam to be without a companion and so he created woman. God designed Adam and Eve for fellowship with himself. He asked only one thing: they could not eat of the Tree of the Knowledge of Good and Evil. It seems such a simple request, but they couldn't obey it. The consequence of their disobedience serves as a powerful motivator for us to do what God says!

go to

Creation
Psalm 8:5

Let's Create a Man

GENESIS 2:7–9 *And the LORD God formed man of the dust of the ground, and breathed into his nostrils the breath of life; and man became a living being. The LORD God planted a garden eastward in Eden [see Illustration #1], and there He put the man whom He had formed. And out of the ground the LORD God made every tree grow that is pleasant to the sight and good for food. The tree of life was also in the midst of the garden, and the tree of the knowledge of good and evil. (NKJV)*

On the sixth day of Creation God, who desired fellowship, made Adam from the dust of the ground by breathing life into him. Adam was created a fully grown man and had everything he needed to survive. Adam did not evolve.

what others say

Allen P. Ross

God's breathing the breath of life into man transformed his form into a living being (lt., "a living soul"). This made man a spiritual being, with a capacity for serving and fellowshiping with God.[1]

Illustration #1
Garden of Eden—
While we don't
know exactly where
the Garden of Eden
was, we do know
four rivers ran
through Eden,
including the Tigris
and the Euphrates.
This area is the
present day location
of Iran and Iraq. The
first civilizations
developed here.

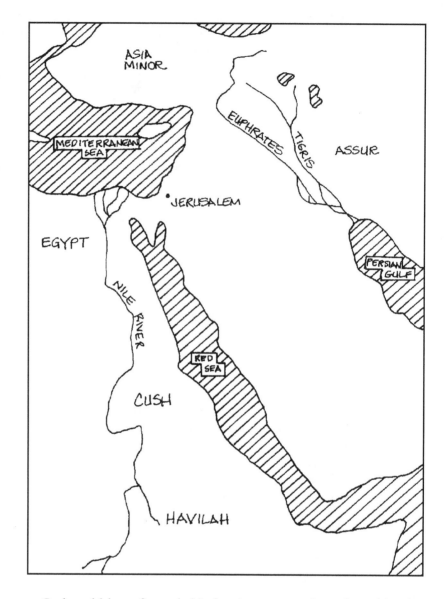

God could have formed this first human creation of anything he
desired in any way he desired. This new creation could have had six
eyes or three legs or any number of other appendages or parts, but
everything created within man's body had a purpose and a reason.
Then God provided for man by placing him in a garden, giving him
all the food and supplies he needed.

Nothing God created was happenstance or by mistake. There was a reason behind everything he did in creation and in the way he created Adam. The word in the Hebrews for formed refers to the work of an artist.

God wants every one of us to feel special, for he created each one of us for a specific purpose. Psalm 139:13–14 says, "You formed my inward parts; You covered me in my mother's womb. I will praise You, for I am fearfully and wonderfully made; marvelous are Your works, and that my soul knows very well" (NKJV).

Each one of your children is not a mistake, accident, or plan of yours apart from God. God is fulfilling his desires for the formation of that child. He knows exactly the plan he has for him or her, and a father should cooperate with God's blueprint for that child. You can't force a child to grow or develop, but you can participate in God's <u>design</u> for him or her.

Let's Give This Man Something to Do

GENESIS 2:15–17 *Then the LORD God took the man and put him in the garden of Eden to tend and keep it. And the LORD God commanded the man, saying, "Of every tree of the garden you may freely eat; but of the **tree of the knowledge of good and evil** you shall not eat, for in the day that you eat of it you shall surely die." (NKJV)*

Right from the beginning, man had work to do. But Adam's work was purposeful and meaningful. Drudgery and trouble would enter the picture only after the **Fall**.

But the plot thickens: there was also a possible **<u>temptation</u>** in the form of a tree that contained the knowledge of good and evil, and there was a consequence for disobedience.

If Adam hadn't been presented with a choice to obey God, he would have been a robot. But with this commandment, God made it possible for Adam to prove his love and devotion to his Creator.

Love without a choice is not love at all.

design
Proverbs 22:6

temptation
Matthew 26:41

tree of the knowledge of good and evil
signified the ability to know right from wrong by personal experience

Fall
the first sin of Adam and Eve

temptation
wanting what God doesn't want

what others say

Charles R. Swindoll
Americans did not invent the idea of freedom. . . . It began with God, way back in the Garden of Eden when he made

test
James 1:13

good
Genesis 1:4, 10, 12, 18, 21, 25

sin
disobedience
to God

devotion
commitment

Adam and Eve. God made them—and he has made you and me—to enjoy the pleasures and responsibilities of freedom. How?

• God made us with a mind . . . that we might think freely.
• God made us with a heart . . . that we might love freely.
• God made us with a will . . . that we might obey freely.[2]

God never tempts you to do evil, but he does give you occasions to prove your love for him. His commandments are not some helter-skelter mistake to trap you in **sin**. They are rules intended for your best and to <u>test</u> your love and **devotion** for your Creator. God created you to have a relationship with him.

Just as God clearly defined the rules and the consequences for disobedience, fathers must clearly communicate the rules of their households to their children. They must express the advantages of obeying, and they must make clear the consequences for disobedience.

The Name Game

> GENESIS 2:18–20 *And the LORD God said, "It is not good that man should be alone; I will make him a helper comparable to him." Out of the ground the LORD God formed every beast of the field and every bird of the air, and brought them to Adam to see what he would call them. And whatever Adam called each living creature, that was its name. So Adam gave names to all cattle, to the birds of the air, and to every beast of the field. But for Adam there was not found a helper comparable to him.* (NKJV)

God created Adam as a thinking, reasoning human with a need to be creative. Naming the animals gave Adam purpose. However, it wasn't satisfying for Adam.

Man was all by himself. And God, the Creator who wanted his creation to be perfectly happy, recognized that this wasn't good. Everything else God had created was immediately labeled "<u>good</u>," but it wasn't good that Adam was alone.

Wow! She's Just Like Me!

> GENESIS 2:21–25 *And the LORD God caused a deep sleep to fall on Adam, and he slept; and He took one of his ribs, and closed up the flesh in its place. Then the rib which the LORD God had*

*taken from man He made into a woman, and He brought her
to the man. And Adam said:*

*"This is now bone of my bones
And flesh of my flesh;
She shall be called Woman,
Because she was taken out of Man."*

*Therefore a man shall leave his father and mother and be
joined to his wife, and they shall become one flesh. And they were
both naked, the man and his wife, and were not ashamed.*
(NKJV)

God created a woman from Adam's rib. Now Adam had a suitable complement for the new task of running Eden. She could walk like him, talk like him, and reason like him. She was just like him. What a relief after dealing with all those animals who couldn't talk. The first marriage was complete, and even though they were not yet parents, God predicted the future of new couples: they should be independent from their parents. But the best thing about this new couple was that they were unashamed of their naked bodies. They had complete acceptance and total love for each other. Ah, Paradise!

what others say

Raymond C. Ortlund Jr.

These are the first recorded human words, and they are poetry. What do they express? The joy of the first man in receiving the gift of the first woman. . . . The man perceived the woman not as his rival but as his partner, not as a threat because of her equality with himself, but as the only one capable of fulfilling his longing within.[3]

Some writers have said about this passage that Adam gave the first wolf whistle when he saw Eve. She must have been a perfect beauty because God would have wanted him to be attracted to her. God knew what would please Adam, and God made sure she fulfilled Adam's expectations, even though he hadn't yet formed any. She was perfectly suited just for him.

Adam found out that humans truly find fulfillment only in relationships. Men may think work will bring satisfaction or that things will bring a sense of completeness. But it doesn't work that way. God designed humans to be fulfilled in relationships—in relationships with other human beings and with their Creator.

God had said that he would make a **helper** suitable for Adam. When Scripture uses the word "<u>helper</u>" in reference to a woman, it isn't meant to be demeaning. God himself is called "<u>Helper</u>." The word *comparable* can also be expressed as "a help opposite him" or "corresponding to him." God intended to provide for Adam exactly according to Adam's needs. That's how God wants a man to view his wife: as someone valuable who completes what he lacks. In fact, God asks men to love their wives so much that they should be willing to <u>give</u> their lives up for them. Now that is a valuable asset.

Illustration #2
Serpent—Satan is described in the Bible as a serpent who led Adam and Eve to disobey God. These poisonous creatures are used throughout the Bible to symbolize sin and evil of many kinds.

Uh-Oh, Trouble in Paradise

the big picture

Genesis 3:1–7

Satan appeared in the Garden of Eden as a serpent [see Illustration #2] and tempted the woman into eating from the forbidden "tree of the knowledge of good and evil." Then she gave some of the fruit to Adam, and he ate too. It didn't take long for them to realize they had disobeyed, for they became conscious of their nakedness. Ashamed, they tried to make their own clothing from fig leaves.

go to

helper
Genesis 2:18

Helper
John 14:16–17

give
Ephesians 5:25

helper
assistant

Satan
the devil

Just imagine the front-page headlines that could have been written after the Fall:

- Why Wasn't Adam Watching the Store?
- First Man Fails; Everyone Else Pays with Their Lives
- Warning Signs Improperly Posted at the Tree of Knowledge; Liability Questioned
- Eve Says, "Adam Never Told Me"

From the biblical account we don't know if Adam was there when Satan tempted Eve, or whether he appeared after she had taken her first bite. Regardless, they both knew that something was wrong. They had never looked at each other before and felt vulnerable. Now clothing seemed like something they could hide behind. Even though Satan had promised something good to Eve, neither she nor Adam saw the promised results.

soul
the immortal, spiritual part of a person

what others say

Herschel H. Hobbs

The devil opened their eyes, but not to becoming as God, but rather to shame. Their physical nakedness suggests their greater nakedness of **soul**. Theirs was the self-consciousness of guilty hearts.[4]

Do you wonder how Adam could have blown it so big? He had it made. He had perfect health, a perfect domain, the perfect job, and the perfect wife. He talked daily with his Creator. He was placed in the Garden to take care of it. It was his service to God, and it was marked by ease and pleasure. Yet it wasn't enough. He thought the forbidden fruit would bring additional satisfaction.

Adam never had to work as you and I do. It was Paradise. Really! With all of this, God placed one condition on Adam's life: don't eat the fruit from one tree. In his complacency, Adam took for granted the overwhelming abundance. He didn't know anything else, and he sacrificed it all because of wanting something he wasn't supposed to have.

Ever since the sin of our first parents, man has hurt himself, his relationship with others, and his relationship with God. Like dominoes, the consequences of sin have tumbled into the present. Marriages and families suffer from selfishness. Society is self-indulgent, and our culture is rotting as sin's poison spreads. The arts, sciences, disciplines, and structures of our world are an apple with a worm in it. And the worm is hungry! What was originally meant to reflect the glory of God became a support mechanism for sin.

something to ponder

We are not to "love the world or the things in the world. If anyone loves the world, the love of the Father is not in him" (1 John 2:15 NKJV). We are not to be insulated or isolated from the things of the world. We are to live in the world without being of the world.

Moses
Exodus 3:11

providence
divine guidance

It's Her Fault!

GENESIS 3:8–13 *And they heard the sound of the* LORD *God walking in the garden in the cool of the day, and Adam and his wife hid themselves from the presence of the* LORD *God among the trees of the garden.*

Then the Lord LORD *God called to Adam and said to him, "Where are you?" So he said, "I heard Your voice in the garden, and I was afraid because I was naked; and I hid myself." And He said, "Who told you that you were naked? Have you eaten from the tree of which I commanded you that you should not eat?" Then the man said, "The woman whom You gave to be with me, she gave me of the tree, and I ate." And the* LORD *God said to the woman, "What is this you have done?" The woman said, "The serpent deceived me, and I ate." (NKJV)*

God knew what Adam and Eve had done, yet he patiently questioned them. This is the first recorded incident where God demonstrates his willingness to have an open relationship with us in spite of our disobedience.

Adam and Eve responded to God's appearance by hiding and then blaming each other and Satan. God tried to reach out to them, but their guilt prevented them from feeling his love. Distance, separation, and fear took their first sneaky steps into the hearts of men. No one wanted to take responsibility. Instead, they pointed fingers, trying to transfer the blame and shame. This is the first buck that was passed—and it'll continue passing for the rest of humanity's existence.

what others say

Alan Redpath

So often the **providence** of God seems to run completely counter to his promises, only that he may test our faith, only that he may ultimately accomplish his purpose for our lives in a way that he could never do if the path were always smooth.[5]

Adam told God he was fearful. Even though his hiding didn't help the situation, at least he expressed his fear, showing he still had an open relationship with God. Moses was another biblical leader who once was filled with enough courage to kill an Egyptian. Yet forty years later when facing God at the burning bush, he fearfully told

God he couldn't deliver the Hebrews. Each man struggled with fear in his daily life but both candidly expressed their feelings to God.

Men today often hide their feelings, but the first man didn't have any trouble describing his emotions. Neither should you.

spiritual tenor
underlying belief

Consequences for Adam

the big picture

Genesis 3:14–4:2

God responded to the sin in the Garden by disciplining the serpent, Eve, and Adam with different consequences for each. Then God provided clothes from animal skins for Adam and his wife. Adam gave the woman the name *Eve* because it means "living" or "life." She would become the mother of all the living. They were finally banished from the Garden.

God referred to his provision of a Savior in the future when he told Satan, "I will put enmity between you and the woman, and between your seed and her Seed; He shall bruise your head, and you shall bruise His heel" (Genesis 3:15 NKJV).

Adam and Eve thought they would experience the freedom of becoming godlike. Instead, they got painful consequences that reminded them even more of their humanness. God rebuked Adam for not being a leader. He should have refused Eve's encouragement to eat the fruit: "Because you have heeded the voice of your wife, and have eaten from the tree of which I commanded you, saying, 'You shall not eat of it': Cursed is the ground for your sake; in toil you shall eat of it all the days of your life. Both thorns and thistles it shall bring forth for you, and you shall eat the herb of the field. In the sweat of your face you shall eat bread till you return to the ground, for out of it you were taken; for dust you are, and to dust you shall return" (Genesis 3:17–19 NKJV). To Adam's credit, he didn't argue, blame his wife again, or try to change God's mind. He accepted his correction like a man.

what others say

Herschel H. Hobbs

The Bible does not say it specifically, but the **spiritual tenor** is that Adam and Eve believed this promise and were saved, looking forward in faith to him who would be the seed of the woman.[6]

go to

giver
James 1:17

supply
Philippians 4:19

key point

Results of the First Sin

Verses	Person	Consequences
Genesis 3:14–15	Satan	Serpent will crawl on belly. Satan will be defeated by Jesus Christ.
Genesis 3:16	Eve	Pain in childbirth. Desire to please husband and be mastered by him.
Genesis 3:17–19	Adam	Work and toil to survive. Physical death and return to dust.

Adam and Eve tried to have their needs met by disobeying God, but it only brought greater pain. Sin is anything we do when we try to meet our own needs in a way that God doesn't want for us.

If we will remember that God only wants the best for us, we'll be more motivated to try to meet our needs in the way he has laid out. God never plans to withhold something good from us. He is the giver of all good gifts and promises to supply all our true needs. If we'll trust his love for us, we'll sin less often.

Chapter Wrap-Up

- God created a man in his own image to rule over the world and because he wanted fellowship with him. He created a perfect world for Adam to rule over. This world involved work, but it wasn't troublesome work; that would come later. (Genesis 1:26–2:7)

- Because animals didn't completely satisfy Adam's need for companionship, God created Eve from Adam's rib. This companionship would be intimate and blessed by God. (Genesis 2:18–25)

- God gave the couple only one thing to avoid: "the tree of the knowledge of good and evil." Adam and Eve disobeyed God by eating of its fruit. (Genesis 3:1–7)

- After sinning no one wanted to accept responsibility. Finger pointing and rationalization rocked Eden. Adam blamed his wife for his sin, and Eve blamed the serpent. (Genesis 3:12–13)

- For Adam, the consequences of sin were that he would have a difficult time working the ground. Work would never be easy again. For Eve, she would experience pain in childbirth and would desire to serve her husband. For the serpent, he would crawl on the ground and be defeated by Jesus Christ on the cross. (Genesis 3:14–19)

Study Questions

1. What instructions did God give Adam about the trees in the Garden? Why were these instructions necessary?

2. What did God call "not good"?

3. What did God create that did not adequately "help" Adam?

4. What consequences did God give Adam, Eve, and Satan?

5. Who named Eve, and why was that name chosen?

Chapter 2: Abraham—Father of Promise

Chapter Highlights:
- Abram Leaves
- Waiting for Isaac
- Name Change
- New Baby
- Test at the Altar

Let's Get Started

Life was never easy for the **patriarch** Abraham. He was tested in many ways. Some tests he passed with flying colors, and others he just barely passed. With a few, he failed completely.

In spite of Abraham's occasional faithlessness, however, God proved himself faithful over and over again. God kept his promises. Abraham didn't always understand God's timing, but in the end Abraham reviewed God's work in his life and saw how God had strengthened his trust and faith.

God wants us to learn, as Abraham did, that trials draw us closer to him. Then we'll have a joy and contentment like Abraham had when he saw Isaac, his son of promise, born.

go to

Jacob
Genesis 28:13

Moses
Exodus 3:4

patriarch
the head or founder of a family

genealogy
tracing family history

A Big Step

the big picture

Genesis 11:27–12:9

Abram's **genealogy** revealed his family background. His ancestors lived in Ur of the Chaldeans. People of that area worshiped many gods, but Jehovah appeared to Abram and gave him instructions to leave his father's country. He was to head out without knowing exactly where he was going or where he would settle.

When the one true God, Jehovah, appeared to Abram and told him to leave the land of his ancestors, he was faced with a big decision. Why did he respond to the God of heaven (as opposed to all the pagan gods of his culture [see Illustration #3])? In the stories of Jacob and Moses we are allowed to see the glory of the meeting, but we have no idea how God revealed himself to Abram. We do know, however, that the experience ignited Abram's faith and trust such that he chose to leave the familiar and walk toward an unknown future (see Illustration #4).

Illustration #3
The Goddess Astarte—Many people in the land of Canaan worshiped the false goddess Astarte. She was associated with Venus and identified as a goddess of sensual love and fertility.

go to

everywhere
Proverbs 15:3

lead
Psalm 25:5

strengthen
Philippians 4:13

what others say

Charles R. Swindoll

Abraham demonstrated faith by moving into an uncharted course with one guarantee—that God was with him. Think about this: Christianity is not complicated. The neglect of your walk is complicated. And the secret is to distill this walk through the filter of simplicity so that you come back to the basics, which is faith. Visit Abraham regarding faith. Learn from him.[1]

We can't fully appreciate the step Abram took without understanding the fact that his culture trusted in many gods because each one had its own function or area of expertise. Each god also had its own designated geographical area. Therefore, to go outside a particular boundary meant leaving the protection of a particular god. Rejecting all of this, Abram chose to believe in the one God, Jehovah. In light of the culture surrounding him, Abram took a tremendous step in believing that this "new" God was one who transcended boundary lines and ruled the whole earth. He had to believe that Jehovah could be <u>everywhere</u> Abram traveled.

God only said he would show Abram the land. He didn't promise to give him the land at this point. Sometimes all we have to go on is God's promise to <u>lead</u> and <u>strengthen</u> us without knowing all the details. Yet, we can depend on the very smallest of his promises.

apply it

Incredible Appearance

As far as the text tells us, this was the first time God had appeared to Abram. It would not be the last. In total, Scripture records seven times that God personally appeared to Abram. In Bible language, such an appearance is called a **theophany**.

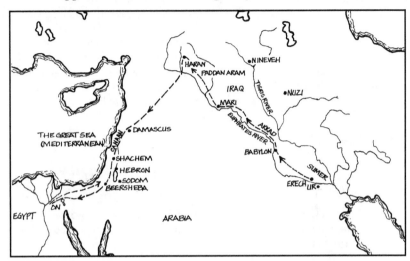

what others say

Harold Ockenga

One of the means used by God in revealing his will unto men in the early stage of divine revelation was by means of a the-ophany.[2]

God's Appearances to Abram

Bible Passage	Circumstances	Promises or Challenge
Genesis 12:1–3	God's call for Abram to leave his area	Abram will be made a great nation. He will have blessings. God will make his name great. He will be a blessing to others. Those who bless him will be blessed, and those who curse him will be cursed. All the families of the earth will be blessed through him.
Genesis 12:7	Abram arrives in land of Canaanites	"To your descendants I will give this land." (NKJV)
Genesis 13:15	After Lot separates from Abram	God promises land to Abram.
Genesis 15:1–5	After Abram refuses reward from Melchizedek	God promises a child who will be a blood heir. God promises descendants as numerous as stars in the sky.
Genesis 17:1–5	When Abram is 99 years old	God establishes his covenant with Abram, and promises to multiply his family into many nations. God changes his name from Abram to Abraham.

half sister
Genesis 20:12

Terah
Genesis 11:24

Haran
Genesis 11:26

chastised
corrected

Semitic
Jewish

God's Appearances to Abram (cont'd)

Bible Passage	Circumstances	Promises or Challenge
Genesis 18	At oaks of Mamre	Three men promise that Sarah will give birth to a child a year from then. Abraham also is given an opportunity to pray for any righteous people at Sodom.
Genesis 22:1–14	Testing of Abraham's dedication	God asks Abraham to sacrifice his son, Isaac. Then, when Abraham is about to do it, an angel stops him.

The Big Lie

the big picture

Genesis 12:10-20

Famine hit Canaan and drove Abram to Egypt. Abram feared for his life when he considered how beautiful his wife, Sarai, was and how the Egyptian king might want to kill him in order to take her as his wife. He told Sarai to lie and say they were brother and sister. The Egyptian took Sarai into his harem, but before he could consummate the relationship, God used a plague to warn Pharaoh and bring riches to Abram.

Abram went to Egypt where there was food. He had proved his faithfulness in his initial move from Ur, but his faith in God's provision and protection collapsed when he suspected someone might kill him to get his beautiful wife. Abram was asking Sarai to give a half-truth since Sarai was a relative of Abram's before she became his wife. Some Bible experts believe she was his <u>half sister</u> (the daughter of Abram's father <u>Terah</u>, but not his mother), whereas some believe she may have been his niece (the daughter of <u>Haran</u>—Abram's brother). Even though Sarai was taken into the king's home, God intervened by giving Pharaoh the sense to see the connection between a plague and Sarai (we don't know how). He returned Sarai to Abram and **chastised** Abram for lying. How embarrassing for a man of God.

what others say

Gene A. Getz

Abraham's fears were not without reason. History records that Egyptian men were very impressed with **Semitic** women. Furthermore, it was rather standard procedure in those days for men to secure women as their wives by murdering their husbands and previous possessors.[3]

If a superstar of the faith can fail so badly, then we must be alert to the possibility that we could also be one step away from surrendering to fear. We will be constantly <u>tested</u> but with God's help, we can be faithful. We haven't seen God in person like Abram did, but we have the <u>Bible</u> and the example of other Christians to encourage us and help us know the right thing to do.

Just as Abram was not counted as unfaithful because of his temporary lack of faith, God doesn't give up on us when we make mistakes or even sin. All our sin was in the future at the time of the cross, and it was nailed there. Of course, that doesn't give us a <u>license</u> to sin, but it can give us hope to turn back to God over and over again. All we have to do is <u>confess</u> sin and receive God's forgiveness.

Lot Walks by Sight, Abram by Faith

the big picture

Genesis 13:1–18

After the famine Abram returned to Canaan a wealthy man. His nephew Lot returned with him. Their shepherds were fighting because there wasn't enough land to support all of the herds. Abram graciously offered first pick of the land to his nephew. Lot chose the best part. After this, God again spoke to Abram and promised him many descendants.

Abram wisely separated from Lot. Both of them were wealthy but conflict was something Abram did not want. Abram was the head of the family and could have dictated the terms of living together or a separation. Instead, he graciously offered Lot first choice. Lot headed for the city of Sodom. Abram met God again and was then promised all the land he could see. God marvelously promised to bless him with countless generations.

go to

what others say

Jamie Buckingham

When Lot said there was not room enough for the two of them, Abram chose again to obey God. Jealous for the integrity of his tribe and its testimony before the corrupt society that was so closely observing him, he determined he

tested
1 Peter 1:6–7

Bible
Colossians 3:16

license
Jude 1:4

confess
1 John 1:9

go to

faith
Romans 4:9

key point

marauding
robbing

should not dishonor God by causing disunity and conflict within his family—a family that had professed a loyalty to God, making them different.[4]

God's promise to Abram was not fulfilled in his lifetime. He didn't own the land and he only had one descendant, Isaac, when he died. Yet, that's why Abram was counted by God as such a man of <u>faith</u>. He trusted that what God said would come to pass, even if he didn't experience it. And it did. "These all died in faith, not having received the promises, but having seen them afar off were assured of them, embraced them and confessed that they were strangers and pilgrims on the earth" (Hebrews 11:13 NKJV). Faith means we believe even if we don't see the results immediately.

Abram's Courage and Humility

the big picture

Genesis 14:1–24

Lot settled in Sodom but was captured by Chedorlaomer, a king and his army. When Abram heard about it, he quickly pursued the **marauding** armies and rescued his nephew. The king of Sodom wanted to reward Abram for his courage, but Abram refused. However, he did receive a blessing and some provisions from Melchizedek, the king of Salem.

The easygoing Abram reacted decisively and formed a rescue party to recover Lot from an invading army. He marched 140 miles north to engage in a night battle. He then chased the enemy for another 100 miles, ensuring victory. Lot and all of the possessions taken from Sodom were returned.

what others say

Charles R. Swindoll

Abraham was willing to sacrifice himself for the sake of others. . . . When Abram heard that Lot was in trouble, he could have reacted with indifference: "So what? I've got my own problems to deal with here." He could have been critical: "Well, he finally got what he had coming." Instead Abram chose to lead the charge to rescue his nephew.[5]

Abram had faith in God's ability to give victory. Abram was also ready because he had 318 men trained for trouble. His faith gave him confidence because God had promised him earlier, "I will bless those who bless you, and I will curse him who curses you" (Genesis 12:3 NKJV).

When the evil king of Sodom wanted to reward Abram, Abram refused. He didn't want others thinking that anyone or anything had made him rich, except God. His faith went beyond any riches the king of Sodom could provide. Abram passed this test of faith. God promised to bless him and that was enough.

As leaders we can trust that the Lord has prepared us for our tasks. He promises to be there and guide us, but we'd better make sure those people depending upon our leadership have been properly trained. We owe them a duty to prepare, plan, and position them for success.

history
Exodus 1–40

solidified
firmed up

covenant
agreement, like a treaty

Waiting for a Son

the big picture

Genesis 15:1–21

God again appeared to Abram and repeated his promise that Abram would have many children, even though Sarai hadn't yet been able to conceive a child. God **solidified** his promise by making a **covenant** with Abram.

God met Abram again and told him not to be afraid because he would be a shield to him. Because so much time had gone by without the promise of a child being fulfilled, Abram wondered aloud whether his faithful servant Eliezer, the current heir of his estate, would actually take over. But God confirmed that a son would indeed be born to Abram—a child from his own body. Then God pointed out the stars in the sky and said Abram's descendants would be as numerous as them. By faith Abram believed God and "He accounted it to him for righteousness" (Genesis 15:6 NKJV). To affirm his promise, God conducted a ceremony called a covenant and gave Abram some other details of his future nation's history.

go to

breach
Ezekiel 17:12–20

help
2 Corinthians 1:3–4

breach
breaking

Abraham's Future Predicted and Fulfilled

Future Predicted	Promise Fulfilled
Abram's descendants would be strangers in a foreign land	Exodus 1:1–7
They would be enslaved for 400 years	Exodus 1:11–14
God would judge the nation they served	Exodus 11:1
They would leave with abundant material goods	Exodus 11:2
Abram would die after a long life	Genesis 25:8
After the fourth generation, Abram's descendants would return to the land of the Amorites	Joshua 4:1
That land was determined as the land from the river of Egypt (Wadi el-Arish) as far as the river Euphrates	Genesis 15:18

what others say

Smith Wigglesworth

Faith is an inward operation of that divine power which dwells in the contrite heart, and which has the power to lay hold of things not seen.[6]

apply it

A covenant is a solemn transaction between a person and God or between people and God. In it each person promises to fulfill certain things and is promised certain advantages. In God's covenant with Abraham, God promised everything and didn't receive anything. This demonstrates his unconditional love and grace. The **breach** of a covenant was and still is a serious offense.

If it seems like God is slow in supplying you with the help you need to overcome some sin or correct a weakness, just know that he has the power and a plan. Only he knows the right timing. In the meantime, you'll learn something that you can use to help others in the future. If you were to have an instantaneous deliverance, you wouldn't learn those things.

A Human Plan Gone Awry

the big picture

Genesis 16:1–16

Sarai still couldn't conceive a child so she suggested to Abram that he have the child through her maid, Hagar. When that happened and Hagar became pregnant, Hagar despised Sarai. That made Sarai so mad she mistreated Hagar and Hagar ran away.

> But an angel of God found Hagar in the wilderness and told her that her son would become a great nation. He also gave her the ultimate challenge: Hagar should return to Sarai and submit to her authority. She did, and in time her son Ishmael was born.

go to

everything
Philippians 4:6–7

Cultural solutions to carry out God's plans don't work! Sarai suggested a solution that was considered appropriate by the surrounding culture, but Abram and Sarai were supposed to be part of God's culture. Unfortunately, their poor choice would have unpleasant consequences. God always has a reason for his delays.

what others say

Gene A. Getz

> But Ishmael's birth began a new chapter in world history that has not yet ended. From Hagar's son have come the great Arab nations who have in recent years plagued the children of Israel, the promised seed of Abraham. They are still suffering from Abraham's mistakes—mistakes born out of a right motive on Abraham's part, but from a wrong method.[7]

Abram showed us again his willingness to avoid conflict when he refused to become involved in Sarai and Hagar's hostility. God had to intervene and provide temporary leadership for the family by meeting Hagar in the desert. Abram might be faithful, but when faced with his wife's suggestion, he seemed to want peace at any cost.

The trouble could have been avoided if Abram and Sarai had asked God to guide them. When we jump at a solution to our problem without praying about it, we are asking for trouble. Nothing is too small or large for us to ask for God's help and viewpoint. The Bible says for us to pray about <u>everything</u>.

apply it

As fathers, we need to remember the poor choices Abram made. As head of the family he had the responsibility of making a righteous choice. As we learn from Abram, our inaction with family problems weakens the impact we have on our children. It makes us distant and disengaged from them. It also weakens the respect and confidence our wives have in us. Wives often say that watching their husbands giving attention to the children strengthens their love for their husbands. That should be a strong motivator for getting involved.

strengthen your family

circumcised
to cut off the
foreskin of a male

A New Name and a Unique Pain

the big picture

Genesis 17:1–27

God appeared to Abram again and repeated his promise to Abram that he would be the father of a multitude of nations. But this time, God did something new; he renamed the patriarch. Abram became Abraham and Sarai became Sarah. Not only that, he gave Abraham something new to do that would show that he and the male members of his household were unique and connected to God. God commanded all the males to be **circumcised**. Though it was painful, Abraham obeyed God's commands.

It was thirteen years before God spoke again to Abram. At that time God gave himself a new name, El Shaddai, which refers to the one who actually causes nature to do the opposite. Abram was ninety years old at this time and God revealed a new name for Abram as well, Abraham. This signified God was giving him a great honor. He then asked Abraham to undergo circumcision to demonstrate the covenant between them. Talk about faith in action! Obeying God might be painful sometimes but it always brings blessings.

what others say

Life Application Bible Notes

Why did God require circumcision? (1) As a sign of obedience to him in all matters. (2) As a sign of belonging to his covenant people. Once circumcised, there was no turning back. The man would be identified as a Jew forever. (3) As a symbol of "cutting off" the old life of sin, purifying one's heart, and dedicating oneself to God. (4) Possibly as a health measure.[8]

A Big Laugh

the big picture

Genesis 18:1–15

God visited Abraham again, this time in the form of a man. With him are two angels disguised as men. These men tell Abraham that in a year, Abraham and Sarah will have a child. Now God was really getting specific. Sarah had been listening nearby and laughed when she heard such an impossible prediction. She was too old for childbearing. When one of the angels pointed out her lack of belief, she denied laughing.

The Smart Guide to the Bible

God didn't withdraw his promise of a son for this old couple even though Sarah's faith was weak. If we have the view of God as an ogre looking for something to get upset about, we would expect him to become offended by Sarah's doubt and take away the promised blessing. But he didn't do that because he's a loving God. Besides, a <u>promise</u> is a promise.

Sarah is nearly ninety years old, and Abraham is no spring chicken at one hundred. Is it any wonder they doubted? Perhaps the Lord delayed this promise because of their disobedience with Hagar. Or perhaps waiting this long would clearly focus appropriate glory on the Lord's provision.

promise
Numbers 23:19

patient
2 Peter 3:9

effective
James 5:16

just
Revelation 15:3

abomination
something loathed

what others say

Herschel H. Hobbs

One may wonder why the Lord delayed the event so long, twenty-five years after the first veiled promise was given. In a sense it was a test of Abraham's faith. Furthermore, when the promise was fulfilled, there must be no question that it was God's doing alone.[9]

God is <u>patient</u> with us. He knows we aren't perfect and don't have perfect faith. "As a father pities his children, so the LORD pities those who fear Him. For He knows our frame; He remembers that we are dust" (Psalm 103:13–14 NKJV). God understands that our earthly perspective can diminish our ability to really believe he can do anything he wants.

When Pleading Won't Work

the big picture

Genesis 18:16–19:38

Not only did the angels tell Abraham and Sarah about their future child, they also told of how God was going to destroy Sodom and Gomorrah. Abraham's nephew, Lot, lived in Sodom, so Abraham pleaded for mercy on the city. God graciously saved Lot and his family, but the sin of Sodom and Gomorrah was too great and the cities were destroyed.

The prayer of a righteous man is <u>effective</u>, but God is <u>just</u>. The situation in these two cities was an **abomination** to the Lord.

Although Abraham asked for mercy for the cities, God and the angels left without giving Abraham an indication of whether they would spare anyone for sure. But God, in his generosity, caused his angels to physically pull Lot and his family out of the city. Lot's wife was killed because she disobeyed the order to not look back at the destruction.

Abraham started out his prayer by asking whether God would destroy the righteous with the wicked. We don't know whether Abraham thought he knew of a certain number of righteous people, but maybe because he couldn't think of too many, he mentioned fifty righteous and then forty-five, then forty, then thirty, then twenty, and finally ten. Each time, God said he wouldn't destroy the city if that particular number were found. We don't know why Abraham stopped at ten. Maybe he sensed that God must destroy the city because of its great wickedness.

Laughter Finally in the House

the big picture

Genesis 21:1–21

When Abraham was one hundred and Sarah was ninety, God fulfilled his promise. Sarah gave birth to Isaac. Their joy was boundless at first. But soon fourteen-year-old Ishmael, who had made fun of Isaac at his weaning party, spoiled it. Sarah was so angry that she insisted Abraham throw Hagar and Ishmael out of their home. God commanded Abraham to do that very thing and, though it grieved him, he did so. As Hagar sat helpless in the wilderness, God again appeared to her and promised to provide for her and her son.

The promise was finally fulfilled. Sarah and Abraham couldn't believe their joy. A baby—born to Sarah, the barren one. Isaac's name meant "laughter," and laugh they did, with joy. Whereas Sarah had previously laughed in doubt, she now laughed from faith. Abraham must have been doubly thrilled to see the son of promise in the flesh and to see the joy on his beloved wife's face. But another kind of laughter occurred several years later at the party celebrating the weaning of Isaac: mocking laughter. Ishmael, Abraham and Hagar's son—the result of disobedience to God—must have felt intense jealousy because of all the attention being given the promised heir. Maybe he had secretly carried the thought he would somehow be the heir after all. Isaac's birth had spoiled that. He didn't laugh out of joy, but out of ridicule.

His mocking made Sarah so angry that she demanded Abraham throw Hagar and Ishmael out of the house. Abraham, loyal even to the son who wasn't the true heir, hated the idea, but God told him to do it. God then promised that he would take care of Ishmael by making a nation of him also. Most likely that comforted Abraham some. He obeyed God.

Patience and faith had paid off for Abraham and Sarah. God delivered just as he promised, even though they'd had imperfect faith, and at times, even disobeyed God's directions. That is just like God's faithfulness! Although he may have to discipline us at times for disobedience, he will still keep his promises.

key point

The Ultimate Challenge

the big picture

Genesis 22:1-24

God commanded Abraham to sacrifice his beloved son, Isaac, on an altar of his own making in the nearby mountains. In full obedience, Abraham made plans to kill his son, but God stopped him right before he did it. God affirmed Abraham's dependence on him and again confirmed his promise that Abraham would be the father of a multitude of people. When Abraham returned home, he learned that his brother, Nahor, was now the father of many children.

Abraham and Isaac traveled fifty miles to reach Mount Moriah. As they approached their destination, Abraham must have been deeply troubled. God had asked him to sacrifice his son! Abraham knew child sacrifice was practiced in the region, but God detested the practice. Pangs of love must have rocked Abraham's heart as every step brought them closer to Moriah and the ultimate surrender. God had given him this child; it didn't make sense that he would want him killed. Abraham no doubt remembered previous tests, but this one was the most painful.

When they arrived at the mountain, he instructed his servants, "Stay here with the donkey; the lad and I will go yonder and worship, and we will come back to you" (Genesis 22:5 NKJV). As

go to

prepare
James 1:2–4

Abraham's hand brought the knife toward Isaac's bound body, God stopped him and provided a ram for the sacrifice.

what others say

Oswald Chambers

Faith never knows where it is being led, but it loves and knows the One Who is leading.[10]

What do you love most? Your children, job, possessions, or reputation? Do you hold on to your future, waiting for one more life experience before really surrendering your heart to God? Abraham had to demonstrate his willingness to sacrifice his greatest love. When someone makes his or her first parachute jump, climbing out the door signals willingness, but letting go proves the commitment. God needed to know Abraham was totally focused upon serving him. Abraham chose to place God before his son when he immediately readied the donkey and left for the mountain. Each step toward Mount Moriah marked his willingness to obey El Shaddai through faith. When Abraham raised the knife, he let go. We must be as faithful. You can give all to the God of heaven, who will transform your life.

A Long Life of Love and Challenge

the big picture

Genesis 23:1–20; 24:1–9, 67; 25:1–10

Sarah died at 127 years of age, and Abraham bought a nearby field from the Hittites to bury his beloved wife.

Abraham did not want Isaac to marry one of the local women who didn't believe in Jehovah so he sent his servant to their distant relatives to find a wife. The servant was successful in bringing home a wife for Isaac. Abraham married another wife in his old age and had children through her. He died at the age of 175.

Abraham's long life was a visual aid demonstrating the reality of God. Through Abraham, we are given these truths:

- God honors our faith but will test it through trials.

- Trials prove our faith is real and <u>prepare</u> us for service.

- God will be glorified through our obedience.
- God is faithful even when we are faithless.

Abraham consistently reviewed God's faithfulness in the past so that he could better deal with his current difficulty. We can do this by reviewing God's faithfulness as recorded in the Scriptures. "Whatever things were written before were written for our learning, that we through the patience and comfort of the Scriptures might have hope" (Romans 15:4 NKJV).

Chapter Wrap-Up

- God told Abram to leave his present country and go to a land that God would show him. God promised to bless Abram greatly if he obeyed. By faith Abram left to follow God. (Genesis 12:1–3)

- God promised Abram that he would have many descendants— so many that they couldn't be numbered. (Genesis 13:16)

- Since God delayed Sarai's ability to become pregnant, she tried to help God's plan by causing Abram to have a son through Sarai's maid, Hagar. That son was named Ishmael. (Genesis 16:1–16)

- To show Abram that he had a unique relationship with God, God changed Abram's name to Abraham and commanded Abraham and his male household to become circumcised. (Genesis 17:5–12)

- In spite of old age and many delays, the son of promise was finally born. He was named Isaac, which means "laughter." (Genesis 21:1–7)

- God tested Abraham by telling him to sacrifice Isaac on an altar in the mountains of Moriah. Abraham was willing to do it but was stopped by God's intervention. (Genesis 22:1–13)

Study Questions

1. What did God promise to Abram when he called him to leave his own country?

2. Since Abram and Sarai were childless, who did Abram initially think would be his heir?

3. How did Sarai encourage Abram to fulfill God's promise for an heir? What happened?

4. What new names did God give to Abram and Sarai?

5. What motivated Abimelech to want to make a treaty with Abraham?

6. What ultimate test did God give to Abraham?

Chapter 3: Isaac—Man of Patience and Submission

Chapter Highlights:
- Isaac Yields to Sacrifice
- Isaac Asks Rebekah to Lie
- Jacob Receives the Blessing

Let's Get Started

Isaac's name meant "laughter," and that's what he brought into his family when he was born. As the son of Abraham and Sarah, Isaac learned of the great God Jehovah, who had appeared to his father, Abraham. In some ways, Isaac was like his father. He avoided confrontation. But unlike Abraham, who rose to the occasion when pressed, Isaac was more interested in peace at any cost.

inability
Genesis 16:1

As a result, Rebekah, the wife found for him by his father's servant, became the powerhouse of the family. Rebekah came into the family as a stranger but quickly stole Isaac's heart and ruled the roost. That didn't bother Isaac. His favored son Esau was a skilled hunter, and Isaac just wanted to enjoy the game Esau brought to him.

Regardless of Isaac's weaknesses, it was God's plan for Isaac to be a great Hebrew patriarch. We can learn much from him because he represents many of us who would rather give in than fight.

Laughter Is in the Family

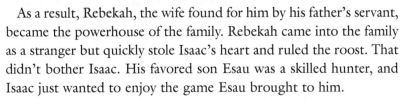

the big picture

Genesis 21:1–7

God had promised for many years that Abraham and Sarah would have a child. Now the son he had promised was born. Abraham was a hundred years old and Sarah was ninety.

Isaac inherited a rich heritage: a home of faith, filled with promise. No child of the Bible, except Jesus Christ, was surrounded by so much promise, expectation, and waiting. Time and again Sarah's <u>inability</u> to conceive seemed to place this longed-for promise in jeopardy. The wait seemed never-ending. Finally, Isaac was born and, appropriately, his name means "he laughs."

go to

born again
John 3:3

new creation
2 Corinthians 5:17

inheritance
Ephesians 1:18

spiritual birth
occurs at acceptance and faith in
Jesus Christ

repents
turns away from sin

born again
receiving Jesus
Christ as savior

Charles R. Swindoll

The home is God's built-in training facility. The home is a laboratory where experiments are tried out. It is a place where life makes up its mind. It is a place where biblical truth permeates everyday life and where children are taught to seek and to follow the way of the Lord.[1]

In a spiritual kind of way, there is just as much anticipation in heaven as the angels wait to celebrate over the **spiritual birth** of each of God's newborn children. "Likewise, I say to you, there is joy in the presence of the angels of God over one sinner who **repents**" (Luke 15:10 NKJV).

The Bible says we each must be "**born again**." That act of spiritual life makes us into a <u>new creation</u> in Christ. As a result, we have a spiritual <u>inheritance</u> just like Isaac. He inherited his father's possession and was raised with the knowledge of his spiritual ancestry.

What Are You Doing, Dad?

Genesis 22:1–19

God spoke to Abraham and told him to sacrifice Isaac. Isaac allowed his father to tie him down on an altar and watched as his father raised the knife. But God told Abraham to stop, and saved Isaac's life.

Scholars believe Isaac was between seventeen and twenty-five when his father tied him to that altar. Imagine yourself in Isaac's place. What compelled him to stay put? Surely, it was a powerful act of his will and faith in God, who he knew was at work in the situation—even if he didn't understand. When his father actually raised the knife, what thoughts flashed through his mind? His willingness to suffer death proved he trusted his father beyond a shadow of a doubt. It also meant Isaac was committed to serving the God of his father. And at that moment, if it hadn't already happened, his father's God became his own God.

go to

forbidden
Isaiah 57:4–5

what others say

Herschel H. Hobbs

Was this question asked out of a child's curiosity, or was the grim reality of the occasion beginning to dawn upon him? Perhaps he had noted the painful ordeal reflected in his father's face, hardly one to be experienced in anticipated worship. Was he himself to be the sacrifice? Isaac must have been familiar with the practice among the **Canaanites**.[2]

Canaanites
people living in the land promised to Israel

heathen
unbeliever in Jehovah God

As Isaac and his father walked toward the place of sacrifice, he said, "My father!" "Here I am, my son," Abraham replied. "Look, the fire and the wood," Isaac said, "but where is the lamb for a burnt offering?" (see Genesis 22:7 NKJV). The tenderness in Abraham's voice must have comforted Isaac. He knew he was loved. He knew his father would never allow anything bad to happen to him. Isaac trusted his father when Abraham replied that God would provide the lamb.

Not only was Abraham commanded to kill Isaac, but he would then have to burn Isaac's body in order for Isaac to become the burnt offering God required. What a horrible thought. Even though the **heathen** of the surrounding area did such despicable things, Abraham knew that such a practice was forbidden by God. Isaac might have believed that his life wasn't actually in danger—until the knife was raised.

Momma Is Gone; I Want a Wife

the big picture

Genesis 23:1–2; 24:61–67

Isaac's mother, Sarah, died. Isaac, as her only son and long-awaited heir, must have felt close to her. Abraham sent a faithful servant back to his home country to find a wife for Isaac from their relatives. The servant brought back Rebekah, Isaac's cousin. When his mother died, Rebekah must have comforted him. Isaac fell in love with Rebekah.

When Isaac was thirty-six, his mother died. He grieved deeply over the loss. Four years later, through his father Abraham's arrangements, Isaac met Rebekah, his wife. When she first arrived, Isaac was found praying and meditating. Isaac may have been seeking God's comfort from the loneliness he felt after the death of his mother. Or he may have been praying for the success of the servant's search for a wife. We don't know, but he most likely considered Rebekah an answer to prayer since she was beautiful and complemented his personality.

Illustration #5
Well and Water Jug—Rebekah probably drew water from a well like this one and carried the heavy jugs by balancing them on her head. She would have had to draw as much as 250 gallons of water for Eliezer's camels, because each camel could drink up to 25 gallons of water.

J. Vernon McGee

Notice that Isaac loved her. He was comforted after his mother's death. Christ loved the church and gave himself for her. This reveals to us that Christ gains a great deal in our salvation. He wants us. He longs for us.[3]

Isaac was the only patriarch to take solely one wife. Where Isaac was compliant and patient, Rebekah was strong-willed and energetic. When Abraham's servant had originally <u>found</u> Rebekah, she brought <u>water</u> from the well to water all his camels—an incredible feat (see Illustration #5). Then she was willing to <u>leave</u> her family and travel many miles with a stranger. She was a risk-taker. Isaac was the exact opposite. Without knowing it, we often marry the opposite temperament to bring balance into our lives.

Isaac's example of praying and meditating is an encouragement to us. It was important to Isaac and it should be important to us. Without it, we cannot know God and we can't grow closer to him. Through prayer, we:

go to

found
Genesis 24:15

water
Genesis 24:19

leave
Genesis 24:58

- Gain courage (2 Samuel 7:27)
- Know God has answered us (Psalm 118:5)
- Know we are heard and cared about (1 Kings 8:28–30)
- Confess our sins (Nehemiah 1:6)
- Ask for success (Nehemiah 1:11)
- Express our faith in God (Matthew 21:22)
- Ask for God's miracles (Mark 9:29)
- Ask for others to be saved (Romans 10:1)
- Overcome anxiety and worry (Philippians 4:6)
- See people healed (James 5:15)

apply it

Favoritism Rules the Roost

the big picture

Genesis 25:8, 19-34

Isaac's father, Abraham, died, and left everything to him. But for a while, it seemed that Isaac would not be able to pass along his inheritance because Rebekah was barren. After much prayer, Rebekah conceived and then gave birth to twins, Esau and Jacob. Isaac favored Esau, and Rebekah favored Jacob. The sons lived out God's prediction that Jacob would be master over Esau when Esau exchanged his birthright for some food.

Rebekah was initially barren like Isaac's mother, Sarah, but eventually bore twins, Esau and Jacob. Isaac avoided the conflict between the brothers, but both he and Rebekah contributed to it by each having his or her own favorite.

Isaac favored Esau because he loved the game that this son brought in from the fields. Esau was a skillful hunter, but he didn't value the spiritual life. Even though he must have seen his father's prayer life and heard of the spiritual journey of his ancestors, Esau was not interested in spiritual things. As a result, he sold his birthright to his brother Jacob for some food.

Rebekah favored Jacob because Jacob stayed more in the tents. Since he fixed a tasty meal that tempted his brother, Jacob must have been a good cook, no doubt trained by his mother. Mother and son were very close.

promise
Genesis 13:14–16

reaction
Genesis 12:11–13

slighted
ignored

William Hendriksen suggests there are at least six ways a father can embitter his children:

1. Over-protection

2. Favoritism

3. Discouragement

4. Forgetting a child has ideas of his own and need not be an exact copy of his father

5. Neglect

6. Bitter words and physical cruelty[4]

How interesting that Jacob was identified as "a mild man, dwelling in tents" (Genesis 25:27 NKJV). That characteristic also described Isaac. Rebekah valued this quality in her son Jacob, because it was the opposite of hers. Isaac valued Esau's aggression as a hunter—something he lacked. Both in marriage and in our children, we tend to value in others that which we need.

Showing favoritism will cause the **slighted** child to feel angry. "Fathers, do not provoke your children to wrath, but bring them up in the training and admonition of the Lord" (Ephesians 6:4 NKJV). When we train them, we must show God's kind of love that loves everyone equally.

Not Another Lie

the big picture

Genesis 26:1–17

God appeared to Isaac and promised to give him the Canaanite land—a confirmation of the <u>promise</u> given to Isaac's father Abraham. As Isaac resided there, like his father's <u>reaction</u> years earlier, he was afraid Rebekah's beauty would cause his death. As a result, he told Rebekah to say they were sister and brother. The king of that area, Abimelech, saw them caressing and confronted Isaac. Isaac then told the truth. Isaac continued to live there and God greatly prospered him.

God had <u>promised</u> a future for Isaac's family in their own land. Without a doubt, Isaac completely embraced his father's God. His life was marked by dedication to God and he proved himself faithful. In spite of this, when threatened by fear of possible death, he <u>sacrificed</u> truth. He lied about his relationship to his wife.

Throughout the Bible, many men of faith struggled with telling the truth. These included:

- The Israelites when Achan kept some of the plunder for Jericho (Joshua 7:11).
- Samson when he teased Delilah with the source of his strength (Judges 16:10).
- House of Judah and Israel when they said God would do nothing to them (Jeremiah 5:10–12).
- Ananias and Sapphira when they claimed they had given all to God (Acts 5:3–4).

Just as heart disease is prevented or reversed through diet and exercise, we need a remedy to reverse the disease that lying can inflict upon our spiritual lives. "Lying lips are an abomination to the LORD, but those who deal truthfully are His delight" (Proverbs 12:22 NKJV). Prayer and studying the Word are the cure. Honestly, earnestly, and humbly seeking God through a knowledge of the Bible is the best medicine for this spiritual heart problem.

go to

promised
Genesis 26:4

sacrificed
Genesis 26:7

venison
deer meat

<u>The Wrong Son</u>

the big picture

Genesis 27:1–29

As Isaac grew older, he grew blind. Since he anticipated his own death, he told his son Esau to prepare one of his favorite **venison** dishes so that he could give his son the blessing. When Rebekah heard of it, she manipulated Jacob into deceiving Isaac so that Jacob would get the blessing.

In order to deceive Isaac, Rebekah dressed Jacob in Esau's clothing, put animal skins on his hands and arms to resemble Esau's hairiness, and then fixed a meal of goat meat to taste wild. When Jacob brought the meal to his father, Isaac believed Jacob was Esau and gave Jacob the blessing.

older would serve the younger
Genesis 25:23

head
Ephesians 5:23

deception
trickery

Isaac was trying to play God, for God said the <u>older would serve the younger</u>, but Isaac wanted nothing of God's plan. He wanted his favored son, Esau, to get the blessing. Isaac was not only physically blind, but he was spiritually blind. Even though he knew God's promises, he made preparations to give the blessing to Esau. He was suspicious because Jacob's voice didn't sound like Esau's, but he still gave the blessing because the meat tasted good. Blinded by the desire of his heart, he sought disobedience; blinded by the hunger in his belly, he unwittingly helped in the final act of a **deception**.

what others say

Charles R. Swindoll

If you are in a position of authority, no matter how small or how large, the temptation to manipulate will never go away. You may have the authority to claim certain honors . . . to call attention to your right to be listened to. Don't yield. Resist at all costs![5]

Even though everyone in the family was at fault, Isaac was supposed to be the spiritual <u>head</u> of them all. He wanted peace at any cost. He didn't even ask a few simple questions when he suspected an impostor.

A Disappointing Ending

the big picture

Genesis 27:30–28:5; 35:23–29

As soon as Jacob left Isaac's presence, Esau arrived and learned that Jacob had already received the blessing. Isaac was shaken to realize what had happened. The only "blessing leftover" he could give was a disappointing prediction of Esau's future. Esau vowed to kill his brother. Knowing that, Rebekah convinced Jacob to go away to her family to find a wife.

Many years later, Jacob returned to show his wives and twelve children to Isaac before he died. Isaac died at age 180. Esau and Jacob, who had patched up their differences just a short time earlier, buried him.

Isaac physically trembled when he realized what had happened. From his perspective, the wrong son had been given the blessing. The blessing he would have for his favored son was a disappointment, for it included living in a more difficult terrain and Esau serving his younger brother's relatives. It must have broken Isaac's heart to know his favored son wouldn't receive great blessings.

Men today can also give a blessing to their children, even if it doesn't include a prediction of their child's future. Such a blessing should be a positive reflection of the qualities God has put within the child and an affirmation of the unconditional love the father has for his child.

go to

serving
2 Kings 8:20

strengthen your family

Chapter Wrap-Up

- Isaac was born after his parents had waited for many years. He was the promised child who would be the beginning of the huge family that God had promised his father, Abraham. (Genesis 21:1–7)

- Isaac demonstrated his faith in God and Abraham when he was offered as a sacrifice. (Genesis 22:1–19)

- Abraham sent his servant away to their relatives to find a wife for Isaac and the servant returned with Rebekah. When she came into the camp, Isaac was meditating on the Lord. (Genesis 24:67)

- Twins were born to Isaac and Rebekah. Isaac favored his son Esau, and Rebekah favored the other twin, Jacob. Such favoritism brought great conflict and sadness into their family. (Genesis 25:27–28)

- Like his father, Abraham, Isaac feared that the same king would kill him to steal his wife so he told Rebekah to lie and say she was his sister. (Genesis 26:9)

- When Isaac knew he would die soon, he told Esau to prepare a meal so that he could bless him. But that was not God's will. Rebekah and Jacob tricked Isaac into giving the blessing to Jacob. That made Esau revengeful. (Genesis 27)

Study Questions

1. What does Isaac's name mean? What is its significance?

2. What was Isaac doing when Rebekah arrived as his wife? What does that say about his character?

3. Why did Isaac favor Esau? What were the consequences of the favoritism?

4. Why did Isaac lie about calling Rebekah his sister?

5. How could Rebekah and Jacob have deceived Isaac in giving Jacob the blessing?

Chapter 4: Jacob–Deceiver Who Learned Dependence on God

Let's Get Started

Jacob can best be compared to the main character in Robert Louis Stevenson's Dr. Jekyll and Mr. Hyde. We see a side of Jacob that is conniving and manipulating. Next, we see a man planning, praying, and wrestling with his God.

Jacob, which figuratively means "he deceives," is an appropriate name. Jacob grabbed his brother Esau's heel at birth, and by the time he fled from home, he had also grabbed his brother's **birthright** and blessing. Throughout his life he continues to deceive others. God disciplines him for this behavior by allowing him to be deceived by others.

birthright
a special honor given to the firstborn son

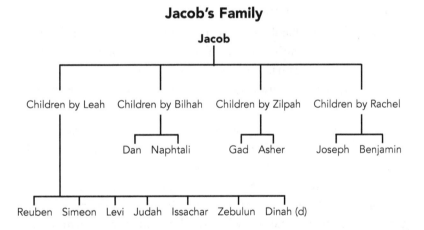

Jacob's Family

Jacob

Children by Leah   Children by Bilhah   Children by Zilpah   Children by Rachel

Dan   Naphtali   Gad   Asher   Joseph   Benjamin

Reuben   Simeon   Levi   Judah   Issachar   Zebulun   Dinah (d)

d = daughter. All others are sons.

As Jacob grows and matures, God forms him into one of the patriarchs of the Jewish nation and the Old Testament. We have much to gain from studying his life.

Early Beginnings Show the Heart

enemies
Numbers 20:14–21

supplants
takes the place
of another, by
treachery

the big picture

Genesis 25:19–34

After Isaac prayed for his wife, who was having a difficult time conceiving, she became pregnant, but it was a difficult pregnancy. God told her that two future nations were warring within her. The two "nations" were born and named Esau and Jacob.

Rebekah birthed twins who had made her pregnancy so uncomfortable that she prayed and asked God why. He told her, "Two nations are in your womb, two peoples shall be separated from your body; one people shall be stronger than the other, and the older shall serve the younger" (Genesis 25:23 NKJV).

In that culture, it was very unusual for the older child to serve the younger, but God was already setting up the future of the Jewish people. Esau's descendants would live in the land of Edom, which was located at the southeast border of Palestine. The Edomites would become one of the Jews' <u>enemies</u>.

When Esau and Jacob were born, Jacob followed Esau from the womb, grasping Esau's heel—as if to say, "I'm going to get you." The second twin was named Jacob because it means "one who takes by the heel," or **supplants**. Jacob grew up to fulfill the meaning of his birth name.

From the very beginning of Jacob's life, favoritism created strife and disunity. Jacob was favored by his mother, Rebekah, because he "was a mild man, dwelling in tents" (Genesis 25:27 NKJV). His father, on the other hand, favored Esau. He was "a skillful hunter, a man of the field" (Genesis 25:27 NKJV). Isaac loved the taste of wild game, so he favored the son who could provide for his own lusts.

Many years later, when Esau returned from hunting, he asked Jacob for some food. Jacob knew his brother's weakness and used it for his own advantage. He offered to feed him in exchange for his birthright. Esau was so hungry that he rationalized, saying his birthright would be no good if he were dead. He promised the birthright to Jacob and then enjoyed his bowl of stew. Even the finest, most expensive restaurant in the world doesn't offer a course that costs as much as this one did.

go to

work hard
Proverbs 10:4

deceit
Proverbs 12:20

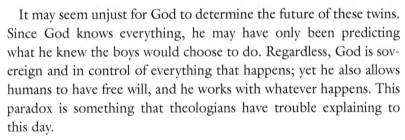
what others say

Herschel H. Hobbs

According to custom, the firstborn was to receive two-thirds of his father's estate, the younger getting only one-third. Furthermore, the older became the head of the family at the father's death. This involved not only family authority but also spiritual responsibility.[1]

Jacob wanted everything out of life he could get. Two rules guided his actions:

Rule One: Avoid work by scheming.

Rule Two: If conflicts arise, refer to rule one.

Our character and integrity never grow until we are deprived of what we want or we are required to work hard for what we have. If we cheerfully accept God's will when something is withdrawn from us that we want, we will develop true contentment. If we choose to work hard, we will develop a godly character that reveals our dignity. In contrast, when we take advantage of others, like Jacob did, the Mr. Hyde side of our lives shows others our ugliness and selfishness. Jacob would soon discover that deceit brings disunity and problems.

It may seem unjust for God to determine the future of these twins. Since God knows everything, he may have only been predicting what he knew the boys would choose to do. Regardless, God is sovereign and in control of everything that happens; yet he also allows humans to have free will, and he works with whatever happens. This paradox is something that theologians have trouble explaining to this day.

The birthright was the right of the firstborn male to be head of the clan. In Esau and Jacob's case, it also included being in the family line of Christ as God had promised their grandfather, Abraham: "In you and in your seed all the families of the earth shall be blessed" (Genesis 28:14 NKJV). Obviously, this birthright had great spiritual importance. When Esau treated it cheaply, it showed the awful condition of his heart. We should be careful lest something temporal take away our desire for spiritual blessings. No matter how important a temporal need seems, it's never important enough to sacrifice a spiritual blessing.

The favoritism of Rebekah and Isaac brought great pain into their family. If we favor one child over another, we'll also experience great

Something to ponder

strengthen your family

patriarchal blessing
the divine approval
of a father

pain. We won't love equally and our children will notice. They will pit the parents against each other, and their feeling of not being loved could create low self-esteem. Although we may naturally prefer the personality of one of our children, we must take steps to love each one with equal attention.

A Hairy Conspiracy

the big picture

Genesis 27:1-29

When Isaac planned to give Esau the blessing, Rebekah intervened and convinced Jacob to trick his father by pretending to be Esau. It took several props to pull it off (dressing up in Esau's clothing, putting an animal's hairy hide on his hands, and serving a cooked goat made to taste like venison), but Isaac was deceived and gave Jacob the **patriarchal blessing**.

Like mother, like son. Jacob's mother hatched a conspiracy to ensure he received the birthright. Even though God had promised this blessing to Jacob, she intervened and made it happen herself. Her willingness to deceive gives us a clue as to how Jacob sharpened his slick-tongued skills. What was Jacob's reaction to Mom's scheme? He only worried about getting caught. The immorality did not trouble him. The fact he would be lying to his father and the Lord did not concern him.

Here's the blessing Jacob received from Isaac:

- He would receive the dew of heaven, the fatness of the earth, and an abundance of grain and new wine.
- People would serve him.
- Nations would bow down to him.
- He would be the master of his brothers.
- His mother's sons would bow down to him.
- Those who cursed him would be cursed.
- Those who blessed him would be blessed.

Fear of getting caught has always been a motivation for keeping our behavior moral. We need to let this fear be a warning. Doing right and living in honesty have small price tags compared to the consequences of lying. Jacob got the blessing and the riches it brought, but paid a huge price for carrying out this dishonest plan. And he got caught: he had to flee from his own family.

God knows dishonesty is not good for us. The Bible gives us convincing reasons for being honest.

hates
Proverbs 6:17

God <u>Hates</u> Dishonesty

Benefits of Honesty	Disadvantages of Dishonesty
You will be trusted by others. (2 Kings 12:15)	Will be punished by God. (Psalm 120:4)
Truth lasts forever. (Proverbs. 12:19)	Shows a person's foolishness. (Proverbs 10:18)
God delights in truthful people. (Proverbs 12:22)	A dishonest person will be destroyed. (Proverbs 12:19)
Honesty gives a clear conscience. (Romans 9:1)	Wealth made through dishonesty won't last. (Proverbs 21:6)
With honest statements, you don't feel compelled to convince people. (1 Timothy 2:7)	Dishonesty reveals you hate people. (Proverbs 26:28)

A Cheating Heart Runs Away

the big picture

Genesis 27:30–28:9

After Esau discovered what had happened, he vowed to kill his brother. When Rebekah heard about this, she manipulated Isaac to send Jacob away to her own family to find a wife.

The price of Jacob's deceit was high. He fled from his own family and never saw his mother again. Imagine the fear of being "Mama's boy" and knowing your brother, the Super Hunter, has vowed to kill you.

Rebekah told Jacob to go to her brother's home and "stay with him a few days, until your brother's fury turns away, until your brother's anger turns away from you, and he forgets what you have done to him; then I will send and bring you from there. Why should I be bereaved also of you both in one day?" (Genesis 27:44–45 NKJV). Both of them thought the separation would be temporary and easy. They had no clue they would never see each other again.

We may think the consequences of our dishonesty will be insignificant, and therefore what we'll gain through our deceit will be worth

mocked
Galatians 6:7

know
Philippians 3:10

hope
Jeremiah 29:11

it. But God is not <u>mocked</u>. If we sow dishonesty, we'll reap the consequences.

Jacob Encounters God's Heavenly Ladder

the big picture

Genesis 28:10-22

Jacob left his home and set out for Haran, his mother's original country. One night, Jacob had a dream that changed his life. Because of it he vowed to remain loyal to God.

Esau took God for granted. Esau easily traded away the truly important things in life. But God could see Jacob was a man ready to <u>know</u> him. As a result, God unveiled his majesty to Jacob in a dream. He showed him a ladder that reached between the earth and heaven. Angels went up and down on it. God was revealing the spiritual realm that he wanted Jacob to experience.

what others say

Bruce H. Wilkinson and Larry Libby

Through the ladder, God is showing Jacob that there is no gulf between heaven and earth for the one who knows him. The ladder and the angels symbolize free access from the believer on earth to the Lord in heaven. The ladder is there; God is there. But the ladder must be used; God must be approached.[2]

Jacob's early life lacked faith, goodness, and grace. Many have wondered how he could be the one to receive promises and blessing. Throughout the Bible, God uses broken, imperfect, and selfish people and in spite of Jacob's past, God awakened a personal knowledge of himself within this deceiver. We, too, can walk away from our past because God can awaken a spirit of <u>hope</u> for our future. As we climb our own ladder of life, God can help us lean it against the right wall!

Jacob had been raised on stories of how his grandfather Abraham was delivered by God from difficult circumstances. He also heard about the personal relationship his father had with God. Until this point there was no evidence such a spiritual awareness existed for Jacob. But in this encounter with God, Jacob made his own commitment. God is not in a <u>hurry</u> to work in someone's life, and he <u>never gives up</u> trying to do that.

Jacob's spiritual heritage eventually paid off. As parents, we should share our own spiritual stories with our children because sharing will bear fruit. Any time, no matter what we're doing, we can make a spiritual application and <u>draw</u> our children's attention to God.

Love at First Sight

the big picture

Genesis 29:1-35

Jacob arrived in his mother's home country and quickly met a beautiful shepherdess named Rachel. It turned out she was the daughter of his mother's brother, Laban. He immediately fell in love with her and agreed to work seven years for Laban in order to earn the right to marry Rachel. But on their wedding night, Laban hoodwinked Jacob by substituting Rachel's less attractive sister, Leah, as the bride. Even though Jacob was angry about it, he agreed to serve another seven years in order to be the husband of Rachel. This was only the beginning of family troubles, because Leah could bear children but Rachel couldn't.

Jacob was a changed man. The desert experience with God had given him a new perspective on life. He walked into his uncle's territory with nothing but a fistful of promises—but that was all right. Within minutes of arriving at a well, he met his beautiful cousin Rachel. Jacob was smitten by the love bug. The problem? He couldn't pay the customary **dowry**, and no scheme or trick would work to win his new bride.

Laban negotiated the dowry to be seven years of Jacob's labor. Jacob agreed and 2,555 days later had earned the right to marry Rachel. But Laban didn't tell Jacob it was the custom for the older daughter to marry first. Laban slipped Leah, Rachel's sister, into the wedding tent. He tricked Jacob into another seven years of hard work. Jacob, the deceiver, received a taste of his own bitter medicine. God says that will happen to us if we "invest" in unrighteousness or crafty schemes. The "interest" paid on our investment will be unpleasant <u>consequences</u>.

hurry
Isaiah 5:19

never gives up
Philippians 1:6

draw
Deuteronomy 6:7

dowry
Genesis 34:12;
Exodus 22:16

consequences
Ezekiel 44:12

dowry
bride price

envy
sad about another's good

prolific
productive

barren
unable to conceive

compensate
make up for

strengthen your family

what others say

Herschel H. Hobbs

How this was done is not stated. Jacob must have been very drunk from the wedding feast. The bridal feast was literally a drinking feast.[3]

Just as God gives consequences for disobedience, parents should give consequences to their children for disobedience. Although it may be unpleasant and even inconvenient to discipline them, following through pays off with a better-behaved child and someone who grows up to appreciate our efforts and consistency. The Bible says, "No chastening seems to be joyful for the present, but painful; nevertheless, afterward it yields the peaceable fruit of righteousness to those who have been trained by it" (Hebrews 12:11 NKJV). God will allow unpleasant consequences for wrong choices.

Lots of Children and Lots of Trouble

the big picture

Genesis 30:1–43

Envy filled Rachel's heart because of her sister's **prolific** childbearing ability. In order to cope with being **barren**, Rachel chose an ungodly but culturally acceptable way to **compensate**. Rachel offered her maid to Jacob to bear children and it worked. But Leah did the same thing, and, as a result, Jacob began to have the many descendants God had predicted he would have. But it brought great family conflict. Jacob made plans to leave the area and be on his own—without Laban benefiting from the blessings that God had given Jacob.

Although the situation is slightly different from his grandfather Abraham's situation, Jacob should have thought of the conflict that resulted when Sarah used the same technique to have a baby. Jacob most likely heard the stories from his father, Isaac, about how Isaac's brother, Ishmael, was conceived through using Sarah's maid and how it brought great trouble to the family.

Jacob's twelve sons were the ancestors of the twelve tribes of Israel. The entire nation of Israel came from these men.

Jacob's Sons and Their Notable Descendants

Son	Descendant(s)
Reuben	none
Simeon	none
Levi	Aaron, Moses, Eli, John the Baptist
Judah	David, Jesus
Dan	Samson
Naphtali	Barak, Elijah
Gad	Jephthah
Asher	none
Issachar	none
Zebulun	none
Joseph	Joshua, Gideon, Samuel
Benjamin	Saul, Esther, Paul

From Deceiving to Working

the big picture

Genesis 31:1-55

Jacob ran away with all his wives and many children, along with the large flock he had amassed. When his father-in-law, Laban, heard about it, Laban chased him. Laban, the deceiver, then accused Jacob, another deceiver, of deceiving him. They eventually worked through their differences and Jacob left in peace.

The deceiver was now a worker. With God's blessings, he became wealthy even though Laban continually tried to siphon off wealth dishonestly. But Jacob went the extra mile to benefit his uncle. When his flocks were attacked, he took the losses rather than splitting them with Laban. He continued to work even after ten separate pay cuts. But God blessed him and his flocks began to multiply. God is in charge of who is successful financially and materially.

A life marked by doing more than expected, or going the extra mile, pays dividends even today. One caution: Our efforts should come from our heart, not grudgingly or greedily.

Terror and Wrestling

go to

fear
Isaiah 21:4

Genesis 32:1–32

Jacob left Laban and Haran behind and made his way toward his home country. Again he had an encounter with God in the night. This prepared him for the next challenge he faced: seeing Esau again after all those years. Terrified that Esau still wanted to kill him, Jacob prayed for God's protection and sent his family ahead of him in the order of the most loved at the back, where there might be protection. Jacob, left alone, had his third encounter with God, which ended with the dislocation of his thigh and being given a new name: Israel.

Every step Jacob took toward home was another step toward Esau's revenge. Jacob's relationship with God had become essential, and he prayed for deliverance and reminded God of the promises given his father and grandfather for success and countless descendants. He then sent his servants ahead with 550 animals as a present to his brother. Next, he split his family into two different groups to ensure that someone survived the coming attack.

Even so, Jacob was not merely fearful; he was terrified. How like God's provision that Jacob would come across an angel (which was the Lord himself) in the darkness of night. Throughout the night, they wrestled and a supernatural blow to the hip crippled Jacob. Just as the light of day broke, Jacob realized with whom he was wrestling. Jacob clung to his opponent, demanding a blessing. He emerged from that night a changed man, with a changed name: Israel.

Smith Wigglesworth

Jacob was not dry-eyed that night. . . . He knew he had been a disappointment to the Lord; he had been a groveler. But with the revelation he received as he wrestled that night, there was the possibility of being transformed from the supplanter to a prince of God.[4]

The darkness of <u>fear</u> often prevents us from clearly seeing God's best for our lives. God might have sent the fear so that we would wrestle with him. In that case, the fearsome circumstance will not fade until it has changed us. God always has a <u>purpose</u> for our good in the things we go through, even the darkness of fear.

Whew! Esau Got Over It

go to

purpose
Jeremiah 29:11

trust
Isaiah 41:13

faith
1 Corinthians 2:5

the big picture

Genesis 33:1–20

Jacob encountered Esau and was surprised to find that Esau no longer wanted to kill him. Instead, Esau welcomed him into the area and even offered to help. But Jacob refused and they parted company.

Jacob's prayer for deliverance from Esau's revenge was answered. Jacob speaks to his brother in humble terms and makes sure his generous gifts are seen as sharing a portion of the blessing he took with him originally.

what others say

Bruce H. Wilkinson and Larry Libby

God shows through the life of Jacob the bankruptcy of manipulating people to get your own way. Jacob had manipulation down to a science but it wasn't God's way. Jacob refused God's way, refused God's timing. In so doing, he refused God's best.[5]

When fear turns into worry, it makes us focus on the problem rather than seeing the opportunity for God's blessings. When Jacob was fearful, he couldn't imagine his brother could be at peace with him. For Jacob and for us, worry enlarges the problem and diminishes God's abilities. Instead, God wants us to <u>trust</u> him. <u>Faith</u> is the ability to look past the problem and focus on God's great power to help us.

key point

Sons Out of Control

the big picture

Genesis 34:1–31

Jacob's daughter Dinah visited the nearby people of the land and was raped by one of the men there named Shechem.

Shechem wanted to marry her but Jacob's sons wouldn't allow it. Instead, Dinah's brothers devised a plan to deceive the men of the country and kill them. Jacob was unhappy about their behavior but seemed **impotent** to control his children.

Jacob missed the opportunity to demonstrate real leadership after his daughter's rape. Justice was needed; however, Jacob was willing to compromise this evil by allowing the rapist to marry his daughter. He failed to take responsibility and exert leadership for his family. As a result, his sons hatched the plan to seemingly permit the marriage. Jacob should have known something was brewing. When his sons acted out their vengeful plan, the result was murderous bloodshed.

what others say

Gene A. Getz

Rather than dealing with his sons' murderous actions, Jacob was primarily concerned about his own status and welfare. Consequently, Jacob left the area of Shechem, traveled to Bethel and eventually Hebron.[6]

As leaders we need to ask the hard questions to ensure the mission and vision for our plans are followed with integrity. Usually those we are responsible for will not directly lie to us, but instead won't volunteer bad news unless directly asked. It is the leader's responsibility to ensure accountability by asking those questions, even if we know the answers will contain information we really don't want to hear.

Housecleaning

the big picture

Genesis 35:1–29

God appeared to Jacob and told him to go to Bethel. Because Jacob intended to worship God there, he told his family to rid themselves of all their idols and lucky charms. He arrived in Bethel with his large family and made an altar in honor of God. God, in return, again promised Jacob he would be the father of many nations. Rachel died there giving Jacob his last child: the beloved Benjamin. Isaac, Jacob's father, also died there.

When Jacob traveled to Bethel with his wife Rachel, he did not know she secretly possessed <u>idols</u>. Fortunately, he took a strong leadership position and ordered his household to get rid of their gods.

go to

idols
1 John 5:21

creating
Proverbs 19:3

what others say

Charles R. Swindoll

Waste no time in asking God to help you realize and remove any idols that are usurping His place in your heart.[7]

Many in his family gave Jacob their earrings, not because jewelry in itself was evil, but because in Jacob's day they were often worn as good luck charms. His family chose to cleanse themselves of all pagan influences, including reminders of any foreign gods of their old country.

What idols do you have? Idols are not just things. They can be jobs, desires, or thoughts. An idol is anything that is more important to us than obeying or loving God. Like Jacob, we should get rid of anything that can stand between God and us. If we don't, it can ruin our faith.

Deceived Again

the big picture

Genesis 37:1-36

Jacob again experienced deception, but this time, didn't know it. His sons sold one of their youngest brothers, Joseph, into slavery because they were jealous of Joseph's standing in the family. The brothers made it look like a wild animal had killed him. They smeared his coat with blood and showed it to Jacob. When Jacob saw it, he deeply mourned.

How many times must Jacob be subjected to painful trials? It happened over and over again because of the inner core of his family. His children were acting just like Jacob when he was young. But Jacob kept <u>creating</u> his own troubles through the favoritism he openly demonstrated to his son Joseph.

peace
Philippians 4:9

what others say

Gene A. Getz

In some respects Jacob knew his sons well. In other respects he did not know them at all. He understood their outward behavior, but he knew little of their inner feelings. If he had, he would not have set Joseph up for such a bad experience.[8]

A parent must consider each child unique and different. There isn't any one response that is appropriate for every child in every circumstance. What is appropriate for one may not be right for the other. However, trying to treat each child appropriately may cause siblings to accuse you of favoritism. The different ways we respond to each child need to be handled with great care.

It may be natural for parents to be drawn toward one child over the other because of a preferred personality or skills, but openly demonstrating those feelings without regard to the other children is damaging to the family.

Family Restored

the big picture

Genesis 42–46

Joseph ended up becoming first in command after Pharaoh in Egypt. When there was a famine in the land, Jacob sent his sons to Egypt to buy grain. They encountered Joseph, and he eventually sent them back to bring Jacob along with all he owned to live in Egypt. Jacob was thrilled to see Joseph again.

Imagine losing your favorite son. Things can't get worse, right? Never say that, because the next thing that happened was a devastating famine that made everything die. Faced with starvation, Jacob sent his sons to Egypt to buy food. When they returned, his youngest son had been held hostage. Reaching the end of his emotional and spiritual rope, Jacob heard God's command to go to Egypt. God reassured Jacob he would be with him and take care of him there.

Most of the time when God is leading us, he will give us an assurance of his will through the supernatural <u>peace</u> that accompanies his guidance. That doesn't always happen, but it can be a sign that he is indeed leading us. But we also need to make sure:

- The guidance we're hearing is in line with the Bible.
- It fits with the circumstances that accompany it.
- The direction has been <u>affirmed</u> as being from God.

affirmed
Proverbs 22:17

Retirement Home Found

the big picture

Genesis 47:1–31

Joseph introduced Jacob to Pharaoh, and he gave Jacob and his family permission to settle in Goshen where they could raise their flocks. Separated from the Egyptians, his family thrived and was not tempted to intermarry with them.

Playing out the last dramatic scene of his life, Jacob was an old man in Pharaoh's court. He had just been embraced by his lost son, Joseph, who was now the number two man in the most powerful country on earth. Jacob's clan had been delivered from the famine, and they had all the food they could eat. He told the pharaoh his years had been "few and evil" (Genesis 47:9 NKJV). Yet Jacob could tell a story of survival:

- God had delivered him from a family model of deceit and manipulation.
- When Esau threatened him, God protected him.
- When Laban tried to destroy him, God prospered him.
- God delivered his wife, Rachel, and family from idolatry.
- God saved his family from famine.
- God promised that his sons would be the patriarchs of a future land and leaders over their own tribes.

The Lord had kept his every word to Jacob.

what others say

Kay Arthur

When you need assurance that God is there, that He will keep His promises without changing—even though you have wavered in your promises to Him—run to your Jehovah. Trust in His name. It can't change because He can't change.[9]

God is <u>faithful</u> and consistent. He <u>never changes</u> or <u>forgets</u> to keep his promises. He can do that because he has the wisdom to promise the right thing and the power to bring it to completion. Just as he was faithful to Jacob, he is faithful to you.

Predicting the Future of the Tribes of Israel

the big picture

Genesis 48:1–50:3

When he was 147 years old, Jacob called all of his sons to him for the patriarchal blessing. He first prophesied over Joseph's sons and then over each of his own sons. Through God's power and insight, Jacob predicted the future of each of these twelve tribes of Israel. Then Jacob died and was buried.

Once a deceitful, independent, and conniving man, Jacob on his deathbed was now marked by total dependence on God. The transformation was complete. Jacob gathered his children and grandchildren around him for a final talk and blessing.

Jacob's life was a constant struggle. As troubles rolled over him, he drew closer to God. Can you trust God when trials are directed at you? Remember, it was the trials that proved God's faithfulness to Jacob. Expect no less in your life. "Many are the afflictions of the righteous, but the LORD delivers him out of them all" (Psalm 34:19 NKJV).

go to

faithful
Deuteronomy 7:9

never changes
Hebrews 13:8

never forgets
Psalm 111:5

Chapter Wrap-Up

- Jacob was born as a twin and demonstrated his true colors right from the start by grabbing his older brother's heel during birth. God declared to his mother that Jacob would someday be the heir to the birthright instead of Esau. (Genesis 25:19–34)

- Favoritism by the parents found each one manipulating circumstances. Jacob tricked Esau into selling his birthright for some stew. (Genesis 25:29–34)

- After Jacob and his mother deceived Isaac into giving Jacob the patriarchal blessing instead of Esau, Isaac had to run for his life because Esau vowed to kill him. (Genesis 27:1–28:7)

- Jacob arrived in his mother's homeland and immediately met and fell in love with Rachel, his cousin. He worked for seven years to gain her as his wife, but was deceived into marrying her sister, Leah, by their father, Laban. Jacob had to work another seven years to gain Rachel. By being married to both of them and their maids, he became the father of twelve sons. (Genesis 28:10–30:43)

- God prospered Jacob so much that he wanted to return to his home country. He left with his family without telling Laban. While running away, Jacob had an encounter with God and was renamed "Israel." His character had been changed. (Genesis 31–32)

- After reuniting with a forgiving Esau, Jacob settled down. He was deceived again when his sons sold their brother Joseph into slavery. Thinking Joseph was dead, Jacob grieved. Years later he found out Joseph was actually alive in Egypt. Jacob was reunited with Joseph and settled in Egypt, where he died. (Genesis 33–50)

Study Questions

1. Of their sons, whom did Rebekah favor and whom did Isaac favor? Why?

2. How were Rebekah and Jacob able to deceive Isaac into giving Jacob the blessing instead of Esau?

3. What explanation did Laban give for substituting Leah for Rachel on Jacob's wedding night?

4. What did Jacob's new name "Israel" mean?

5. Why did Jacob think Joseph had died?

Chapter 5: Joseph–Obedient Servant

Chapter Highlights:
- Joseph Is Sold into Slavery
- Joseph Interprets a Dream
- Joseph Reunites the Family

Let's Get Started

No one likes trials. They try our patience and make us wonder if God really loves us (or even likes us). Joseph, the great-grandson of Abraham, could have had those thoughts many times, because he was tested to the ultimate.

Joseph was hated by his brothers, sold into slavery, falsely accused of rape, and forgotten after giving good news. Time after time bad things happened to him, and he never did anything wrong. Talk about being misunderstood!

Yet, Joseph consistently trusted God, didn't complain, stayed pure, and forgave those who meant him harm. In the end, he summarized his life by saying God had it all planned out and meant it for his good and the benefit of many people. Talk about faith! Joseph had a lot of it, and we'll be inspired to have more of it as we learn about him.

wife
Genesis 29:25

given
Genesis 30:3

A Future Prime Minister Is Born

GENESIS 30:22–24 *Then God remembered Rachel, and God listened to her and opened her womb. And she conceived and bore a son, and said, "God has taken away my reproach." So she called his name Joseph, and said, "The LORD shall add to me another son." (NKJV)*

Jacob and Rachel had been married a long time, but Rachel hadn't been able to have children. Leah, Jacob's first <u>wife</u> and Rachel's sister, had given birth to many children and this caused Rachel to feel jealous. She'd even <u>given</u> her maid to Jacob so that she could claim to have children, but she'd never had the satisfaction of holding her own baby. Finally, Rachel became pregnant, and the favored child of the favored wife became a reality. That was Joseph.

Leslie Flynn

For twelve years he was not only the only son of Rachel, but the youngest of all Jacob's sons. He undoubtedly received a lot of attention, for with his half-brothers grown, father Jacob had more time to enjoy the little lad.[1]

key point

God always knows his purposes for everything he does and allows. He doesn't **capriciously** plan to bring harm or trials upon certain people for the fun of it. Instead, "I know the thoughts that I think toward you, says the LORD, thoughts of peace and not of evil, to give you a future and a hope. Then you will call upon Me and go and pray to Me, and I will listen to you. And you will seek Me and find Me, when you search for Me with all your heart" (Jeremiah 29:11–13 NKJV). Always, his intention is to draw us closer to him with everything he does.

Joseph, the Naive Dreamer

the big picture

Genesis 37:1–11

Jacob favored Joseph above his other children. That wasn't lost on those other sons. Joseph made the situation worse by voicing his dreams that symbolized his father, mother, and half brothers would one day bow down before him.

Young people often speak their thoughts without realizing the impact their words have on others. Joseph knew his father favored him. As a teenager he likely reminded his brothers of that fact. Who would mentor him toward maturity and gracious behavior? His brothers were older but wouldn't; they were angry because he was the one who was always right. His love of the Lord had caused him to tell his father about his brothers' immoral lifestyle. His heart was sensitive to the God of heaven and was appalled at the sin in their lives. But his report further angered his brothers.

His father, Jacob, was unable to mentor him because he was fueling the conflict with favoritism. Jacob just threw gasoline into the fire by giving Joseph a multicolored robe. This publicly signified that Jacob favored Joseph and intended to give him all or a larger portion of the inheritance.

go to

steadfast
1 Corinthians 15:58

speaking
1 Peter 3:15

affliction
1 Thessalonians 3:7

reproach
reproof

Allen P. Ross

God's sovereign choice of a leader often brings out the jealousy of those who must submit. Their actions, though prompted by the belief that they should lead, shows why they should not have led.[2]

Joseph might have contributed to his brothers' envy, but they had already rejected everything their father held dear. In that day, God-given dreams were synonymous with hearing the voice of God. His brothers only heard bitter complaints from each other—blocking out God's voice.

When our hearts are focused on the righteousness of God, some resent it. When we make known all that is spiritually dear to us, it may become a **reproach** to others. That shouldn't prevent us from remaining <u>steadfast</u> in godliness and <u>speaking</u> meekly of our faith. We know we will suffer <u>affliction</u> in this life. Therefore, we shouldn't stop telling what God has done in our lives; however, the apostle Paul recommends, "Let your speech always be with grace, seasoned with salt, that you may know how you ought to answer each one" (Colossians 4:6 NKJV). If we focus on bitterness toward another, we won't hear God.

apply it

Sold for Eight Ounces of Silver

Genesis 37:12–36

The jealousy of Joseph's brothers had increased to the point where they wanted to kill him. They saw their opportunity when Joseph came looking for them out in the wilderness. First, they intended to murder him, but because of Reuben's intervention, they decided to just leave him helpless in a pit. When a train of Midianites passed by, they saw the opportunity to gain some money, and they sold Joseph into slavery. The brothers put goat blood on his multicolored robe and presented it to their father. In great grief, Jacob assumed a wild animal had killed his son. In the meantime, the Midianites sold Joseph to Potiphar in the land of Egypt.

In obedience to his father, Joseph walked sixty-five miles to find his brothers. Even though he knew his brothers hated him, he went to find them because he wanted to please his father.

deceived
Genesis 27:16

Joseph was sold for twenty shekels, which is eight ounces of silver. Once Joseph was sold to the Midianites and then later to Potiphar's household, Joseph began not only slavery, but on-the-job training in maturity and graciousness. He must have wondered how the dreams God had given him squared with being an Egyptian's slave.

what others say

Billy Graham

[Envy] erodes through the soil of the soul, marooning the man who indulges in it on an island of selfishness. In the chemistry of the spirit, no sin is so devastating, no sin can so quickly mar the sweet fellowship between man and God.[3]

How ironic that Jacob was <u>deceived</u> by the goat blood. As a young man, Jacob deceived his father with goat fur to cheat his brother, Esau, out of a blessing. The tables are now reversed. "Whatever a man sows, that he will also reap" (Galatians 6:7 NKJV).

Favor Brings Power

the big picture

Genesis 39:1–6

Joseph served in the home of Potiphar, the pharaoh's officer and a captain of the bodyguard. Because of God's blessings and divine plan, Joseph had great favor with Potiphar and rose to the position of Potiphar's household manager.

Joseph brought success and wealth to Potiphar's home. His management skills were unsurpassed, and he was given control over everything. Potiphar trusted him completely. As Potiphar gave him more power, God blessed Potiphar with more wealth.

what others say

Gene A. Getz

It is clear that Potiphar understood that there was a direct cause-effect relationship between Joseph's devotion to God and his successful career as a servant in his household. Consequently, Potiphar looked very favorably on Joseph and promoted him.[4]

When God has a plan in mind that requires you to find favor and value in another person's mind, he can influence that person. Nothing is impossible for God to do—even changing someone's heart and mind. God knew exactly where he wanted Joseph to end up, and it was at the pharaoh's palace. The favor with Potiphar was one of the steps he was taking to make that possible. No one can escape God's influence, even Pharaoh's officer or a <u>king</u> himself.

king
Proverbs 21:1

<u>Run, Don't Walk</u>

the big picture

Genesis 39:7-23

Potiphar's wife was attracted to Joseph's handsomeness and purity, but when he rebuffed her sexual advances by running away from her, she accused him of raping her. Potiphar believed his wife rather than his servant and threw Joseph into jail. But even in jail, God gave Joseph favor. He became second in command to the chief jailer.

Joseph loyally served Potiphar for ten years. The temptation offered by Potiphar's wife was powerful and persistent. He tried to reason with her. He had a duty to Potiphar, and it would be a sin against God. Joseph tried to avoid this woman but ultimately had to run away from her. She struck back. If she couldn't have him, no one would.

what others say

Charles R. Swindoll

Lust is no respecter of persons. No one is immune. You're not. I'm not. And beware—lust never gives up. It never runs out of ideas. How do you handle such an aggressive intruder? Try this: When lust suggests a rendezvous, send Jesus Christ as your representative.[5]

The accusation by Potiphar's wife was likely intended to lead to Joseph's death. Such a betrayal of trust by a slave would normally mean execution. However, Potiphar must have had some doubts because he allowed Joseph to live. Even in jail, his managing prowess caused the chief jailer to promote him. The process started again.

flee
1 Corinthians 6:18

When Joseph first faced temptation he spoke against it. He let Potiphar's wife know that what she proposed was wrong because it would violate the trust her husband held for both of them. He also stressed that it would be an insult and offense to God. When temptation continued to pursue Joseph, he ran! Sometimes reason, prayer, and Scripture-quoting are not enough to make people stop tempting us. We must turn, not look back, and flee.

Don't Forget Me When You're Restored to Your Position

the big picture

Genesis 40:1–23

While Joseph was serving in the Egyptian jail, Pharaoh's baker and cupbearer were thrown into jail. They had dreams they couldn't interpret, but Joseph could. He predicted the baker would be hanged, but the cupbearer would be restored to the pharaoh's favor. Joseph asked the cupbearer to remember him when that happened because, he explained, he had been sold into slavery and imprisoned without just cause. Just as Joseph predicted, the cupbearer was restored; but he forgot about Joseph.

Another evidence of God's favor upon Joseph was his remarkable gift of interpreting dreams that no one else could understand. Joseph clearly sought to faithfully serve others, deriving his sense of significance from his relationship with God. And despite his incredible hardships, Joseph must have sensed that God was truly with him. Joseph's on-the-job training was painful, yet he remained faithful. God wants us to be faithful even when life isn't fair.

what others say

Patrick M. Morley

The difference in men is in how we go about satisfying our need to be significant. Some men, eager for the spoils of this life, pursue significance by gratifying only their own ambitions. Others, trained by the scriptures, find it by obeying God.[6]

Like Joseph, we often face troubles in our own lives that are unfair. Just when we think our heartfelt contribution will be graciously accepted, it is misunderstood and thrown back in our faces. In those times we are faced with a choice. Everything inside us wants to defend and explain our actions. Our hurt seems to take precedence and self-interest takes over. Joseph was more interested in God's interests. God was with him and gave him strength to persevere. It is no different for us. God promises to be with us and never leave us. When we can set aside our self-interest, we will walk with integrity.

apply it

Come—You're Going to See the Pharaoh!

the big picture

Genesis 41:1-36

Two years later, Pharaoh had dreams that his magicians couldn't interpret. The cupbearer then remembered Joseph and told the king about how Joseph interpreted his and the baker's dreams correctly. Joseph was immediately called to Pharaoh's presence and the king explained his dreams to Joseph. Joseph knew God was communicating something important to the pharaoh and gave God credit for being able to tell him the interpretation of the dream: seven years of bounty and then seven years of famine. Joseph also gave wise advice for managing the coming disaster.

Joseph put up with two more years of confinement in that stinking, rotten jail before God answered his prayer. Without Joseph's knowledge or influence, God reminded the cupbearer of his experience with Joseph. It was finally the right time for Joseph's deliverance and suddenly he was called before the pharaoh himself. Joseph must have been relieved but tentative. Was this another ray of hope that would turn disastrous?

what others say

Matthew Henry

Great gifts appear most graceful and illustrious when those that have them use them humbly, and take not the praise of them to themselves, but give it to God. To such, God gives more grace.[7]

Joseph took a great risk by speaking of Jehovah, the Hebrew's God, when Pharaoh didn't believe in him. Pharaoh could have scoffed at such nonsense and immediately thrown the Israelite back into prison. But Joseph's integrity remained intact, and he again faithfully told the truth as he had so many times before.

When bringing problems to others, particularly your superiors, give some thought to the solution. Be willing to offer your suggestions to resolve the issue. Ask if they would be interested in your opinion. This accomplishes four things:

- It dilutes the appearance of finger-pointing.
- It demonstrates your willingness to work as a team member.
- It shows respect for the other person.
- It allows you the opportunity to contribute to the success of the job or project.

From Prison to the Palace

Genesis 41:37–57

The pharaoh recognized Joseph's wisdom and godliness and made him second in command to manage food for the coming fourteen years. Additionally, Pharaoh gave Joseph the daughter of one of his priests in marriage and two sons were born to him. Just as Joseph predicted, the seven years of bounty arrived and then the seven years of famine. It affected all the known earth.

Pharaoh asked his advisers, "Can we find such a one as this, a man in whom is the Spirit of God?" (Genesis 41:38 NKJV). When everyone admitted no one was as wise as Joseph, Pharaoh promoted Joseph by:

- Giving him his signet ring
- Dressing him in expensive clothes and jewelry
- Naming him second in command
- Giving him permission to ride in the second chariot and receive everyone's adulation
- Presenting his daughter, Asenath, to him as his wife
- Giving him an Egyptian name, Zaphenath-Paneah

All this happened when Joseph was only thirty years old.

68 ——————————— The Smart Guide to the Bible ———————————

dwells
Romans 8:11

complete
Philippians 1:6

Merrill F. Unger

A seal is a portable instrument used to stamp a document or other article, instead of or with signing manually. The impression made therewith had the same legal validity as an actual signature, as is still the case in the east. Indeed, the importance attached to this method is so great that, without a seal, no document is considered authentic.[8]

Picture standing in front of the president of the United States. He points at you and tells his advisers that the Spirit of God is in you, then appoints you to a cabinet post. What an honor for you and God. The Bible tells us the Spirit <u>dwells</u> within us when we accept Christ. It is only when we yield our will and behavior to the Spirit that God will use us to influence others as he did with Joseph.

It took thirteen years for Joseph to go from slave to servant/ manager, then to inmate/manager, and finally to prince/manager. The on-the-job training was over and God was ready to <u>complete</u> his plan through Joseph. He had been faithful in all the little things he experienced throughout the long years that he'd been separated from his home and family. Now his integrity and faithfulness were paying off with great interest. God always rewards his children who serve him faithfully; if not here on earth, for sure in heaven.

The Testing of the Brothers Begins

Genesis 42:1–24

The famine also affected Jacob and his family back in Canaan. When they heard there was food in Egypt to be bought, Jacob sent his ten oldest sons to buy grain for them. When they arrived, Joseph saw his brothers and recognized them, but they didn't recognize him. (He would have been groomed in Egyptian fashions, including face makeup.) He accused them of being spies and put them in prison. Later, he released them, ordering that one of the brothers must remain to guarantee the other brothers would return later. Plus, the youngest brother must return with them if they wanted any future grain purchases. While there, the brothers became sorrowful for what they had done to Joseph many years earlier.

go to

dreams
Genesis 37:6–8

ambivalence
simultaneous
contradictory
feelings

What went on in Joseph's emotions when he saw his brothers? **Ambivalence**? Joy? Defensiveness? He must have been greatly suspicious when his full brother, Benjamin, wasn't with them. Had the brothers attacked—even killed—him too?

Since his half brothers did not recognize him, Joseph devised a plan to return the family to Egypt and test the hearts of his brothers. Joseph caused them to experience what he had experienced—prison, false accusations, and fear.

what others say

Leslie Flynn

Some argue that Joseph could have dispatched a messenger to tell Jacob that he was alive, but such news might have incited revenge by the father on the brothers. Also, didn't Joseph's dreams indicate his family would some day bow down to him? Joseph suspected that sooner or later the famine would drive the brothers down to Egypt to come knocking at his door for grain. Then he could seek reunion with his father.[9]

When the brothers appeared before him and bowed down to him as ruler, Joseph's <u>dreams</u> from many years earlier were fulfilled. The brothers had mocked him for his "foolish" notions of grandeur, but Joseph carried the confidence all those years that God's revelation to him would be carried out. And it was.

The Return Trip with Benjamin in Tow

the big picture

Genesis 42:25–43:15

When Joseph dismissed the brothers from Egypt, he kept Simeon imprisoned and put the money they paid for the grain back into their sacks. One of the brothers discovered it while returning home; the rest found theirs when they arrived home. They told their father about their experience and wanted to go back to get Simeon, but Jacob refused to allow his youngest son to be taken from him. Eventually, the grain the brothers brought from Egypt ran out, and they were forced to return. Jacob finally agreed to allow Benjamin to join them, but only after one of the brothers, Judah, guaranteed he would bring Benjamin home safely.

The insight, courage, and thoroughness Joseph put into his plan was remarkable. His arrangement of the money in the sacks guaranteed the brothers would feel the same kind of fear he had experienced when sold into slavery. The tables had turned. Suffering and conflict found their way into the lives of his brothers. Joseph used this opportunity to effectively bring them to a point of **repentance** with the threat of a spying conviction. The final exam was about to be administered. Guilt is God's way of motivating us to repent and seek forgiveness.

what others say

Patrick M. Morley

Men suffer for seven reasons:
- An innocent mistake
- An error in judgment
- An integrity problem
- The environment changes
- Evil happens
- God disciplines
- God tests.[10]

The brothers were being tested as Joseph had been tested over the years. Would they refuse to return to Egypt, sacrificing the brother left behind? When they found the money in their sacks, would they take it for themselves or report it to Joseph? They were beginning to make right choices. They were willing to return to Egypt with Benjamin, and they reported finding the money to Joseph.

Another Test

the big picture

Genesis 43:16–44:34

Back in Egypt, Joseph saw the brothers arrive, with Benjamin. Joseph commanded that they be brought to his home for the noon meal where he accepted their gift and asked them about their father. Seeing his blood brother, Benjamin, made Joseph cry, and he had to excuse himself. But after controlling himself he returned to finish the meal. Joseph dismissed all the brothers but arranged for one of his silver cups to be put into Benjamin's sack. When they had gone a short distance, Joseph sent his

father
Genesis 37:34

steward to intercept them, find the cup in the sack, and accuse Benjamin of stealing. This was a test of the brothers' loyalty to their stepbrother, something they'd lacked with Joseph. When they were brought before Joseph again, Judah demonstrated he had changed because he offered to become a slave in Benjamin's place.

When Joseph's servant made the accusation against Benjamin, the brothers were shocked. They tore their clothes in grief, the very thing their <u>father</u> had done when he learned of Joseph's bloodied coat. Judah, who promised Jacob he would be responsible for Benjamin, begged Joseph to take him as a slave in the place of the youngest brother. It had been Judah who suggested selling Joseph into slavery years before. Now he willingly sacrificed himself. There was no finger-pointing from any of the brothers. They didn't try to justify what had happened. God's plan to bring them to a point of submission, sorrow, and ultimately repentance for selling Joseph into slavery was effective.

what others say

Gene A. Getz

Joseph had no doubt instructed the steward to tell them before he conducted his investigation that whoever had the cup would become a slave and the rest were free to go. Twenty-two years before, there was no question what they would have done. And Judah would have taken the lead in suggesting that Benjamin bear the blame and become a slave. But their reactions this time were different. Together they returned to Egypt.[11]

We have sinned against God time and again. But each time God graciously forgives us if we turn from our sin. "As the heavens are high above the earth, so great is His mercy toward those who fear Him; as far as the east is from the west, so far has He removed our transgressions from us" (Psalm 103:11–12 NKJV).

Joseph's Shocking Revelation

the big picture

Genesis 45:1-20

At Judah's sacrificial offer, Joseph became emotionally overwhelmed and revealed himself to his brothers. He immediately

> tried to comfort them, knowing they would be upset with themselves over their past choices. He didn't want them to mourn past sins. He expressed his faith and knowledge that God had used their cruelty for the good of the people of the land by giving him the wisdom to deal with the famine. He told them to bring his father, Jacob, to him in Egypt so that they all would be safe in the remaining five years of the famine.

go to

cross
Matthew 27:38

salvation
Luke 1:77

sympathize
Hebrews 4:15

intercessor
Romans 8:27

stronger
James 1:2–4

Joseph told his brothers that God was behind all these events! "But now, do not therefore be grieved or angry with yourselves because you sold me here; for God sent me before you to preserve life. . . . So now it was not you who sent me here, but God" (Genesis 45:5, 8 NKJV). What a scene that must have been. Like a deer frozen in approaching headlights, the brothers probably stood with open mouths. They heard the words, but I doubt they grasped their significance. Even though Joseph kissed and hugged them, deep down inside they probably still feared him. Everything that happens to us is a part of God's supernatural plan.

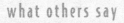
what others say

Max Lucado

> Because Jacob's boys are as greedy as they are mean, Joseph is sold to some southbound gypsies and he changes history. Joseph eventually stands before his brothers—this time with them asking for his help. And he is wise enough to give them what they ask and not what they deserve.[12]

As a symbol of Christ, Joseph represented how Jesus was willing to endure the great suffering of dying on a <u>cross</u>, knowing it was all part of his Father's plan for the <u>salvation</u> of the people of the world. It also gave Jesus the ability to <u>sympathize</u> with the temptations and difficulties that humans face. As a result, he is better able to pray for us as our <u>intercessor</u> before God's throne.

Remember: the ugliest, most painful, and most ragged spots in our lives can be changed into glory for God. The failures we face today are often the foundation God uses to build a positive impact in the lives of others. Rarely do we reflect on how the good times shaped our lives. It is always the trouble we walk through that makes us <u>stronger</u>.

key point

go to

share
2 Corinthians 1:3–4

comprehension
Isaiah 55:8–9

Moving Time

the big picture

Genesis 45:21–47:12

The brothers returned home and gave the amazing news to Jacob that his son Joseph was still alive. Jacob was shocked to find out Joseph was second in charge in Egypt, and overwhelmed with joy to know he would see his favored son again. Jacob took his family to Egypt where he saw Joseph again and rejoiced in God's blessings. Joseph arranged for his family to meet Pharaoh. Taking advantage of an Egyptian prejudice, Joseph ordered his clan to say they were shepherds. That way, they would live separately from the other Egyptians. The pharaoh placed them in charge of his own livestock.

Jacob moved everything he owned from the land he knew to Egypt. He saw Joseph, the son he thought long dead, for the first time in thirteen years. The fulfillment of God's plan was occurring just as intended. All that had happened was God's way of pulling his chosen people out of the land of the Canaanites, so he could grow them into a huge nation without evil influence. And grow they did! For the next two centuries the Israelites lived in Goshen while their population grew to about two million. God used Joseph's faithfulness and willingness to work for the greater good of others.

what others say

Philip Yancey

Through all his trials, Joseph learned to trust, not that God would prevent hardship, but that he would redeem even hardship.[13]

Although God can give instantaneous deliverance from the struggles we face, it is often his plan to have us go through pain and slowly learn ways of deliverance from the journey. As a result, we'll gain more and have something to share with others in their journey. God's ways are mysterious and sometimes beyond our comprehension.

A Drive Down Memory Lane

go to

sermon
Acts 7:13

Hall of Faith
Hebrews 11

review
Romans 15:4

the big picture

Genesis 47:13–49:33

Joseph continued to prove himself an effective and efficient manager, bringing great wealth into Pharaoh's administration as people from all over the world came to Egypt to buy food. Eventually, as the famine got worse, the people were forced to sell their land to Joseph. Joseph then rented the land back to them to farm it.

Canaan
the territory promised to Abraham's descendants; thus, "the promised land"

Before Joseph died, he requested that when his father's descendants returned to **Canaan**, his bones be carried back to be buried there. This confirmed his belief that the children of Israel would one day fulfill God's promise to Abraham that they would own a great amount of land and be a great nation of people.

Joseph was trained in pain. He was strengthened by deception and became patient through imprisonment. Troubles seemed to wash over Joseph most of his life. After all the affliction and his rise to power, he was faced with the emotionally painful challenge of testing and reuniting his family. Yet faith, skill, and integrity marked his life. God gave him favor and under the Lord's guidance, Joseph developed the character to persevere.

what others say

Edwin Louis Cole

Every man is limited by three things: The knowledge in his mind. The strength of his character. The principles upon which he builds his life.[14]

Stephen, one of the New Testament followers of Jesus, used an example from Joseph's life in his <u>sermon</u> to defend his faith before the Jewish High Council. Joseph is also mentioned in the <u>Hall of Faith</u> in the book of Hebrews. Just as Joseph's example of integrity and trust in God has inspired many through the ages, God wants to use our lives to represent him.

One of the keys for building our spiritual strength is to <u>review</u> how God has been faithful in the past. That will strengthen our faith and dependence upon him. The Bible is basically a record of God's workings and a revelation of his character. As we review what he did in the lives of biblical characters like Joseph, and then what he has done in our own lives, we'll become spiritually strong, knowing we can face any situation, just like Joseph did.

Chapter Wrap-Up

- Joseph's father, Jacob, favored him over his brothers. Joseph had a dream that indicated his father and brothers would bow down to him, and he told them about it, making the brothers jealous. (Genesis 37:3–11)

- All that favoritism poisoned the family relationships and created distrust, unhappiness, and anger. Without Jacob's knowledge, Joseph's brothers sold him into slavery for eight ounces of silver. (Genesis 37:18–28)

- From slavery Joseph rose to managing an important household. He was falsely accused of rape by his employer's wife and thrown into prison. While there, he interpreted the dreams of some of the pharaoh's employees, and when Pharaoh had a dream, Joseph was brought to the palace to interpret it. Through all the difficulties Joseph faced, he didn't complain to God. (Genesis 39–41)

- While in charge of Pharaoh's food program during a famine, Joseph saw his brothers come to buy grain. He tested them to make sure they had changed their attitudes. He engineered a plan that revealed that the brothers were willing to sacrifice themselves for each other. (Genesis 42–44)

- When Joseph knew they had changed, he revealed himself as their long-lost brother and restored the family by bringing everyone together in Egypt. After Jacob died, the brothers feared Joseph would take revenge on them. But Joseph showed his faith by telling them God meant everything that had happened to work for their good. (Genesis 45–47)

Study Questions

1. Why did Jacob love Joseph more than his other sons?

2. How did Reuben save Joseph's life?

3. What means did God use to bring Joseph to the attention of Pharaoh?

4. In what two ways did Joseph cause his brothers to come to a point of surrender?

5. When Joseph revealed himself to his brothers, what were they afraid of?

Chapter 6: Moses—Man of Humility and Strength

Chapter Highlights:
- Moses Saved
- Moses Meets God
- Moses Confronts Pharaoh
- Moses Leads the Israelites

Let's Get Started

Humility and strength are elusive yet important character traits that develop while we're not even trying for them. God performed that kind of development in Moses by taking him through many difficult trials. He had an encounter with God, was challenged to become a leader when he didn't believe he could, led a huge group of people who didn't want to follow, and communicated God's important Law to a skeptical, burgeoning Israelite nation.

Yet, in the midst of so many challenges, Moses stayed faithful and true. Of course, he had his ups and downs, at times feeling discouraged and even wanting to quit, but he was always willing to do what God wanted. Because he was more concerned about God's reputation than his own, God called Moses the most humble man on earth. What a distinction—one we all should shoot for.

serve
Exodus 1:14

From Death Row to the Palace

the big picture

Exodus 2:1–10

A Levite and his wife gave birth to a son, who, according to Pharaoh's instructions, should have been killed. But they courageously kept him hidden until he was too old to hide any longer. Moses's mother, Jochebed, put him in a basket and then into the Nile River. The pharaoh's daughter found him on the river and adopted him as her son, calling him Moses.

The Israelites in Egypt had grown to such proportions that they were perceived as a threat by their Egyptian neighbors. Therefore, they were put into bondage to <u>serve</u> as brickmakers and field hands. They continued to multiply anyway. To stop this, Pharaoh made a law that all of the male babies born to the Hebrew women must be killed. Abraham's descendants cried out to God to help them. That's why God raised up Moses.

what others say

Bruce H. Wilkinson and Larry Libby

At the age of 40, when Moses faced a major crossroads, the simple values instilled by his Hebrew mother when he was still a young child outweighed the influence of a prestigious education.[1]

Moses's mother, Jochebed, was brave in hiding her son and then trusting God enough to let him float down a river. After he was plucked from the river and made the son of the pharaoh's daughter, Jochebed became his wet nurse. We don't know how many years she had contact with him, but evidently she must have instilled in him some of her courage. Plus, she must have instructed him in the ways of the Lord because Moses <u>knew</u> he was really a Hebrew and not an Egyptian in his early years.

<u>**Courage**</u> is a sometimes subtle and elusive characteristic that can't be developed without having an opportunity to choose it. Courage grows only through facing danger or discouragement and then choosing to continue. Courage is developed as we face difficult choices.

go to

knew
Exodus 2:11

courage
Deuteronomy 31:6

courage
bravery in the face of danger

From Prince to Shepherd

the big picture

Exodus 2:11–25

Moses knew of his heritage. When he had grown, he tried to defend a Hebrew who was being beaten by an Egyptian. He killed the Egyptian and hid the body. Later two Hebrews confronted him about it; then Pharaoh tried to kill him. Afraid, he ran for his life. He ended up in Midian where he found favor with Reuel and married his daughter, Zipporah. In the meantime, the Hebrew people, the Israelites, were tired of being slaves to the Egyptians and kept asking God to deliver them.

go to

forty
Exodus 16:35

patience
1 Timothy 6:11

Privilege and power marked Moses's life. However, when he was faced with the brutal beating of a Hebrew slave, principle overcame preference. In that moment, his passion moved his comfort and position into secondary priorities. When he rescued the slave, Moses knew he put his preference for the palace on the line. But he wasn't quite ready to forsake that privilege and power. He tried to hide the evidence of his crime, hoping to maintain his lifestyle.

But when the crime was revealed and his life was in danger, Moses ran over three hundred miles to Midian. At a well there, he rescued several women from some aggressive shepherds. Those women turned out to be the daughters of Reuel, also known as Jethro. Moses married one of them, Zipporah. As a result, Moses began his family life as a shepherd, far from his destiny in Egypt.

what others say

Jamie Buckingham

Jethro, with warm, simple hospitality, helped the former prince of Egypt emerge from his shell of grief and self-pity and enter a world of preparation, a world designed by God to train him for the time he would return to Egypt for a far greater purpose.[2]

Moses's <u>forty</u> years in the wilderness taught him the topography of the land. It would be that very same kind of land that he and the Israelites would travel through during their forty years of wandering in the wilderness. The knowledge he had gained as a shepherd would be valuable. In the same way, the difficult things we learn as lowly employees later become the valuable information God uses to empower us as leaders.

Moses must have been discouraged when he ran for his life. But God had a bigger plan, unimaginable to Moses. In the same way, when you and I are discouraged and feel like we've let ourselves or others down, we need to have <u>patience</u> with God's pruning of our

something to ponder

character and skills. It takes time to become who God wants us to be. And God isn't impatient about doing that.

Sometimes we forget that our children need to develop slowly. We become <u>impatient</u> with their growth and maturity, thinking they should be like our neighbor's brilliant daughter or our brother's athletic son. <u>Comparing</u> our children to others won't encourage them to grow. We can't force it. All we can do is encourage them with praise and give them consequences for poor choices.

From Shepherd to Seeker

the big picture

Exodus 3:1–11

God unexpectedly appeared to Moses one day while Moses was up on Mount Horeb tending his flocks. God identified himself as he spoke from a bush that was on fire but didn't burn up. God told Moses that he had picked him to deliver the Israelites from their Egyptian bondage. Moses replied, "Who am I . . . ?" (Exodus 3:11 NKJV).

Moses spent his first forty years as a prince and the next forty as a shepherd. That made him eighty years old the day he walked toward the fire of the burning bush. Moses knew something **supernatural** was happening because the bush wasn't **consumed**. Through it, God revealed a portion of his glory to Moses. He told him to return to Egypt and deliver the Hebrews. Moses's reaction? He asked, "Who, me?" Moses immediately recognized even his princely training had not prepared him for this role.

impatient
Ephesians 6:4

comparing
Galatians 6:4

supernatural
something outside the normal

consumed
burned up

what others say

Bruce H. Wilkinson and Larry Libby

In this, Moses' second glimpse of God, he saw a God of grace. A God who not only remembered the anguish of his people back in Egypt, but also the discarded dreams of a discouraged servant. Moses had wanted so much to do something for God. Tried so hard. And failed so miserably. But God hadn't written him off as an impetuous bumbler—a hopeless case. Instead, he sent Moses to school.[3]

Jamie Buckingham

At the age of forty, Moses entered God's graduate school. The next forty years were spent in the deprivation of the wilderness. These were years in which his rough edges were sanded smooth. The literal blast of the furnace of the Sinai refined the character of a man God was going to use. There he learned to pray and learned the value of solitude. There, sitting with a few sheep and goats, he learned the principles of leadership.[4]

Forty years in Midian prepared Moses for this meeting. Forty years of relative obscurity had readied Moses for a change. Forty years of tending sheep had developed patience and meekness. Those are perfect qualities to lead a multitude for God. The prince turned shepherd was ready to depend upon something other than his own wits.

In the hard-charging world of business we hear little of building character traits like patience and meekness. Humility is not embraced by many. However, looking at the enormous job asked of Moses, it was a good thing that those traits were so ingrained they became foundational in his character. On this foundation the strong, confident, and bigger-than-life leader developed. It should be no different for us.

apply it

Not Me, Lord

Exodus 3:12–4:17

Moses was shocked that God had picked him to be the Israelites' deliverer. He argued with God that he wasn't qualified. God answered all his arguments patiently and insisted that Moses would indeed be the person he used.

Moses said, "Here I am" (Exodus 3:4 NKJV), but then he argued with God about how he chose to use him. Moses developed argument after argument against the very goal he'd originally wanted to see happen. Yet God was persistent and didn't give up on Moses. God did end up getting angry with him because Moses's final arguments were no longer out of fear but disobedience.

go to

faithful
Deuteronomy 7:9

How God Dealt with a Reluctant Leader

Scripture	Moses's Objection	God's Answer
Exodus 3:11–12	I'm not anyone special.	I will be with you.
Exodus 3:13–22	Who shall I say sent me?	Say, "I AM WHO I AM" sent you.
Exodus 4:1–9	What if they won't believe me?	Take your staff, and I will use it to perform miracles.
Exodus 4:10–12	I am slow of speech and slow of tongue.	I will teach you what to say.
Exodus 4:13–17	Send someone else, please!	Your brother, Aaron, will assist you, but you will do it.

Although it shouldn't make us feel free to argue with him, we can count on God being persistent and <u>faithful</u> as he works in our lives. But we'll be happier if we add to our "Here I am," an immediate, "I'll do whatever you say." Arguing will only make us miserable. Why not obey instantly and see God's blessings sooner?

what others say

Max Lucado

Do something that demonstrates faith. For faith with no effort is no faith at all. God will respond. He has never rejected a genuine gesture of faith. God honors radical, risk-taking faith.[5]

Stepping Out in Faith

the big picture

Exodus 4:18–31

Moses obeyed God, and, after informing his father-in-law of his intentions, took his family back to Egypt. On the way, God almost killed him because Moses hadn't yet circumcised his son. When he wanted to do it, Zipporah became angry and did it herself. As they continued traveling, Aaron met Moses in the desert as God had said he would, and when Moses explained what had happened, Aaron joined him to call the elders together. Those Hebrew leaders believed Moses's account.

God assured Moses that the pharaoh who had wanted to kill him was now dead. That may have given him more courage to go back. Moses asked for his father-in-law's permission to take his daughter and grandsons with him. Jethro agreed. As Moses traveled, God explained more of the plan that he had in mind. He said to Moses:

- You will perform miracles and wonders.
- I will harden Pharaoh's heart so that he won't let you go.
- You will say to Pharaoh to let the Israelites serve me.
- I will arrange for Pharaoh's firstborn son to be killed.

All those things happened.

sovereignty
Habakkuk 3:19

sovereignty
totally in control

what others say

John Hercus

Moses was to learn, but he hadn't then learned, that if God asks a man to do something, it is up to God to provide the equipment needed.[6]

When God said he would harden Pharaoh's heart, he was predicting Pharaoh's natural and selfish reaction. He would use that to give Moses an opportunity to perform miracles and thus have God glorified. God didn't remove the ability of Pharaoh to make his own decisions but he knows the condition of everyone's heart, including Pharaoh's. As the encounters between Moses and Pharaoh went along, God would then harden Pharaoh's heart so that further miracles could be done. Eventually, though, when God's purposes were fulfilled, Pharaoh's heart softened, and he let the Israelites leave. Everything that happens in Exodus and in all of our lives is controlled by God's <u>sovereignty</u>, while at the same time, he gives us freedom to make our own choices. It's a paradox no one can explain.

Crisis in the Desert

Many commentators are uncertain about the meaning of the experience when Zipporah circumcised Moses's son. But many agree that Moses became sick, and God revealed that it was because Moses had not circumcised his son. Since he was going to die, Zipporah circumcised the boy herself even though she didn't agree with the practice. She threw the boy's foreskin at Moses's feet, and that symbolized a sort of substitution: obedience for the previous disobedience.

One of the ways God empowered Moses was to assure him that the pharaoh who had wanted to kill Moses was now dead. God often deals with our real fears and gives us assurances of how he wants to help us. But if he has answered our fears, and we are being disobe-

go to

prediction
Exodus 4:21

dient, God usually isn't quite as quick to give us assurances. He just wants us to obey!

From Shepherd to Deliverer

Moses knew God had brought him before Pharaoh to deliver the

the big picture

Exodus 5:1–23

Moses and Aaron went to Pharaoh and demanded that God's people should be allowed to travel three days into the wilderness to sacrifice to their God. But the king didn't like the idea of the Hebrews leaving their work, so he refused and put even more strict requirements upon them. Now they had to find their own straw for making the bricks while keeping the same production quota. When the people's work increased, they blamed Moses, and Moses cried out to God. He couldn't understand why he was encountering obstacles to God's plan.

Hebrews from slavery. It was pretty heady stuff and he expected quick results. Moses marched up to Pharaoh, and in the name of the Lord, asked him to free the Hebrews. Shock and dismay swept over Moses when his intervention caused more harm to those he came to help. Not only was Pharaoh resisting him, but also his own people became angry and questioned his mission.

Moses's prayer to God demonstrated how he wanted a smooth deliverance and a quick fix to this problem. He couldn't understand why he'd encountered this glitch. He must not have remembered God's previous prediction. God had already told him that Pharaoh's heart would be hardened to the point that his firstborn son would be killed. That hadn't happened yet. To his credit, Moses did immediately seek God.

When leading others, sometimes your choices will make things worse. The results of discipline, cutbacks, and even dumb decisions will test your leadership resolve or weaken your confidence. The principles of obedience in Moses's leadership were momentarily overshadowed by this setback even though those principles had moved Moses to Egypt from Midian. When we suffer bad outcomes, we need to make sure our moral compass is still pointing toward the principles and values that honor justice, service, and integrity. If not, correct your course.

apply it

From Deliverer to Reluctant Leader

the big picture

Exodus 6:1-12

God replied to Moses's complaint that he was indeed God and in charge of what was happening. God confirmed that he would deliver the Israelites and take them to a new land. When Moses tried to tell the elders about it, they couldn't listen because they were so depressed. So when God told Moses to go back to Pharaoh, Moses again objected, saying he wasn't skilled in his speech.

God quieted Moses's complaints with detailed instructions on how to lead the children of Israel and deal with Pharaoh. Moses was devastated and his confidence weakened after his attempts to rally the Israelites failed. Moses wasn't the most articulate speaker and again pointed this out to God.

Losing hope creates spiritual deafness. Depression weakens our resolve and makes circumstances appear larger, darker, and more powerful than even God can handle. The Israelites heard a direct promise of deliverance, yet were unable to believe it. We must never allow circumstances to make us deaf to the Word of God. If we'll listen, God will tell us his plan. Our job is to stick to it.

Reluctant Leader Sends the Message

the big picture

Exodus 7:1-11:10

God reassured Moses that he would indeed use him even with unskilled speech, and Aaron would help him. God also explained that even though he would empower them, they would still encounter difficulties because God intended for Pharaoh to be stubborn. That way, God would receive greater glory as he performed miracles that would show his own great power.

Moses and Aaron began their effective ministry to Pharaoh with a string of ten miracles. One of them turned the Nile River's water into blood. With each miracle, the power and influence of God were revealed. Moses's reputation with the Egyptians grew while he led this miracle campaign. The Egyptians worshiped many gods and each miracle revealed how weak their gods were. Since the masses believed that Pharaoh was also a god, the miracles demonstrated his weaknesses. The ten miracles came after Aaron's rod swallowed Pharaoh's magicians' rods. This represented God's superior power.

Throughout God's work in the miracles, Moses maintained a consistent trust in God, going back again and again to Pharaoh to tell God's next judgment. Whereas he had been discouraged in the past when God's plan didn't bring immediate results, Moses had developed a strength that believed God was truly in control of everything that was happening. Here is a summary of the miracles and their meaning as God worked through Moses to bring Pharaoh to the point where he would release the Israelites.

The Miracles of Moses

Scripture	The Miracle	The Egyptian God(s) the Miracles Defeated
Exodus 7:14–25	The Nile's waters turned to blood and all the fish in it died.	Isis and Khnum, who were in charge of the Nile
Exodus 8:1–15	Frogs covered all of Egypt.	Heqet, the goddess of birth, who had a frog head
Exodus 8:16–19	Dust became lice.	Set, god of the desert
Exodus 8:20–32	Flies swarmed across Egypt, yet they didn't go into Goshen where the Israelites lived.	Uatchit, who is believed to be represented by a fly
Exodus 9:1–7	A severe pestilence caused all the livestock of Egypt to die.	Hathor and Apis, the fertility god, who had heads of a cow and a bull
Exodus 9:8–12	Boils broke out on bodies of both man and beast.	Sekhmet and Isis, who had power over disease and healing
Exodus 9:13–35	Hail destroyed everything that was ready to be reaped, along with trees and plants. There wasn't any destruction in Goshen.	Nut (sky), Osiris (crops), and Set (storms)
Exodus 10:1–20	Locust swarms ate everything left by the hail.	Nut (sky) and Osiris (god of crops and fertility)
Exodus 10:21–29	Darkness covered all of Egypt for three days so thickly that no one would move.	Re, the sun god

The Miracles of Moses (cont'd)

Scripture	The Miracle	The Egyptian God(s) the Miracles Defeated
Exodus 11:1–10	The firstborn son of every Egyptian household died, including the Pharaoh's son.	Isis, goddess who protected children and Pharaoh's own firstborn son, who was regarded as a god.

(Chart adapted from *The Bible Knowledge Commentary*.[7])

what others say

Charles R. Swindoll

The attack on the Nile struck even deeper at Egypt's spiritual roots. The Nile god, Hapi, was their supreme deity, and the Egyptians, including Pharaoh, often came to the river to worship him. By turning this life source into a bloody stream of death, the Lord stated unequivocally that He was superior to Egypt's greatest deity.[8]

The most important purpose of these miraculous plagues was revealed when God said, "My signs . . . I have done among them, that you may know that I am the LORD" (Exodus 10:2 NKJV). God yearns for relationship with his creation. Miracles and deliverance throughout history are evidence of his efforts to reach out to mankind. Though the deliverance of the Hebrews was mighty, God's greatest act of deliverance came fourteen hundred years later when he allowed Jesus Christ to die on our behalf. When God does miracles, they are intended to reveal him as Sovereign God.

Moses had become strong in his faith and endurance because of the trials he had faced. God wants us to experience the same thing— even to the point of looking positively on our struggles. "My brethren, count it all joy when you fall into various trials, knowing that the testing of your faith produces patience. But let patience have its perfect work, that you may be perfect and complete, lacking nothing" (James 1:2–4 NKJV).

something to ponder

Death and Deliverance

the big picture

Exodus 12:1–13:16

Even though God caused the firstborn sons of the Egyptians to die, he spared the Israelites' homes when they obeyed him and

Passover
when God "passed over" the Hebrew homes and spared their firstborn sons

shedding
pouring forth in a stream

performed the **Passover** feast. Each family sacrificed a lamb and covered the doorposts of their houses with the lamb's blood. Additionally, they performed a ceremony of eating unleavened bread and other food in a specific way. These ceremonies became a festival the Israelites celebrate to this day.

When Pharaoh realized his own son and the firstborn sons of all the Egyptians had died, he allowed the Israelites to leave Egypt. The Israelites quickly packed up everything and left Egypt, bringing along some who weren't Hebrews. God gave Moses further instructions about the Passover and how he wanted it to remind them of what God had done in delivering them from their bondage.

The Hebrews were to kill a male lamb that was one year old and put its blood on two doorposts of each home. Then they were to eat the meat with unleavened bread and bitter herbs. They were to dine with all their clothes on—ready for the deliverance God was about to do. The blood on the doorposts caused God's Spirit to "pass over" those homes when God's judgment of death for the firstborn sons in the Egyptian homes came through the towns.

Not only did God give the Hebrews instructions for fleeing from Egypt, but the instructions included future observance of the Passover Festival. They were instructed to celebrate it every year as a memorial of God's great work on their behalf. Moses made sure the Israelites followed God's command both then and in the future.

The use of blood on the doorposts and the Passover celebration all pointed to the coming Messiah, who would shed his blood for the sins of the world. That is why Jesus is called the "Lamb of God." "According to the law almost all things are purified with blood, and without **shedding** of blood there is no remission" (Hebrews 9:22 NKJV). Jesus shedding his blood on the cross made our forgiveness possible.

Leader Challenged Again

Exodus 13:17–14:31

Moses led the Israelites out of Egypt, but Pharaoh changed his mind and tried to catch them at the Red Sea. It looked like the

> Israelites were trapped. God directed Moses to use his staff to divide the waters of the Red Sea. The Israelites crossed over on dry ground. The Egyptians tried to follow, but they drowned when the waters covered them. The Israelites were again saved.

Two million people were trapped between the Red Sea and the Egyptian army. Duty pressed the Egyptian army forward, but fear and loathing filled most of their hearts. During the past nine months, ten different miracles had convinced these Egyptians that the God of Abraham, Isaac, and Jacob was the Hebrews' protector. The facts were clear to them. Their belief was echoed by the fear in their hearts.

The Hebrews were also filled with fear as they looked one way and saw the Red Sea and then looked the other way and saw the dust of the massive army closing in. Unlike the Egyptians, they forgot God's miracles and angrily confronted Moses. Fear feeds on forgetfulness. Remember God's past faithfulness. Imagine the many times he had proved God was with them. Once more his own people turned against him. Moses spoke up and told them, "Do not be afraid. Stand still, and see the salvation of the LORD, which He will accomplish for you today. For the Egyptians whom you see today, you shall see again no more forever. The LORD will fight for you, and you shall hold your peace" (Exodus 14:13–14 NKJV). As soon as we start fearing, like the Israelites, we are replacing our faith in God with doubt.

The importance of Moses's years of humbling in Midian becomes evident, as time and again Moses is the focus of attack. His patience can be explained only as God-inspired. All leaders must be prepared for the criticism, judgment, and anger from those following them. It will come. Just like a toad in a hailstorm, we will have to dodge those missiles of critical comments. To have the strength that Moses had, we need to realize that the comments are not usually personal, but reflect the discomfort of the people.

The Challenges Never Stop Coming

the big picture

Exodus 15:1–40:38

When Moses and the sons of Israel saw God's deliverance in another miraculous way, they composed a song of praise to

God. The women joined them in singing and by playing the tim-
brel and dancing. Everyone rejoiced because they were finally
set free from their bondage in Egypt. Moses continued to lead
the Israelites toward the land that God had promised them, a
land with "milk and honey." As they traveled, they encountered
many difficulties that were trials sent by God to make them seek
him and depend upon him. Because of that, Moses, as their
leader, was challenged over and over again. Each time he asked
God for guidance. God always helped him to deal with each situation. During this time in the desert, God also delivered the
Ten Commandments to Moses on Mount Sinai (see Illustration
#7).

Illustration #7
Map of Wilderness
Wanderings—When
the Israelites left
Mount Sinai they
traveled to Kadish
Barnea, where they
rebelled against
God. After wander-
ing in the desert for
thirty-eight years
they traveled north
to the plains of
Moab. There, just
across the Jordan
River from the
Promised Land,
Moses reviewed
God's law.

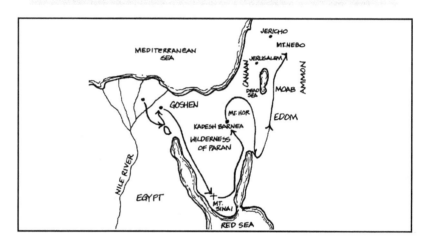

As the Israelites traveled, they weren't a happy group. They complained and blamed Moses for everything. They were unhappy when
they didn't have water or food, and they disobeyed God repeatedly.
Yet, Moses stayed consistently faithful in representing God and
responding to the people with patience and humility. He resisted
taking on the responsibility that only God could shoulder. That's
hard to do. If he hadn't resisted, he would have shifted the focus off
God and onto himself.

what others say

Max Lucado

I know what it's like to set out to serve God and end up serving self. I've spoken to conference audiences about the sufferings of Christ and then gotten frustrated that the hotel
room wasn't ready. It's easy to forget who is the servant and
who is to be served. Satan knows that. This tool of distortion
is one of Satan's slyest.[9]

As the Israelites traveled, God communicated with Moses and gave many guidelines for his people, who would occupy the future land of Israel. In each case, Moses passed those rules along to the people clearly and honestly.

I Want to Quit, Now!

Numbers 11:1-15

The Israelites continued to travel, and they easily slipped into a negative mind-set when they weren't comfortable or happy. In this instance, God disciplined them with a fire that only stopped when Moses prayed. After that, those who weren't Israelite by birth created problems when they affectionately recalled (no doubt with some exaggeration) the different foods that were available to them back in Egypt. They had grown tired of eating the wonderful sweet manna, which God provided daily. Moses also grew tired—tired of the complaints of God's people. He even asked God to kill him so that he wouldn't have to deal with it anymore.

It's hard to understand why the Israelites continued to be so unhappy. All their physical needs were met by God's direct provision. They were marching to the Promised Land. They could remember miracle upon miracle where God had freed and delivered them, and lit their path. Everything God had promised came true, yet still they grumbled. As a result, Moses was sick of the whining, sniveling malcontents he was leading. He wanted to die rather than lead this ungrateful mob one more step. The only thing that had changed was Moses; the people had grumbled all along. He had hit a dead end (see Illustration #7).

Oswald Chambers

We may have a vision of God, a very clear understanding of what God wants—wrongs to be righted, the salvation of sinners, and the sanctification of believers; we are certain we see the way out, and we start to do the thing. Then comes something equivalent to the forty years in the wilderness: discouragement, disaster, upset, as if God has ignored the whole thing. When we are thoroughly flattened out, God comes back and revives the call.[10]

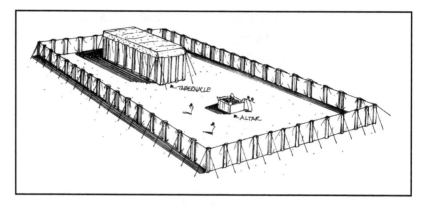

Moses cried out to God (Numbers 11:10–15). His discouragement had the common symptoms of burnout and depression:

- Exaggerating the problem
- Blaming God
- Taking responsibility for something that he shouldn't
- Thinking he is responsible to provide for the people
- Focusing on himself
- Forgetting who God is
- Forgetting God's original purpose, provision, and promises

Moses was ready to remove the mantle of leadership that God had given him. He even wanted to die. But God wouldn't allow it. And at times, a leader wants to give up and resign from his position. But if that's not God's will, he shouldn't. Instead, by seeking God as Moses did, he will find God's renewed <u>strength</u>.

Most Humble on Earth

strength
Philippians 4:13

the big picture

Numbers 12:1–16

Miriam and Aaron, Moses's sister and brother, also began to complain. They were dissatisfied with Moses's leadership because they were jealous that he was in control and honored. God corrected them in person and caused Miriam to have a skin disease that required her to be in solitude outside the camp. She was healed only when Moses prayed for her healing.

Throughout all the trials and troubles of the past, Aaron and Miriam, Moses's brother and sister, had stood at his side. Aaron was the high priest and Miriam a prophetess. They were both joint-commissioners with Moses for the deliverance of Israel. Yet, these trusted siblings and co-laborers chose to criticize Moses's wife instead of dealing with the real issue—their jealousy. God reacted immediately because the core of his leadership team was about to come apart. This affront demonstrated poor character and poor role modeling because this team led a people who were disposed to rebellion. He brought all three together and spoke of his special relationship with Moses. Then he dealt with Aaron and Miriam.

go to

golden calf
Exodus 32:4

what others say

Gene A. Getz

Moses' response to this false criticism immediately revealed who was right and who was wrong. Self-defense is not necessarily wrong, but there are times when it's better to let the truth win out in other ways. Because of his humility and meekness, he did not try to justify himself or to put his brother and sister down.[11]

Moses had boldly defended the honor of God during the golden calf incident. But in this incident, Moses reacted mildly when his own character was attacked.

"Seek the LORD, all you meek of the earth, who have upheld His justice. Seek righteousness, seek humility. It may be that you will be hidden in the day of the LORD's anger" (Zephaniah 2:3 NKJV). Moses was content to battle for the Lord's honor but let his own honor rise or fall on its own merits. Real strength of character is demonstrated when we spend more time building up others, rather than defending ourselves.

Keep on Keeping On

the big picture

Numbers 13–36

Moses faithfully guided the Israelites toward the Promised Land even though they disobeyed God many times. They should have immediately gone into the Promised Land, but because of their lack of faith in God's power, they were destined to wander for 40 years in the wilderness. During the wandering, Miriam and Aaron died. Moses continued to lead alone, even though originally he feared he could not.

Just before entering the Promised Land, Moses sent twelve leaders into the area to spy out the territory. Ten of them returned with scary tales of giants. The Hebrews grew fearful and had a great meeting where they talked about getting a new leader. Moses and Aaron fell on their faces and only two of the spies, Joshua and Caleb, spoke against the rebellion and challenged the crowd to enter the Promised Land. Their words fell on fearful, deaf ears. The crowd talked of stoning them. Only God's intervention once again saved the faithful few. For their unbelief, God promised that the rebellious adults would never enter the Promised Land. They would die in the desert.

key point

If anything should be remembered about Moses, it's that he persevered! He was a faithful servant of God who was more interested in God's reputation than his own. Even though the Israelites continued to rebel, Moses kept going, until the very end.

Sit Down for Some Long Sermons

the big picture

Deuteronomy 1–34

This book of the Bible is a record of three sermons that Moses gave to the Israelites as they prepared to enter the Promised Land of Canaan. Because all the Israelites who had started out from Egypt had died, a new generation was entering the land God had promised to Abraham so many years earlier. Moses's three sermons reminded that new generation of what God had done in the past, what God expected of the Israelites, and what God wanted to do in the future.

The unfaithful parents of those about to enter Canaan were gone. Moses was faithful to the end and in his final acts as a leader, reminded the Hebrews of God's mighty deeds and the covenant obligations.

Moses's Three Sermons in Deuteronomy

Scripture	Sermon Topic
Deuteronomy 1:1–4:43	A reminder of what God had done in the past
Deuteronomy 4:44–26:19	A review of the laws God expected the people to keep in the new land
Deuteronomy 27:1–34:12	A revelation of what God promised to do for Israel in the future

An outline of Moses's last words to the Israelite people:

Moses's Final Comments

Scripture	Final Comment
Deuteronomy 31:1–30	A final challenge to the Israelites
Deuteronomy 32:1–43	A final song of praise to God
Deuteronomy 33:1–29	A final blessing of the tribes of Israel

what others say

Gene A. Getz

Perhaps the greatest lesson we can learn from Moses' final days is that a person never gets too old to fail. Therefore we must be on guard against Satan and his subtle attacks at all times.[12]

It has been said Moses spent forty years in Pharaoh's court, learning he was somebody. Then he spent forty years in Midian, learning he was nobody. Finally he spent the last forty years of his life learning what God can do with a somebody who finds out that he is a nobody.

God called Moses his faithful servant and a friend. Moses the lawgiver and leader of a nation also modeled a type of Christ. Look at the parallels in their lives in the following chart.

Similarities Between Moses and Jesus

Similarity	Moses	Jesus
Threatened as infants	Exodus 2:2	Matthew 2:14
Tempted by but overcame evil	Exodus 7:11	Matthew 4:1
Controlled the sea	Exodus 14:21	Matthew 8:26
Fasted for 40 days	Exodus 34:28	Matthew 4:2
Fed a multitude	Exodus 16:26	Matthew 14:20
Radiant face	Exodus 34:35	Matthew 17:2
Endured grumbling	Exodus 15:24	Matthew 7:2

Similarities Between Moses and Jesus (cont'd)

Similarity	Moses	Jesus
Discredited at home	Numbers 12:1	John 7:5
Mighty men of prayer	Exodus 32:32	John 17
Spoke as oracles of God	Deuteronomy 18:18	John 7:46
Had 70 helpers	Numbers 11:16	Luke 10:1
Established memorials	Exodus 12:14	Luke 22:19
Reappeared after death	Matthew 17:3	Acts 1:3

The traits of Moses's life are rarely found in today's leaders. There are plenty of confident and powerful leaders who feign humility, but their motives are so evident that nobody believes their false modesty. It is difficult to fake humility. Just as courage springs spontaneously from the heart, humility flows freely because it represents an inward commitment that transforms the outward behavior.

Chapter Wrap-Up

- Moses's life was in danger as soon as he was born because all Hebrew boys were to be killed. His mother, Jochebed, had great faith in God, and rather than see him die, she put him in the river in a basket. Downstream, he was found by Pharaoh's daughter and adopted as a prince of Egypt. (Exodus 2:1–10)

- Moses killed an Egyptian who was attacking an Israelite and then ran away because Pharaoh wanted to kill him for it. Moses became a shepherd with the Midians and in the solitude of the desert, God prepared him for future leadership. (Exodus 2:11–22)

- God appeared to Moses in a burning bush and told him he would deliver the Israelites out of their Egyptian bondage. Even though Moses argued, God won and Moses agreed to lead the Israelites. Moses learned God could enable him. (Exodus 3–4)

- Moses performed many miracles in God's power in order to convince Pharaoh to release God's people from their bondage. When Pharaoh finally let the Israelites leave Egypt, Moses led them through the desert and Moses had to constantly use God's power to keep them in line. (Exodus 5–18)

- The people rebelled against going into the Promised Land, so Moses had to lead the Israelites around in the wilderness for forty years until the unbelieving generation died out. God entrusted Moses with his Law for the people to follow, starting with the Ten Commandments. (Exodus, Leviticus, Numbers, and Deuteronomy)

Study Questions

1. Why did Moses run away from being a prince in a palace?

2. What were some of the objections Moses gave for not wanting to become Israel's deliverer?

3. What are some of the miracles God did to deliver the Israelites from the Egyptians?

4. When Moses was burned out and wanted to quit what solutions did God provide?

5. How did Moses show his humility when God struck Miriam with leprosy?

Chapter 7: David—Man After God's Own Heart

Let's Get Started

David, an ordinary shepherd, was chosen by God to be king of Israel. Saul, the current king, had disobeyed God. Therefore, even before Saul died—which was the usual way a king was replaced—God directed the prophet Samuel to anoint David as the new king. David was a gifted king. But he was not a perfect man. He lied, committed adultery, and murdered. He was responsible for the suffering of many people. Still, God used him in incredible ways, and the Scriptures ensure he'll always be remembered as a man <u>after God's own heart</u>.

go to

after God's own heart
Acts 13:22

Bad King, Good Shepherd

the big picture

1 Samuel 16

Because the first king of Israel, Saul, had displeased God so greatly, David was chosen by God to replace him (see Illustration #9). God directed his prophet, Samuel, to anoint David king even though the shepherd boy's appearance and stature were not kingly looking. Saul became emotionally unbalanced. David was called to the palace to play his harp to calm him. Saul, not knowing of David's anointing, delighted in David and assigned him as the king's own armor bearer.

Saul, who physically was a superior man, made a poor king. Anger, depression, and open disobedience to God marked his reign.

God sent a message to Saul through the prophet Samuel. "You have done foolishly," Samuel said. "You have not kept the commandment of the LORD your God, which He commanded you. For now the LORD would have established your kingdom over Israel forever. But now your kingdom shall not continue. The LORD has sought for Himself a man after His own heart, and the LORD has commanded him to be commander over His people, because you have not kept what the LORD commanded you" (1 Samuel 13:13–14 NKJV).

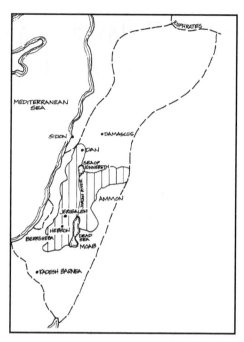

Illustration #9
Israelite Territory Before and After David's Reign—King David expanded Israel's borders to give his people ten times as much land as they occupied when Saul became king. The striped area of land indicates the extent of Israel's kingdom before David's reign. The dashed line indicates the extent of Israel's kingdom at the end of David's reign.

The prophet Samuel was sent to David's family home to pick out the next king. He looked at each of David's impressive brothers, but God said, "Do not look at his appearance or at his physical stature, because I have refused him. For the LORD does not see as man sees; for man looks at the outward appearance, but the LORD looks at the heart" (1 Samuel 16:7 NKJV). It turned out that David was "ruddy, with bright eyes, and good-looking" (1 Samuel 16:12 NKJV), but appearances didn't interest God. He looked into David's heart.

David, the youngest son in the family of Jesse, trained in solitude to be a king. While tending sheep in the isolated plains and mountains, this musician, songwriter, and godly man developed a heart for God. His psalms of praise scattered throughout the book of Psalms reflect a man who longed for God. His songwriting and musical skills brought him to the palace as Saul's harpist.

David's isolation was used to build his spiritual life. To know God's heart, we must spend time alone with him. Although corporate worship in our church is great and fellowship with other Christians is encouraging, time alone with God is essential. It's in the times of being <u>still</u> and focusing on him that our hearts get to know him best.

still
Psalm 46:10

He Is Too Big to Miss

go to

ridiculed
1 Samuel 17:33

the big picture

1 Samuel 17

David's father sent him to check on his brothers who were at the battlefront in Israel's fight with the neighboring Philistines. When David arrived, he found the battle was at a stalemate because the Philistine giant, Goliath, had challenged the Israelite army to fight him. David couldn't understand why his countrymen were so afraid. He used his slingshot and killed Goliath with a single stone (see Illustration #12). As a result, the Israelites were victorious in the battle.

The solitude that surrounded David's early life also taught him responsibility and gave him courage. As a shepherd, it was necessary to protect the flock from predators. Standing toe-to-toe alone with a lion put steel into the backbone of this little shepherd. One sage said, "Not the size of the dog in the fight, but the size of the fight in the dog determines the outcome."

what others say

F. B. Meyer

You may have nothing in the outward semblance, nothing in your surroundings or circumstances, to indicate the true royalty within; but if you bare your heart to God, you shall stand revealed as his son, as a priest and king unto himself.[1]

King Saul was a seasoned warrior, and he was taller than most Israelites. He should have been the man to face Goliath. When David offered to fight Goliath, Saul ridiculed David because of his size and youth.

As a leader, it is your responsibility to encourage and challenge those who are under your leadership. If you belittle the faith or courage or vision of your "troops" like Saul did David, you may find they lack courage and the ability to think for themselves. When facing fearful giants in our lives, we normally draw upon our experience. Take a lesson from David and remember our real strength comes from knowing Whose we are, rather than what we are.

apply it

Illustration #10
How Tall Was Goliath?—At six cubits and a span, Goliath was over nine feet tall!

Illustration #11
What Did a Sling Look Like?—It looked like a doubled rope with a leather pocket in the center.

Illustration #12
How Heavy Were Sling Stones?—Sling stones found on Israelite battlefields were the size of tennis balls.

strengthen your family

Don't belittle your children for their awkwardness, sports inability, struggle with academics, or tender heart. You may crush their spirits and make them fear trying new things. If you give them the feeling that they can never please you no matter how much they try, they'll give up trying.

Spears Keep Whizzing by My Head

the big picture

I Samuel 18–24

When introduced to King Saul as Goliath's conqueror, David met Saul's son, Jonathan, and they became best friends. Everyone in the country heard about David's courage, and they lifted him up in song as a great hero, even above Saul. That made Saul so jealous that he tried to kill David by spearing him.

Failing in this, he developed another plan. He would give his daughter Michal's hand in marriage to David, if the upstart warrior brought back the foreskins of a hundred Philistines. David successfully completed his task and married Michal. Over time, Saul tried various ways to have David killed. Yet God always protected the up-and-coming shepherd king from the down-and-sinking coward king.

The prophet Samuel had already anointed David as the next king, but while he waited in the wings for the promotion, David found himself dodging spears chucked by a demented Saul. David fled and gathered a loyal following of six hundred fighters. His relationship with Jonathan gave him intelligence information from inside the palace.

David must have lived a stressful life. Saul threw spears at him, tricked him into potentially getting killed by Philistines, commanded his servants to kill him, sent messengers to kill him in bed, and arrived at Samuel's house to do it himself. He even commanded his son, Jonathan, David's best friend, to kill him. Talk about pressure! David was forced to grow closer to God.

Labor-Management Conflict

the big picture

1 Samuel 25

After David's trusted friend, Samuel, died, he moved out into the desert. As David traveled around trying to keep his distance from Saul, he encountered the servants of a man named Nabal. When he sent his servants to ask for a donation in exchange for helping Nabal's sheep shearers, Nabal rebuffed him. An angered David determined to destroy Nabal and all he owned. But Nabal's wife, Abigail, heard about the situation, intercepted David, and placated him by apologizing and providing food and drink. David relented from his deadly plans. When David later heard that Nabal had suddenly died of heart failure, David proposed marriage to Abigail and she accepted.

David had been providing protection for Nabal and so David sent some of his men to the rich rancher requesting provisions. Nabal rudely rejected this request, even though he benefited from David's protection. David was so furious that he took four hundred armed men to kill Nabal. David, the man after God's heart, had lost it.

what others say

Alan Redpath

David! David! What is wrong with you? Why, one of the most wonderful things we have learned about you recently is your patience with Saul. You learned to wait upon the Lord, you refused to lift your hand to touch the Lord's anointed, although he had been your enemy for so many years. But now, look at you! . . . Your self-restraint has gone to pieces and a few insulting words from a fool of a man like Nabal have made you see red? David, what's the matter?

> "I am justified in doing this," David would reply. "There is no reason why Nabal should treat me as he has. He has repaid all my kindness with insults. I will show him he can't trifle with me. It is one thing to take it from Saul, who is my superior at this point, but this sort of man—this highhanded individual must be taught a lesson!"[2]

David's anger at Nabal is what most of us feel when we are rejected or mistreated. Yet, it's not the way God wants us to respond. We will show more forcefully that we are Christians by responding with kindness and gentleness. Besides, more people are convicted of their sin by our gracious response than an angry one.

David Pours Out His Fear

While David was on the run from Saul and his life was in danger, he expressed his emotions by writing more songs and verse. These portions of poetry were David's way of dealing with his fear and of continuing to develop his trust in God. Many of his psalms also expressed his joy at knowing God would protect him.

Today, these songs and poetry have become what we call the "Psalms" in Scripture. David didn't write all of the 150 psalms in our Bible, but he wrote the majority. People through the centuries have identified with David's heartfelt cries. They have found that joyful moments are enhanced and sorrowful ones softened. Many who feel their lives are spent on the run have found comfort in the book of Psalms.

Psalms of Comfort

Psalm	Situation	How David Comforted
34	David had pretended to be insane before Abimelech.	David praised God's greatness. He trusted in angels protecting him.
56	The Philistines had seized David in Gath.	David realized that men couldn't do anything to him without God's approval.
59	Saul had sent men to watch David's house in order to kill him.	David remembered God's love along with God's power and mercy.
142	David was hiding in a cave.	David depended upon God as his refuge and believed God would deliver him.

Returning Good for Evil

the big picture

1 Samuel 26–27; 29–31

For a second time, David had the opportunity to kill Saul, but he refused to dishonor God. When Saul realized what had happened, he acknowledged his guilt in trying to kill David. But David, knowing Saul's moods were changeable, joined the Philistines. But they didn't trust him, so they wouldn't let him fight with them. That was God's plan. When David's family was captured by the Amalekites, he was available to rescue them. Shortly after that, King Saul and Jonathan were killed.

David resisted the temptation to kill Saul, faithfully waiting for God's timing to place him on the throne. This demonstrated David's commitment to God.

David had every opportunity to accelerate God's plan. The throne had been promised to him, and this man Saul was out to kill him. He had opportunity, just reasons, and loyal followers to take the kingdom. He resisted those ungodly temptations.

David's Victories

the big picture

2 Samuel 1–8; 10

Although Saul had died, David didn't take the throne in both Judah and Israel without opposition. He was easily crowned king in Judah because that was where he was from. But in the land of Israel, Saul's relatives crowned Saul's other son, Ishbosheth, to be king over them. In time, some of Ishbosheth's commanders turned against him and killed him. That opened the door for David to become king over all of Israel. Years earlier, Saul had given Michal, David's first wife, to be another man's wife. Now, David demanded that she be returned to him. She was, but her heart was no longer entwined with his as at the beginning. Later, she grew to hate him, especially when she saw him dancing in the streets of Jerusalem over the return of God's ark.

After Saul died, you might expect David to march into the palace and fulfill his destiny. Instead, we find a man who was in a hurry to know more of his God. "It happened after this that David inquired of the LORD, saying, 'Shall I go up to any of the cities of Judah?' And the LORD said to him, 'Go up.' David said, 'Where shall I go up?' And He said, 'To Hebron'" (2 Samuel 2:1 NKJV).

Notice the statement "It happened after this." Saul is dead and David takes the time to ask God what he should do. The humility and patience developed in the pastures have cashed in dividends. Success was at hand, but David didn't let this future power go to his head. David lived in Hebron for seven and a half years, where he reigned over Judah.

But the darker side of David started to appear. He married six women, and six children were born to him in Hebron. David's move into polygamy started him down the road of poor choices.

One of his top army commanders, Joab, began killing potential opponents against David's wishes, yet David seemed unwilling to deal with this skilled but ruthless leader.

David's conquests brought power and prestige to his kingdom. General prosperity arrived for all his people.

what others say

Thomas Carlyle

But for one man who can stand prosperity, there are a hundred that will stand adversity.[3]

David began his reign with a wonderful heart for God. He wanted God's will to be done, and he became highly successful against the enemies of Israel. When peace came because of those victories, David wanted to build a house for God. But God communicated to him through the prophet Nathan that David wouldn't build such a house—but his son would. David obeyed God instead of forcing his own will.

That's What Best Friends Do

the big picture

2 Samuel 9:1–13

Many years earlier, David had promised Jonathan, his best friend and Saul's son, that they would take care of each other. Now that Jonathan was dead, David asked if there were any of Jonathan's relatives to whom he could show kindness. That could be a dangerous step, because any of Saul's relatives could be called upon to be king. Yet David found out about Jonathan's son, Mephibosheth, and called him to his presence. He restored him to honor by welcoming him to his own table. David took care of him for the rest of Mephibosheth's life.

In David's time, the families of their rivals would be killed to prevent any attempts to reclaim the throne. But David vowed to show kindness to all of Jonathan's descendants. David sheltered and protected Mephibosheth, whose grandfather was King Saul. This was also a wise move politically, for it would help unite Judah and Israel under David's rule.

During his reign, David penned many songs and poetry that have become part of our Bible as the Psalms. Like the other songs he wrote while fleeing from Saul, these songs represent the emotions he experienced while facing a particular situation, although we don't necessarily know the circumstance.

David's Psalms of Different Emotions

Emotion	Psalms
Anger	7, 36
Guilt over sin	32, 51
Fear or anxiety	23, 64
Loneliness	25
Stress	31
Weakness	62
Envy	16

David wrote about life and the insights he received from God.

Additional Psalms of David

Subject	Psalms
Requesting wisdom	37
Referring to the coming of the Messiah	22, 110
Calling upon God to judge his enemies	35, 58, 109
Complaining to God	4, 12, 26, 57
Thanking God for his deliverance	18, 30
Praising God for who he is	103

go to

complete
Colossians 2:10

dead dog
2 Samuel 9:8

Charles R. Swindoll

Grace is God giving himself in full acceptance to someone who does not deserve it and can never earn it and will never be able to repay. And this is what makes the story of David and Mephibosheth so memorable.[4]

Mephibosheth represents every Christian, sitting at King Jesus's table of spiritual blessings because of Jesus's sake, not because of their own worthiness. We each are spiritually crippled, like Mephibosheth was physically crippled, yet God views us as perfect and <u>complete</u> through Jesus. Mephibosheth called himself a "<u>dead dog</u>," and because of our sin, we each are like that. But God offers us abundant and eternal life, enabling us to be victorious over sin as we lay hold of his power.

Moments of Pleasure, Years of Pain

the big picture

2 Samuel 11–12

One spring when David should have been on the battlefield fighting, he was walking on the roof of his palace and saw a beautiful woman on a neighboring rooftop bathing. He called for her. Her name was Bathsheba and they committed adultery. When she sent word that she was pregnant, David called her husband, Uriah, home from the battlefield, hoping Uriah would sleep with Bathsheba and believe he was father of the coming child. When Uriah wouldn't go home to be with her, David had him put into a position on the battlefield where he would be killed. Then David took Bathsheba for his wife. Their son was born, but God disciplined them by causing the child to die. David repented of his sin after Nathan, the prophet, confronted him. A second son was born to him and Bathsheba. They named him Solomon.

David was on top of the world. In younger years he had written, "I will behave wisely in a perfect way. . . . I will walk within my house with a perfect heart. I will set nothing wicked before my eyes; I hate the work of those who fall away; it shall not cling to me" (Psalm

101:2–3 NKJV). But now he was around fifty years old and had been king for twenty years. Everything was going his way. That godly desire began to slide when he began taking more wives and concubines. In Deuteronomy 17:14–17, God set three rules for the kings of Israel. They must not multiply horses for themselves, they must not take multiple wives, and finally, they must not enrich themselves with silver and gold. David failed the second requirement. David's lust for women began to weaken his ability to make wise, godly choices.

His next slide into sinful passion came with one glance at Bathsheba's beautiful body. The next thing he knew, he was telling his ruthless commander Joab to arrange the death of her husband. After the news of Uriah's death reached David, he took Bathsheba as his wife. The cover-up worked, except that the secret sin ate away at a heart that once was only devoted to God. David wrote of that time, "When I kept silent, my bones grew old through my groaning all the day long. For day and night Your hand was heavy upon me; my vitality was turned into the drought of summer" (Psalm 32:3–4 NKJV).

After Nathan's finger of blame pierced David's heart, the king repented and finally found forgiveness. However, the consequences of the sin rocked David until his death.

David's **contrite** heart existed because it hadn't suffered "hardening of the attitudes" yet. His conscience was still tender and open to identifying the sickness of sin. He felt spiritual chest pains with every pulse of God's conviction coursing through his heart. David had a godly sorrow! How about you? Are you numb to the things you know are wrong? Is there a small corner in your heart still soft enough to feel the pain of conviction? God is ready to finish the heart surgery for your soul. Humbly approach the Great Physician and admit, "I have sinned."

The healing touch of forgiveness comes only from a contrite heart. We can escape the penalty of sin through forgiveness, but the painful consequences of our sin will often follow us. We will remember our sin and so will those we hurt. Only God will <u>forget</u> it.

go to

contrite
Isaiah 57:15

forget
Psalm 103:12

contrite
repentant

Like Father, Like Sons

2 Samuel 13–15:12

After David sinned, his life and reign began to crumble. His son Amnon raped his stepsister Tamar, the sister of Absalom. Two years later, Absalom, who had vowed to take revenge on Amnon, murdered him. David, crushed by all this conflict, wept along with all his sons. Absalom fled and for three years, David refused to reach out to him. Only after Joab concocted a plan to force David to see his error did David allow Absalom to return to the area. Still David wouldn't see him personally. Two years later, Absalom rebelled against his father and set himself up as king.

David saw his sins mirrored in the lives of his children. Consequences of adultery are costly. The Bible says, "Do not be deceived, God is not mocked; for whatever a man sows, that he will also reap. For he who sows to his flesh will of the flesh reap corruption, but he who sows to the Spirit will of the Spirit reap everlasting life" (Galatians 6:7–8 NKJV). David's life began to spin deeper into trouble.

what others say

John W. Lawrence

When David sowed to the flesh, he reaped what the flesh produced. Moreover, he reaped the consequences of his action even though he had confessed his sin and been forgiven for it. Underline it, star it, mark it deeply upon your conscious mind: Confession and forgiveness in no way stop the harvest. He had sown: he was to reap. Forgiven he was, but the consequences continued. . . . What we sow we will reap, and there are no exceptions.[5]

Greg Laurie, author of *The Great Compromise*, says there are six reasons to avoid the compromise of adultery:

key point

1. You damage your spouse.

2. You damage your self.

3. You damage your children.

4. You damage your church.

5. You damage your witness, as well as the cause of Christ.

6. You sin against the Lord.[6]

Although we can always receive forgiveness from God's gracious hand, we won't be able to avoid the consequences of our sin.

Let's Just Throw in the Towel

the big picture

2 Samuel 15:13–19:43

David was so upset by Absalom's disloyalty that he surrendered his reign to his son and left with his entire household. Absalom set up his reign in Jerusalem and demonstrated his newfound power by having sex with his father's concubines on top of a roof, in the sight of all Israel. He also took counsel from one of David's former counselors, Hushai, who was secretly loyal to David. Hushai told him to delay in pursuing David. Absalom followed his advice and lost the advantage. As a result, David had time to organize his defenses. Absalom eventually pursued David. Joab, thinking he would please David, killed Absalom. Instead, David was grieved. But after Joab reproved him for being insensitive to the needs of his loyal followers, David addressed them. David was restored to his kingly position and forgave those who had treated him badly when he was forced to leave.

In direct violation of David's orders, Joab killed Absalom. David's earlier neglect and unwillingness to control his military commander contributed to the death of his son.

what others say

Charles R. Swindoll

Absalom is dead—murdered. This happened before [David] had a chance to clear up several unresolved conflicts between father and son . . . before he and his son could sit down and come to terms with their differences. Even before David could tell him how sorry he was for being so busy, so preoccupied, so negligent as a dad—BOOM! The news of Absalom's death hits him in the face.[7]

David's inability to hold others accountable weakened his authority. His conflicting emotions overwhelmed his management skills. Now with Absalom dead, David's grief had built a wall between him and the warriors who fought for him. So great was the affront and rebuff to these loyal troops that Joab feared another rebellion could occur. As the military leader, Joab knew the king must address his troops. Joab challenged the king to do his duty and shake off his grief. David obeyed even though his heart wasn't in it.

David Was Dangerous to Be Around

the big picture

2 Samuel 20–24

David was reinstated as king. A famine, caused by Saul's mistreatment of the Gibeonites years earlier, was corrected when David cooperated with the Gibeonites' demand that Saul's sons by his wife Rizpah be hanged. Israel was again victorious against the Philistines even though the Philistines had more giants like Goliath. David remembered God's provision over the years and wrote a song of thanksgiving. Then, against God's specific command, David insisted on making a census of the people to discover how many warriors he could draft. When he realized that was a sin, he accepted God's discipline of a plague that killed seventy thousand Israelites. It stopped only after David offered a sacrifice on an altar built at the threshing floor of Araunah the Jebusite.

In 1 Chronicles 21:1, we get another glimpse into this census story. We learn that Satan planted this little temptation in David's mind. Satan whispered to David's prideful side, "You are the great king of Israel; why don't you find out just how big you are?" This census amounted to a draft for the army. There was no need to enlist men because Israel was at peace, and David was solidly in power. But David's pride wanted it done. Even Joab knew the idea of a census was wrong and advised against it. David ignored Joab and ordered it done.

David's pride had caused his downfall in the past, and now God was giving him another opportunity to show he had changed. Unfortunately, he hadn't.

Steve Farrar

The Lord disciplines every one of us as a father would discipline a young, immature son. God is disciplining us because
He wants to give every one of us spiritual responsibilities. But
first we have to take some character examinations. If you
don't pass on the first try, you'll take it again, and again, and
again, until you do pass and God can entrust leadership into
your hands.[8]

After David's disobedience, we find him conscience-stricken. "I
have sinned greatly in what I have done; but now, I pray, O LORD,
take away the iniquity of Your servant, for I have done very foolishly"
(2 Samuel 24:10 NKJV). His heart troubled him and soon we find him
on his knees again confessing his foolish sin. This time the consequences led to a plague for his people. David was in great distress.

Throwing a pebble into a calm pond causes a rippling of waves.
The foolish choices we make are like that point of impact. Just one
peek into the consequences of our choices would restrain our impulsive side. In fact, we are allowed that peek through the life of David.
Great success, painful sin, and profound forgiveness marked his life.
Each time he sinned, a price was paid that compounded in misery
and troubles—even in the lives of others.

"A Heart After God" Dies

1 Kings 1–2:11

David was dying and Adonijah, a son of David's through his wife
Haggith, declared himself the next king, even though David had
previously determined that Solomon would follow him as king.
When Bathsheba saw what was happening, she recruited the
prophet Nathan to help her establish Solomon as the rightful
heir. After David died, Solomon became king.

David was near death. Another son attempted to take the throne
instead of Solomon. David pulled Solomon to his side for some
kingly advice. David encouraged a spiritual dependency within
Solomon so that his son would walk in God's ways. Interestingly, he

then asked Solomon to do what he had been unwilling to do: hold Joab accountable for murder. David had been willing to keep Joab near for his skills as an army commander, but he knew justice required Joab's death.

David charged Solomon as the next king to:

- Be strong
- Prove himself a man
- Keep the charge of the Lord your God
- Walk in his ways
- Keep his statutes and commandments

David told Solomon that if he would do those things, he would "prosper in all that you do and wherever you turn" (1 Kings 2:3 NKJV).

David's instructions to his son for his kingship could also be applied to a father blessing his son or daughter (with some appropriate word changes for a female). As we encourage our children to obey God and be strong in the Lord, and we model it ourselves, they will want to seek him like we do.

Chapter Wrap-Up

- David was chosen as king to replace Saul even though David was young. God chose David as the next king because David trusted him, demonstrated when David killed Goliath. (1 Samuel 16–17)

- Once Saul knew David would replace him as king, he tried many times to kill David. David trusted God so much that when he had the opportunity to kill Saul, he didn't. David believed God would install him as king in his own timing. (1 Samuel 24:1–22)

- When Jonathan died, David kept his promise to care for Jonathan's family by taking Mephibosheth into the royal household. David proved he kept his promises and was a loyal friend. (2 Samuel 9:1–13)

- When David stayed home from the battlefield, he saw Bathsheba bathing, and committed adultery with her. When she became pregnant, he had to have her husband, Uriah, killed in order to take her as his wife. David fell hard, but repented harder. (2 Samuel 11:1–27)

- When Absalom, David's son, staged a rebellion, David meekly submitted, trusting God to reestablish him if God still wanted him as king. Later, David won back his position. David still loved Absalom so much that he was saddened to hear that his son had been killed. (2 Samuel 16–18)

- David died after forty years of serving as Israel's king. He was considered a man after God's own heart, even though he made many mistakes. (2 Kings 2:10–11)

Study Questions

1. What was Saul's response to David's offer to fight Goliath?

2. Who became David's best friend and helped to protect him?

3. How did David keep his covenant with Jonathan after Jonathan died?

4. Where should David have been when he was tempted to have adultery with Bathsheba?

5. What advantage did David have when he fled from Jerusalem because Absalom had staged a rebellion?

Chapter 8: Men of Strong Faith–Lessons in Perseverance

Let's Get Started

Two men with great faith stand out among the men of the Bible, even though they didn't hold prominent positions, nor were they patriarchs of the faith. But they believed God would fulfill his purposes through them. Noah labored for 120 years at a God-given task everyone laughed at. Job suffered under the most incredible personal and physical difficulties, and yet he kept his faith in God's goodness.

Both of these men had enough faith to hold firm in God's promise until they experienced God's solution. That attitude gave them the power they needed to take action as God directed. We'll be able to do the same if we learn from these men of faith.

Noah—120 Years of Faithfulness

the big picture

Genesis 6:5-12

After God created the earth and mankind, and as men became more numerous on earth, their sins multiplied. God grieved over their disobedience but saw in Noah a man who served him and was righteous.

We are first introduced to Noah when he was nearly five hundred years old. For five centuries, he had a good relationship with God. Yet sin was running rampant around him, and God saw Noah as the only one faithful to him. Because the people were so wicked, God decided to wipe out everyone except Noah's family.

Try to imagine you are the only person on the earth who believes in God. That is what Noah faced. The Bible tells us, "Noah was a just man, perfect in his generations. Noah walked with God" (Genesis 6:9 NKJV). Now this doesn't mean he never sinned, but it does mean he loved, obeyed, and most importantly, walked with God.

key point

God was seeking those who were faithful to him. Throughout the Bible, there are examples of God <u>looking</u> for a relationship with his created. During Noah's time, the rest of the world was filled with evil men and women seeking fulfillment apart from God. But anyone who <u>seeks</u> God sincerely can <u>find</u> him.

Noah must have felt lonely in his faith. His immediate family may have helped, but he didn't have any friends to share the Lord with. If we feel that way too, we can be encouraged that when we face spiritual isolation, we can still walk with God. Thankfully, other Christian men are available and God wants to provide Christian friendships. Be sure to attend <u>church</u> and ask God to guide you to those who can offer godly encouragement.

Midlife Career Move

the big picture

Genesis 6:13–22

God told Noah to build an ark of very specific materials and dimensions (see Illustration #13). He wanted to provide protection for those who were righteous on the earth, but he intended to destroy everything and everyone else.

Noah started his boat-building career out of obedience to God. God told him to build a boat—but this was no ordinary boat. It was made of "gopher" wood, 450 feet long, 75 feet wide, and 45 feet tall. It was the length of one and a half football fields and as tall as a four-story building. No wonder Noah took 120 years to build it. This project announced God's coming judgment.

go to

looking
Psalm 14:2

seeks
Jeremiah 29:13

find
Matthew 7:7–8

church
Hebrews 10:25

what others say

Herschel H. Hobbs

The word *gopher* appears nowhere else in the Bible, and its meaning is uncertain. Since the Phoenicians used cypress for shipbuilding due to its lightness and strength, this probably was the wood used. To make it watertight, the ark was to be covered inside and out with "pitch," a material that abounded in the area, evidence of the oil deposits that are so plentiful there today.[1]

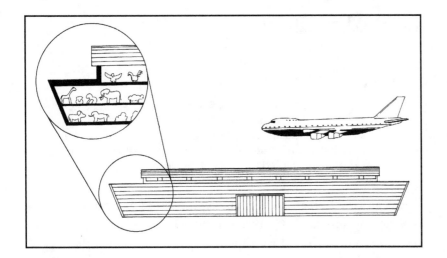

Illustration #13
The Ark—Noah's ark was a wooden boat that was 450 feet long, 75 feet wide, and 45 feet high. It took Noah and his sons 120 years to build, but when finished, the ark was roomy enough for Noah's family, all the animals, and food for everyone. This floating zoo would be home to Noah's family for over a year.

Each year, Noah's obedience demonstrated God's <u>patience</u> with those who continued to rebel. Every board, every beam, and every bucket of pitch signaled God's intentions. There's nothing like one righteous man building a huge boat on dry land to send a message. During that time, he told those around him of God's coming judgment. But his comments fell on deaf ears. He only heard laughter and ridicule.

The ark was exactly six times longer than it was wide. Today, modern shipbuilders use that same ratio because the engineering efficiencies are maximized. How amazing that when man's engineering skills were more primitive, God was already a master shipbuilder!

Noah persisted building the ark over 120 hot summers and cold winters. The only thing colder than the winter chill was the icy comments from those around him. In today's jargon, this would be a "hostile work environment." We may need Noah's <u>faithfulness</u> at times because when our lives reflect a relationship with God, we may hear critical comments. Our commitment to the Lord and the tasks he gives us will strengthen our resolve to work regardless of the loneliness.

patience
2 Peter 3:15

faithfulness
Matthew 24:45

go to

hatred
Proverbs 6:16

covenant
Hebrews 9:15

covenant
a promise

Rain? What's Rain?

the big picture

Genesis 7:1-24

At the right time, God directed Noah to take his family and enter the ark, along with seven pairs of every clean animal and two pairs of every unclean animal. For the first time, rain fell on the earth. It lasted until the earth was completely flooded, and everyone on the earth died—except for Noah's family.

Except for one man and his family, the entire world was in open rebellion against God. God's creation was now so corrupt, he was morally required to deal with those in rebellion. "When the wicked are multiplied, transgression increases; but the righteous will see their fall" (Proverbs 29:16 NKJV).

As a result, God created the first flood. The Bible isn't the only source that refers to a great flood. There are approximately one hundred references to a great flood in the stories of different people groups around the globe.

Like a contagious disease, sin was spreading. More sinners emboldened more men toward more sin. Justice required action so God sent his judgment upon the earth. He would start anew by building the population from Noah's family.

There are times when we also are required to express our opinion of sin in this world. It takes a great deal of wisdom to know how and when to do it. But because God is a God of justice, he may want us to communicate his <u>hatred</u> of sin in this evil world.

Man of Worship, God of Promise

the big picture

Genesis 8:1-9:19

God made the waters recede after a while, and Noah tested the depth of the water by sending out birds at different times. Eventually, the waters receded enough that Noah and his family could leave the ark. On the fresh earth, Noah built an altar and God blessed Noah and his family. Plus, he established a **covenant** with Noah and his sons that he would never cause a similar flood to come upon the earth again.

Chronology of the Flood

Summary	Details	Scripture
Waiting in ark	Noah enters ark; 7 days later the rain begins falling.	Genesis 7:7–9 Genesis 7:10–11
Water for 150 days	40 days later the heavy rains stop; 110 days later waters recede and the ark runs aground on Mount Ararat.	Genesis 7:12 Genesis 7:24; 8:4
Water receded in 150 days	74 days later mountaintops are visible; 40 days later a raven is sent out, and then a dove is sent out and it returns; 7 days later a dove is sent out and returns with leaf; 7 days later a dove is sent out a third time and does not return.	Genesis 8:5 Genesis 8:6–9 Genesis 8:10 Genesis 8:12
Earth dried in 70 days	Noah saw dry land; land is completely dry, and Noah leaves ark; 377 days were spent inside the ark.	Genesis 8:13, 14–19

intrinsic
belonging to the real nature of a thing; inherent

transcendent
separate, beyond or apart from the material

The water was gone and the ground was dry, but Noah waited until God told him to leave the ark. Noah entered the ark in obedience, and he exited the same way. Once released from the confines of the ship, Noah made an altar and worshiped God. Noah blessed God with this act of worship. Then God blessed Noah, the second father of the human race, and made the first covenant with man. God promised never to destroy all of life again. He created a rainbow as a sign of that promise. Noah was told to be fruitful and multiply but was warned against killing men.

Even though God had killed the people of the earth, God explained to Noah that murder was wrong: "Whoever sheds man's blood, by man his blood shall be shed; for in the image of God He made man" (Genesis 9:6 NKJV). It's wrong because man was made in God's image, and we are valuable in ourselves. The rainbow tells us God will never destroy the people of the earth again.

Charles Darwin claimed we are evolved animals. He believed that since the creation never occurred, there wouldn't be a creator to have a claim on the created. Darwin argued that we only possess biologic value as a highly developed species. God doesn't look at us that way. Unlike animals, man has the capacity for morality, reason, and worship because we are made in God's image. Because of what God has done, we are more than physical beings. We possess **intrinsic** and **transcendent** value.

Job—Gaining a Godly Perspective of Suffering

the big picture

Job 1:1-22

Job was a man who lived in the land of Uz and was considered blameless and a worshiper of Jehovah God. He had family and worldly blessings. Satan appeared before God in his throne room and accused Job of impure motives for following God. To prove Job's purity, God gave Satan permission to attack.

Job was a rich man who feared and served God. He had a loving wife and seven sons and three daughters, who regularly met together to have fun. Job prayed for them and offered sacrifices on their behalf.

Satan appeared before God's throne to accuse God's followers. God pointed out Job as one of his loyal servants, saying, "Have you considered My servant Job, that there is none like him on the earth, a blameless and upright man, one who fears God and shuns evil?" (Job 1:8 NKJV). Satan accused Job of only serving God because God had blessed him. God gave Satan permission to remove Job's possessions, so Satan caused everything he owned to be destroyed. Even his children were killed as they feasted together. Job still stayed loyal—even as he grieved deeply. At the end of round one Satan was knocked down, but Job was still standing.

what others say

Oswald Chambers

In the case of Job, Satan asked permission to play havoc with his possessions and God gave him permission, and every possession Job had, even to his bodily health, went. But Job proved that a man would remain true to his love of God though all his possessions went to rack and ruin.[2]

From Job's story, we learn:

key point

1. God knows everything about the people on the earth.

2. Satan has access to God.

3. Satan is looking for ways to accuse us and for the ways we fail.

4. God put limits on what Satan can do to God's servants.

5. It is possible to grieve deeply and yet not sin through blaming God.

accuse
Revelation 12:10

wept
John 11:35

Satan loves to find something in God's children that he can <u>accuse</u> us about before God. Even if there is nothing, Satan will scheme so that there can be something. That's why Jesus called him "a liar and the father of it" (John 8:44 NKJV).

In the Asian custom of grieving, Job tore his robe, shaved his head, and fell to the ground. He also worshiped God, saying, "Naked I came from my mother's womb, and naked shall I return there. The LORD gave, and the LORD has taken away; blessed be the name of the LORD" (Job 1:21 NKJV). Although some people think that Christians shouldn't grieve because they will see their dead again, it is possible to grieve and still trust God. God allows us to express our emotions even as we continue to believe God knows what he's doing in our lives.

At times of difficulty or grief, we can ask "Why?" without being unrighteous. The account of Job's grief said, "In all this Job did not sin nor charge God with wrong" (Job 1:22 NKJV). Job faced his deep loss, but he didn't believe God had made a mistake. Even Jesus grieved over Lazarus's death and <u>wept</u>.

Sickness Will Break Him

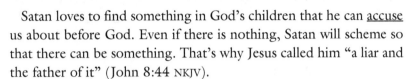

the big picture

Job 2:1–10

Satan again stood before God. This time, he alleged Job stayed true to God only because Job's health hadn't been touched. God broadened his permission so that Satan could bring disease upon Job. But even with great painful sores on his body, Job still trusted God's will. Unfortunately, Job's wife didn't share his faith and wanted him to curse God. He refused.

In round one, Job's heart was broken. Now his body is broken with painful sores. But we quickly see why Job's wife didn't die with the children. Her loss couldn't have been more painful than her reckless comment to Job. "His wife said to him, 'Do you still hold fast to your integrity? Curse God and die!'" (Job 2:9 NKJV). Her faith

go to

schemes
Ephesians 6:11

loved
Jeremiah 31:3

send
John 3:16

empower
Ephesians 3:16

problems
John 16:33

was shattered and she held God responsible. She wanted someone to blame, and she wanted Job to join her in accusing God. Even Job's wife recognized he was still standing at the end of round two.

In the story of Job, everyone is accusing and blaming everyone else, except God and Job. That's how Satan's <u>schemes</u> work. He wants to sow seeds of discord and faultfinding. He uses trials and difficulties to make us think God isn't treating us right. Then if we manage not to blame God, we blame others.

Blaming others—or God—is a warning sign of spiritual heart disease. Blame springs from a heart that believes, "I deserve better. I know what is best for my life. I want it my way." That's like standing before God and wagging your finger in his face. But the same God who <u>loved</u> you enough to <u>send</u> his Son to die for your sin is the same God who allows struggles in your life but also provides the Holy Spirit to fill and <u>empower</u> you to cope with it all.

Many people approach their relationship with God with the expectation things will always get better. But Job had the right attitude, even though his wife didn't. He replied, "'You speak as one of the foolish women speaks. Shall we indeed accept good from God, and shall we not accept adversity?' In all this Job did not sin with his lips" (Job 2:10 NKJV). Job proved his heart was grateful to Jehovah God at all times, and he honored God through trusting him. We can do the same thing if we truly understand that in this world we will always have <u>problems</u>. It's only in heaven that we won't.

something to ponder

strengthen your family

When most couples marry, the statement "for better or worse" is often repeated in their vows. There is an expectation that marriages will experience good and bad times. Evidently Job and his wife didn't have that phrase in their wedding vows because Job's wife wasn't prepared for this onslaught on their family. She was overwhelmed by grief. Job stayed true and was a spiritual leader in his family.

But You Must Have Sin in Your Life!

the big picture

Job 2:11–31:40

Three of Job's friends came to comfort Job in his deep affliction. But they weren't much help because they tried to convince Job he was being attacked because of some sin in his life. Job argued back, saying he didn't have any hidden sin. Their conversation went back and forth, but Job remained unconvinced of their perspective about suffering.

Finally three friends joined Job in his battle: Eliphaz, Bildad, and Zophar. When they saw Job's deep grief, they could only sit with him in silence. Their mere presence must have been refreshing, like a boxer's corner attendants. Job finally broke the silence and complained about his situation, even saying he wanted to die. That opened the door. The blame game was about to raise its ugly head again. Job was facing the greatest battle of his life, and his friends were cheering against him! Job was now reeling in the ring. The crowd had turned against him, but he lasted another round.

what others say

Charles Colson

Job lost his home, his family (except for a nagging wife), his health, even his hope. The advice of friends was no help. No matter where he turned, he could find no answers to his plight . . . though it appeared God had abandoned him, Job clung to the assurance that God is who He is.[3]

At God's throne, Satan accused Job of being too innocent. Now Job's friends were accusing him of being guilty. The man couldn't win. But Job was convinced he had no sin he had not already confessed and that suffering can also happen to the godly. But the three men believed the innocent did not suffer.

Eliphaz, Bildad, and Zophar were like accusers who:

1. Give pat answers without compassion.

2. Don't ask, they tell.

3. Assume a person hasn't sought God's viewpoint.

4. Assume a person's theology is wrong without examining their own.

5. Misunderstand and twist what is said.

6. Believe it's impossible for a man to be acceptable in God's eyes.

7. Don't listen.

compassion
1 Samuel 23:21

listening
Proverbs 11:12

With these men as his "friends," Job didn't need enemies! True friends will listen more than talk.

In the book of Proverbs, a wise communicator is described as:

1. Able to accept commands (10:8).

2. Understanding (10:13).

3. Honest (10:17).

4. Using few words (10:19).

5. Encouraging (12:25).

6. Giving input at the appropriate time (15:23).

Ephesians 4:15 tells us to speak the truth in love. Sometimes truth is better left unsaid if it can't be done in love.

Eliphaz, Bildad, and Zophar may have thought they were leading Job toward righteousness, but their leadership skills were lacking. Instead of leading with compassion and listening, they tried to force their opinions upon a hurting man. If we want to be effective in the lives of those who hurt, we must resist the temptation to "fix" the problem—especially if we don't truly understand the problem.

the big picture

Job 32–37

After Job and his friends finished with all their great theological discussions, another friend, Elihu, began to talk. He had heard what they all said but hadn't been introduced into the story yet. Elihu shared with them a more balanced perspective: that suffering wasn't always a punishment for sin.

A Fresh Idea

Elihu was younger and had refrained from speaking, out of respect for his four older friends. But finally, he couldn't contain himself any longer. He believed suffering wasn't always a punishment for sin. Instead, God in his goodness uses it to draw people closer to himself—whether there is sin in a person's life or not. He said, "God works all these things, twice, in fact, three times with a man" (Job 33:29 NKJV). Elihu told Job the suffering wouldn't stop until he realized his arrogant defense of his innocence. Although Elihu's speech didn't attack as ferociously as the other three friends, he still wrongly assumed that suffering was always connected in some way to sin.

identified
John 9:3

what others say

Jessie Penn-Lewis

Elihu . . . perceived as he listened, that Job was becoming more and more concerned about clearing his own character, rather than justifying the love and wisdom of God in laying His hand upon him.[4]

Elihu portrayed God as:

1. Never doing wrong (34:10).

2. Seeing all of man's steps (34:21).

3. Mighty and understanding (36:5).

4. Exalted and a great teacher (36:22).

Whether a person is suffering because of sin or not, God still wants to help solve problems, deliver from sin, and correct weaknesses. Jesus identified the purpose of one man's suffering as an opportunity for God to be glorified. That's always the purpose of any of our struggles—whether it's a result of sin or not.

Job's Day in Court

the big picture

Job 38–41

Without warning, God himself intervened into the discussion. We aren't told how he communicated or if he appeared in visual form, but a "whirlwind" was mentioned. He ignored the four friends standing nearby and questioned Job in order to show that he was sovereign over everything, even suffering in the world.

beyond
Isaiah 55:8–9

Job was trying to sort out the issues of suffering when God came to him to demonstrate his love for Job. As God revealed his own greatness and sovereign authority over all the earth, Job lost all desire to proclaim his own innocence.

God asked Job to consider the following questions:

1. Where were you when I created the universe?

2. Did you help me create the morning?

3. Have you walked in the depths of the ocean?

4. Do you know when mountain goats give birth?

5. Who takes care of an ostrich egg when its mother leaves it abandoned?

How would you have answered those questions? Job said, "I am vile; what shall I answer You? I lay my hand over my mouth. Once I have spoken, but I will not answer; yes, twice, but I will proceed no further" (Job 40:4–5 NKJV). That would be a good thing for us to keep on the tip of our tongues.

God never did directly address the issues that Job and his friends had covered. It's as if God was saying all that wasn't important. What was important was that they knew he was sovereign and in control of everything. He communicated that his ways are <u>beyond</u> human comprehension. Even if he explained his actions, people wouldn't understand.

key point

If we try to figure out God and his way of thinking, we will only become frustrated. God knows the big picture and we can only see one small puzzle piece. When he makes decisions or answers our prayers in a certain way, he is basing it on everything he knows, not on the little we know. How much better to trust that he knows best.

<u>Vindication!</u>

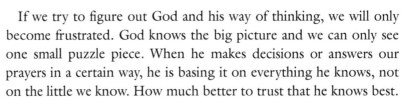

the big picture

Job 42:1–17

Job gave a final answer to God's revelation by affirming his belief that God could do anything he wanted and always knew the right thing to do. God then rebuked the original three friends for not speaking of him the way Job had. He commanded them to allow Job to pray for them so they wouldn't be punished. God then restored Job's fortunes and allowed him and his wife to have children again.

Although God didn't answer Job's concerns directly, Job had the satisfaction of having a direct conversation with him, which is what Job asked for in the first place. He cried out, "Oh, that I had one to hear me! Here is my mark. Oh, that the Almighty would answer me, that my Prosecutor had written a book!" (Job 31:35 NKJV). In the end, he was satisfied.

what others say

Larry Richards

The book of Job does not tell us why God allows good people to suffer. It does remind us that people of faith respond to suffering differently than those without faith.[5]

Some people think that the story of Job is a fable, but James, the brother of Jesus, referred to Job's experience in the book he wrote about the Christian life. He wrote, "Indeed we count them blessed who endure. You have heard of the perseverance of Job and seen the end intended by the Lord—that the Lord is very compassionate and merciful" (James 5:11 NKJV). That would seem to be a confirmation of Job's story actually happening.

God never rebuked the comments of Elihu. He never even referred to what Elihu said. We can most likely assume, therefore, that God thought Elihu's ideas were acceptable and truthful; otherwise, he would have rebuked Elihu along with Job's other friends.

Just like Job, when we are suffering, we want to know God hasn't forgotten us or forsaken us. We want to know he's aware of our pain. Even if we don't learn why we are suffering, if we know he cares, that can be enough.

key point

Aaron—Moses's Spokesman

EXODUS 4:27–31 *And the LORD said to Aaron, "Go into the wilderness to meet Moses." So he went and met him on the mountain of God, and kissed him. So Moses told Aaron all the words*

go to

years
Exodus 7:7

of the LORD who had sent him, and all the signs which He had commanded him. Then Moses and Aaron went and gathered together all the elders of the children of Israel. And Aaron spoke all the words which the LORD had spoken to Moses. Then he did the signs in the sight of the people. So the people believed; and when they heard that the LORD had visited the children of Israel and that He had looked on their affliction, then they bowed their heads and worshiped. (NKJV).

Aaron's and Moses's lives were intertwined over many years in both good and bad ways. Aaron was Moses's big brother by three years. We aren't given much information about how God appeared to Aaron, but Aaron immediately responded to God's call to find his long-lost brother, Moses, even though he hadn't seen him for forty years.

God placed a strong team together with Aaron and Moses. Moses relied on Aaron for the one skill he lacked, public speaking. Their efforts blended powerfully to lead two million people out of bondage and out of Egypt. However, leadership requires vision, and Aaron lacked vision for the future. He relied on Moses for that inspiration and direction.

Aaron was a good follower but a poor leader. When he represented God with Moses's guidance and direction, he did a great job. But without Moses's leadership, he often failed. Whenever Moses wasn't there to be followed, or whenever Aaron set out on his own, he made wrong decisions.

something to ponder

A walk through life without vision is like a helium balloon with a slow leak. It quickly rises into the sky but falls back empty to the earth. Men who rely on their eloquence, skill, or power to inspire and motivate others are destined to fail unless they know where they are going and believe in its purpose. Whether you are trying to influence your family, your job, or your relationships, you must get a handle on this. We find our real purpose in God's will for us by seeking him through the Bible. Whenever you are feeling weak, God promises to bring the support you need, just as Aaron was built up through his association with Moses.

called
Hebrews 5:1–4

<table>
<tr><td colspan="2" align="right">what others say</td></tr>
</table>

what others say

Rick Warren

[lists the benefits of knowing your purpose this way]
1. Gives meaning to your life
2. Simplifies your life
3. Focuses your life
4. Motivates your life
5. Prepares you for eternity[6]

God's Strength

How You Are Strengthened by God	Scripture
Reading God's words in the Bible	2 Timothy 3:16–17
Being guided through advice from wise counselors	Proverbs 27:9
Sensing his presence and love through prayer	Psalm 66:20
Circumstances confirming his leading	Acts 21:2
Putting on the full armor of God	Ephesians 6:10–17
Claiming the promises of God	Romans 4:20
Being alert	1 Corinthians 16:13
Choosing to be content	2 Corinthians 12:9–10

A Very Important Role

EXODUS 28:1–3 *Now take Aaron your brother, and his sons with him, from among the children of Israel, that he may minister to Me as priest, Aaron and Aaron's sons: Nadab, Abihu, Eleazar, and Ithamar. And you shall make holy garments for Aaron your brother, for glory and for beauty. So you shall speak to all who are gifted artisans, whom I have filled with the spirit of wisdom, that they may make Aaron's garments, to consecrate him, that he may minister to Me as priest.* (NKJV)

Aaron and his sons were chosen as the high priests. Over the following forty years, God proved Aaron was his choice for high priest of his people. Many challenged that sovereign choice, but they paid with their lives. God <u>called</u> Aaron into an area of authority to provide spiritual leadership for the Hebrews and He protected His chosen one.

To help the people know of a priest's high position, the priests were given special clothing and were provided for by all the people's offerings.

go to

sacrifice
Hebrews 10:10

afraid
Exodus 20:19

confidently
Hebrews 4:16

understand
Hebrews 4:15

Aaron and the other priests were responsible for sacrificing the offerings that the people brought to God's temple. But because Jesus was the ultimate <u>sacrifice</u> for all the sins of the world, we no longer have to sacrifice animals or give bread offerings in order to be counted righteous by God or to have our sins forgiven.

As a child of God, we now have a priest in Jesus. We do not need to go through any human priest to have access to God, unlike the Israelites, who had to go through Aaron and his sons. We can have direct access to Jesus, who resides in the heavenly throne room and intercedes for his children. "Now this is the main point of the things we are saying: We have such a High Priest, who is seated at the right hand of the throne of the Majesty in the heavens, a Minister of the sanctuary and of the true tabernacle which the Lord erected, and not man" (Hebrews 8:1–2 NKJV).

The Israelites were <u>afraid</u> of God and sent Moses and Aaron to hear God's words, but we don't have to be afraid. Because of Jesus, our High Priest who sits at the right hand of God the Father, we can come boldly and <u>confidently</u> before the throne. God cares about us and wants us to have access to him.

Jesus as our High Priest can <u>understand</u> everything we struggle with because he also was tempted in the ways that we are. Therefore, he will represent us to his Father with passion and enthusiasm because he knows what it feels like to be human.

Aaron Takes Charge?

EXODUS 32:1–4 *Now when the people saw that Moses delayed coming down from the mountain, the people gathered together to Aaron, and said to him, "Come, make us gods that shall go before us; for as for this Moses, the man who brought us up out of the land of Egypt, we do not know what has become of him." And Aaron said to them, "Break off the golden earrings which are in the ears of your wives, your sons, and your daughters, and bring them to me." So all the people broke off the golden earrings which were in their ears, and brought them to Aaron. And he received the gold from their hand, and he fashioned it with an engraving tool, and made a molded calf. Then they said, "This is your god, O Israel, that brought you out of the land of Egypt!" (NKJV)*

Moses was gone for forty days communing with God up on the mountain. He left Aaron in charge. The people knew Aaron was now their substitute leader, and they pressured him to build idols. They were tired of waiting for Moses, and they wanted to be in the Promised Land immediately.

Forty days without movement made the Israelites restless for a new god to lead them. Forty days without Moses made them yearn for a new leader in Aaron. And forty days without God's intervention drove them to replace God with their golden calf. In less than seven weeks they forgot whom they belonged to.

Maybe the pride of being the primary leader went to Aaron's head. He may have thought this was his opportunity to get out from under the authority of Moses. <u>Later</u>, he, along with his sister, Miriam, would complain verbally about Moses's leadership. But it may have been that the seeds of comparing himself to Moses were growing this early. Thus he took this feeble opportunity to distinguish himself by giving the people what they wanted. What a low point in his life. His pride, impatience, and fear motivated his disobedience.

Without one word of rebuke or any effort to challenge their evil suggestion, Aaron fell into the habit of many modern leaders. He placed a moist finger in the air, sensed the wind direction of popular thought, and made a decision. Aaron caved under pressure. In modern jargon, the polls proved everyone wanted it this way. Who was he to deny the will of the people? He led them into idolatry. We must beware that we as leaders in our jobs and homes don't do the same thing. Wanting to be popular with other people will usually lead to disaster. We should only care about one person's opinion: God's. If he is <u>pleased</u> with us, then the popularity polls don't matter.

later
Numbers 12:1–2

pleased
2 Corinthians 5:9

key point

<u>Just Like Magic, the Golden Calf</u> <u>Suddenly Appeared!</u>

EXODUS 32:21–24 *And Moses said to Aaron, "What did this people do to you that you have brought so great a sin upon them?" So Aaron said, "Do not let the anger of my lord become hot. You know the people, that they are set on evil. For they said to me, 'Make us gods that shall go before us; as for this Moses, the man who brought us out of the land of Egypt, we do not know what has become of him.' And I said to them, 'Whoever has any*

Adam
Genesis 3:12–13

disobedience
Numbers 14:23

gold, let them break it off.' So they gave it to me, and I cast it into the fire, and this calf came out." (NKJV)

Aaron tried to paint an incredible story. He backpedaled wildly. "The people pressured me. I didn't have a chance. They are rotten at the core. This is just like them." Just as <u>Adam</u> and Eve didn't want to take responsibility for their actions, Aaron attempted to deflect attention away from his failed leadership. What a cowardly act!

what others say

Gene A. Getz

Aaron's reaction to Moses' confrontation was almost humorous—a lesson to us all! His rationalization was a classic example of man's tendency towards self-deception and dishonesty. What an indication of a man with his back against the wall while being confronted with his irresponsible actions.[7]

Leadership requires accountability. Accountability equals responsibility. Integrity and strong character are only proven when things go wrong. Then true leaders will willingly accept responsibility for any failure. If they do, they will find legions of willing followers. It is never so important, especially in our families, to take responsibility for the mistakes we make. We may think that admitting our failures will take away our wife's respect and our children's love, but the opposite is actually true. They will love and respect us more.

Remaining Silent About Sin

LEVITICUS 10:1–3 *Then Nadab and Abihu, the sons of Aaron, each took his censer and put fire in it, put incense on it, and offered profane fire before the LORD, which He had not commanded them. So fire went out from the LORD and devoured them, and they died before the LORD. And Moses said to Aaron, "This is what the LORD spoke, saying: 'By those who come near Me I must be regarded as holy; and before all the people I must be glorified.'" So Aaron held his peace.* (NKJV)

As the Israelites traveled in the wilderness, a consequence of their <u>disobedience</u>, God revealed his plan for their worship of him. A place of worship was set up in a tent, and Aaron was appointed as the first priest. Both Aaron's sons assisted him with the temple duties. But they showed great disrespect for God and the rules for the temple when they arrogantly overstepped their duties. These verses do not state exactly what "profane fire" meant. Commentators can only suggest several possibilities.

tabernacle
tent of worship

Possible Reasons for the Defiant Acts[8]

Possible Reason	Scripture
Used coals in their censers that didn't come from the altar.	Leviticus 16:12
Offered at the wrong time of day.	Exodus 30:7–9
They may have tried to go into the most holy place, which was only allowed on the Day of Atonement.	Leviticus 16:12–13
Drunkenness could have been a factor.	Leviticus 10:9

Perhaps the thrill of acting like a high priest rushed through Nadab's and Abihu's minds. When they approached God, they sought to honor themselves, not him. As a result, they demonstrated contempt for God's holiness, authority, and justice. Their defiant act demanded immediate justice. "But the person who does anything presumptuously, whether he is native-born or a stranger, that one brings reproach on the LORD, and he shall be cut off from among his people. Because he has despised the word of the LORD, and has broken His commandment, that person shall be completely cut off; his guilt shall be upon him" (Numbers 15:30–31 NKJV).

Aaron was stricken with silence at his sons' deaths. Guilt and sadness paralyzed his tongue. Two of his four sons, who were raised to assist him in the temple, had died. Thoughts of what he didn't say to those men probably raced through his mind. His reflective silence seems to suggest that for the first time he accepted responsibility for a bad outcome.

Facts About the Priesthood

Fact	Scripture
Aaron and his sons were the first priests to serve God in the newly built **tabernacle**.	Exodus 28:1
The food sacrifices of the Israelites provided for Aaron and his family's needs because they served in the temple.	Leviticus 2:10
Aaron and his sons had special assignments as God's representatives and were required to teach the Israelites how to honor God.	Leviticus 11–15
Aaron and his sons were to supervise the Levites in their duties in the temple.	Numbers 4:27

We need to guard against casual attitudes creeping into our hearts and homes when approaching God in prayer. Respect, gratitude, and reverence should mark our words and actions because our children watch and listen. The things we carelessly say or do have an impact upon our families. What we treat with respect and honor will be learned by those young minds.

Envy Raises Its Ugly Head

NUMBERS 12:1–2 *Then Miriam and Aaron spoke against Moses because of the Ethiopian woman whom he had married; for he had married an Ethiopian woman. So they said, "Has the LORD indeed spoken only through Moses? Has He not spoken through us also?" And the LORD heard it.* (NKJV)

Moses's sister and brother have shared leadership with him for a long time now. They grumbled about his wife, but there was another issue simmering in their hearts. It wasn't that Moses was providing poor leadership, but that in their eyes the role his leadership took was too large. They resented their subordinate position. They argued that God also spoke through them.

God became angry and confronted Miriam and Aaron. Their attempt to be equal with Moses was ridiculous. He said to them, "'Not so with My servant Moses; he is faithful in all My house. I speak with him face to face, even plainly, and not in dark sayings; and he sees the form of the LORD. Why then were you not afraid to speak against My servant Moses?' So the anger of the LORD was aroused against them, and He departed" (Numbers 12:7–9 NKJV).

Aaron and Miriam already possessed great authority and respect from the people, but they wanted more. They desired more stature in the eyes of others. It was more important to them to have the Israelites' approval than God's.

God struck Miriam with leprosy, maybe because she started the grumbling. When Aaron saw her illness, he apologetically appealed for Moses's intervention. Moses prayed, and Miriam was healed of the disease. But she was disgraced by being banished from the camp for a week.

go to

counselors
Proverbs 12:15

Bible
Psalm 119:24

Gene A. Getz

No doubt Zipporah, Moses's first wife, had died, and he had remarried. And this was not wrong, for the woman, though not an Israelite, was surely a believer. If she had not been, God himself would have judged Moses. Aaron and Miriam were really not concerned about Moses; they wanted others to know that they too were capable of leading Israel. So they made their accusations public, using Moses's marriage to a Cushite as a basis for demonstrating their wisdom before others.[9]

Complaining and whining never accomplish anything. Of course, there's a difference between complaining about our problems and sharing them with others with the hope of getting support and help. Complaining means we just want to vent our feelings without any desire to change them. Sharing our feelings means we want help. God does want us to get help through wise <u>counselors</u>, but we must be willing to change ourselves in order for it to be effective. We should also remember that the <u>Bible</u> is our wisest counselor.

key point

<u>Aaron Learns to Humble Himself</u>

NUMBERS 14:1–5 *So all the congregation lifted up their voices and cried, and the people wept that night. And all the children of Israel complained against Moses and Aaron, and the whole congregation said to them, "If only we had died in the land of Egypt! Or if only we had died in this wilderness! Why has the LORD brought us to this land to fall by the sword, that our wives and children should become victims? Would it not be better for us to return to Egypt?" So they said to one another, "Let us select a leader and return to Egypt." Then Moses and Aaron fell on their faces before all the assembly of the congregation of the children of Israel. (NKJV)*

Twelve spies were sent into the Promised Land. They returned, and ten of them reported that the land was filled with giants. The fearful report sent a mutinous spirit over the crowd. They actually wanted to kill Moses and Aaron. Both of them fell on their faces to demonstrate the seriousness of the rebellion and to stop the murmuring. The people were now a rebellious mob, and Moses and Aaron were praying for God's intervention. Aaron was now faced with the threat of death. God intervened and protected Moses and Aaron.

Ironically, Aaron had previously wanted a larger share of Moses's position and role, but now he was quickly learning the consequences of being a leader. He realized he would have to take the good with the bad, the responsibility of sharing God's heart. All of a sudden, leadership wasn't all that it was cracked up to be.

Being a leader isn't always a great job. People are more apt to criticize and misunderstand you when you are in charge. As a result, you will need more strength. But most of all, you'll need the humility to fall on your face and ask God for his help and protection.

Aaron's Obedience Saves Lives

NUMBERS 16:46–48 *So Moses said to Aaron, "Take a censer and put fire in it from the altar, put incense on it, and take it quickly to the congregation and make atonement for them; for wrath has gone out from the LORD. The plague has begun." Then Aaron took it as Moses commanded, and ran into the midst of the assembly; and already the plague had begun among the people. So he put in the incense and made atonement for the people. And he stood between the dead and the living; so the plague was stopped. (NKJV)*

Aaron and Moses had just handled a rebellion by Korah, one of Aaron's Levite assistants. The result was death for the rebels as God intervened to reinforce Aaron's high priest role. The next morning rebellion broke out again. The crowd was angry with Aaron and Moses for how God judged the rebels. God's anger burned against the rebels, and a plague started among the people. Moses sent Aaron into the crowd to make atonement for their sin and prevent the spread of God's growing judgment. God was avenging the rebellious who were opposed to Aaron's authority as priest. Yet, to his credit, Aaron worked to turn back God's wrath.

It took courage for Aaron to run into the midst of the rebellious crowd. They could have easily killed him to take revenge on whoever was available to blame for their problems. Maybe his courage showed that Aaron had grown in his abilities to be a leader and to trust God.

Guilty by Association

NUMBERS 20:7–12, 24 *Then the LORD spoke to Moses, saying, "Take the rod; you and your brother Aaron gather the congregation together. Speak to the rock before their eyes, and it will yield its water; thus you shall bring water for them out of the rock, and give drink to the congregation and their animals." So Moses took the rod from before the LORD as He commanded him. And Moses and Aaron gathered the assembly together before the rock; and he said to them, "Hear now, you rebels! Must we bring water for you out of this rock?" Then Moses lifted his hand and struck the rock twice with his rod; and water came out abundantly, and the congregation and their animals drank. Then the LORD spoke to Moses and Aaron, "Because you did not believe Me, to hallow Me in the eyes of the children of Israel, therefore you shall not bring this assembly into the land which I have given them. . . . Aaron shall be gathered to his people, for he shall not enter the land which I have given to the children of Israel, because you rebelled against My word at the water of Meribah." (NKJV)*

It has been forty years since Aaron, Moses, and the Israelites left Egypt. After thirty-seven years of walking through the wilderness, nearly everyone who rebelled after the spies returned was now dead. Little is written of the last thirty-seven years, but nothing has changed for Aaron in his leadership role. The people went against him and Moses with the same grumbling as before. This time the reason was a lack of water.

Rebellion always drove Aaron and Moses to the door of the tabernacle to meet God on their faces. Together they sought direction, and together they walked toward the rock. But instead of demonstrating faith in God's provision by speaking to the rock, Moses struck the rock. Moses then said, "Hear now, you rebels! Must we bring water for you out of this rock?" (Numbers 20:10 NKJV).

Out of frustration, anger, or exhaustion, Moses took the focus away from God and put the spotlight on Aaron and himself. Notice the word *we* in his statement. This shows that Aaron felt the same way and thus would also have to share the consequence. Like Moses, he would not enter the Promised Land.

Aaron didn't do the striking, but he shared the penalty. Aaron didn't complain, argue, or point the finger because he agreed with Moses's

action. Years earlier, he would have tried to squirm out of taking responsibility, but he had gotten better over the years. He had grown in his spiritual life and leadership skills. There may be times when you as a leader, under the leadership of someone else, will have to pay the penalties of your superior. Be like Aaron, and don't try to squirm out of it.

Enoch—He Walked with God

GENESIS 5:18–24 *Jared lived one hundred and sixty-two years, and begot Enoch. After he begot Enoch, Jared lived eight hundred years, and had sons and daughters. So all the days of Jared were nine hundred and sixty-two years; and he died. Enoch lived sixty-five years, and begot Methuselah. After he begot Methuselah, Enoch walked with God three hundred years, and had sons and daughters. So all the days of Enoch were three hundred and sixty-five years. And Enoch walked with God; and he was not, for God took him. (NKJV)*

Enoch walked with God and "was not." He vanished, but we don't know how. We know little of Enoch's life except that he walked with God and was taken from this world alive. Six short verses document 365 years of a man who raised a family and saw his society as corrupt and wicked. Still he walked, pleased, and served God.

The kind of walk that Enoch had with God is closely related to the "abiding" that Jesus refers to in John 15:4–7. In those verses, Jesus says that if we walk in his power, we will bear fruit and have our prayers answered.

This Enoch is different from the Enoch mentioned in Genesis 4:17. That Enoch was the son of Cain and was in a line of wicked people. The Enoch who walked with God was in the line of Seth, which had many godly people in it.

apply it

Jesus also stressed in John 15:4–7 that we cannot bear fruit as a Christian without "abiding" in him or operating in his power. If we are trying to overcome a problem without looking to him and surrendering to the way God wants us to cope, we will fail.

Enoch Hated Sin

> JUDE 1:14–15 *Now Enoch, the seventh from Adam, prophesied about these men also, saying, "Behold, the Lord comes with ten thousands of His saints, to execute judgment on all, to convict all who are ungodly among them of all their ungodly deeds which they have committed in an ungodly way, and of all the harsh things which ungodly sinners have spoken against Him."* (NKJV)

Elijah
2 Kings 2:11

church
Hebrews 10:25

Enoch is quoted in the book of Jude making a prophecy about Christ's return. He strongly denounced the selfish acts of false teachers seeking their own way. Enoch walked with God every single day. At that time, there were no Christian books, Bibles, or DVDs to support his relationship with God. Yet week after week he rejected the evil in his world to stay strong in his commitment to God. He lived in victory, and God took him from this world.

Enoch vanished and was immediately in heaven with God. He didn't experience death. The only other man who never tasted death was Elijah. Both Enoch and Elijah walked with God and hated sin. They were richly rewarded for it.

Who was Enoch's mother, since Adam and Eve were the only people alive who could produce children? Obviously, Cain had to marry one of his sisters. Only later was such a union forbidden because of the physical ramifications down the line. But in the beginning it was necessary.

Enoch had God's perspective about life; we can too. Although Enoch didn't have support for his spiritual life, we have an abundance of support available: seminars, Bible studies, Sunday school, worship services, and many other opportunities. We need to take advantage of those and especially make sure that going to church is a regular habit.

"Beam Me Up, God!"

> HEBREWS 11:5–6 *By faith Enoch was taken away so that he did not see death, "and was not found, because God had taken him"; for before he was taken he had this testimony, that he pleased God. But without faith it is impossible to please Him, for he who comes to God must believe that He is, and that He is a rewarder of those who diligently seek Him.* (NKJV)

Enoch knew God! No one mentored him into this special relationship. No man helped him walk in victory. Enoch set his heart to know God. He rose above the wicked times he was in and pleased God, and God rewarded his godly character by removing him from this world.

If we want to walk with God as Enoch did, we must love the things God loves and hate the things he hates. All the trappings of today's society will not satisfy us anyway. We gain much more by seeing life through God's eyes and by obeying him.

Enoch sets a winsome image for all who desire to walk with God and please him. "Can two walk together, unless they are agreed?" (Amos 3:3 NKJV). Only by faith can we seek to please our heavenly Father. Human effort alone can't do it. We can walk with him only when we reject our own rule and agree to allow God to control our lives.

God longs for us to have a relationship with him. To walk with him requires setting his standards before us and following them. God rewards our faith by removing us from the dominion of sin through faith in Jesus Christ. Just as Enoch was taken out of this world, our relationship with God will be transformed when we allow him to take the world out of us.

Knowing God as Enoch did is something that doesn't just happen; it's something we choose to work at. Not in the sense of striving and gritting our teeth, but in the sense of making time to read the Bible, pray, meditate on Scripture, and look for God moving in our daily lives.

Although daily life gets hectic and overwhelming and we must think about it all the time, knowing God is a far greater thing to dwell upon. Even in the midst of our hectic lives, we can keep him at the forefront of our thinking by constantly shooting "arrow" prayers up to him. "Arrow" prayers are those prayers that are short and fast and meaningful.

go to

high places
Leviticus 26:30

what others say

Max Lucado

Change your definition of prayer. Think of prayers less an activity for God and more as an awareness of God. Seek to live in uninterrupted awareness. Acknowledge his presence everywhere you go.[11]

Jehoshaphat—Learning to Make Wise Alliances

the big picture

2 Chronicles 16:13–17:1–19

Jehoshaphat reigned in Judah as king after his father, Asa, died. He served God and wanted the people of his kingdom to also follow God, so he took down the high places of worship of foreign gods. He also arranged for the book of the Law to be taught to the people, and they responded with renewed faith. The nation and its culture were transformed by the king's decisions.

Jehoshaphat started his reign over Judah when he was thirty-five years old. He recognized the religious weakness in the land and instituted a kingdom-wide campaign to learn God's laws and understand how those laws should affect the Israelites' lives. He desired that the people put God first in their hearts and minds. As a result, his efforts turned the corner for the people. The religious decline was reversed. In addition to the religious instruction, he also improved the judicial system for his people.

Jehoshaphat also knew there was idolatry in the land, and his heart burned with the desire to do something about it. So he destroyed the altars located on hills, which were called "<u>high places</u>," where Canaanite worship occurred.

We have high places in our world today that are just as dangerous and corrosive to our souls as in the time of Jehoshaphat. Jobs, things, and image, among others, show our desire to serve or wor-

apply it

ship something outside ourselves. The lesson learned back then applies to us today. When we find obstacles to serving God, we must tear them down. Obstacles often become idols and prevent us from fully trusting him. Not convinced? Paul expands the definition of idolatry in his letter to the Colossians. He included "fornication, uncleanness, passion, evil desire, and covetousness, which is idolatry" (Colossians 3:5b NKJV).

When we remove these idols from our lives, it signals a yielded heart and demonstrates our desire for his rule and reign over our own. It also shows to others our resolve to be fully committed to God's kingdom, thus building their confidence in our partnership with them.

We also learn the importance of God's Word from this man's actions. Jehoshaphat believed if the people would study God's word, their behavior would be holy. When we study the Bible, the same thing should happen to us. "All Scripture is given by inspiration of God, and is profitable for doctrine, for reproof, for correction, for instruction in righteousness, that the man of God may be complete, thoroughly equipped for every good work" (2 Timothy 3:16–17 NKJV).

In those days, the Law, which was a set of rules, was the Israelites' "Bible." But today, we have our Bible, and it contains both the Jewish Law in the first five books of the Bible (Genesis through Deuteronomy) and the words and works of Jesus. The entire Bible documents God's redemptive plan for his creation, and we can have confidence in the historicity of this precious book.

Bad Partners, Bad Decisions

the big picture

2 Chronicles 18:1–34

King Jehoshaphat aligned himself with the evil king of Israel, Ahab. He did that through marrying one of Ahab's daughters and also by fighting alongside him against enemies of their countries. But before they went to battle, Jehoshaphat suggested he and Ahab seek the counsel of a prophet of God. That prophet, Micaiah, predicted dire results for Ahab. Jehoshaphat aligned himself with Ahab anyway and almost died because of it.

King Jehoshaphat was one of the most godly kings to sit on the throne of Judah, but he made a grave error when he joined forces with one of the worst kings in Israel's history. He was invited by the evil King Ahab to join in reclaiming a city from a previous battle. It seems that it may have been an unsanctified or misapplied mercy to make this decision. He agreed to go to war before the Lord gave his approval. This signals a possible weakness in Jehoshaphat's character, possibly the first symptom of wanting to look good and decisive to his peer.

This decision cost him dearly. He nearly lost his life, it opened Judah up to idolatry, and it resulted in the murder of most of his family.

When we make alliances or partnerships with unbelievers, compromise and trouble can slip into our lives. The Bible strongly warns against teaming with unbelievers. "Do not be unequally yoked together with unbelievers. For what fellowship has righteousness with lawlessness? And what communion has light with darkness?" (2 Corinthians 6:14 NKJV).

go to

require
1 Timothy 4:15

acknowledged
1 Corinthians 3:12–15

charge
Philippians 1:6

God Forgives Jehoshaphat's Bad Decisions

apply it

> **the big picture**
>
> ## 2 Chronicles 19:1–11
>
> Jehoshaphat was rebuked by the seer Hanani for his connections to Ahab, but God also gave him credit for the righteous things he did. As a result, he seemed to be motivated to do more godly things for his country.

Jehoshaphat appointed more judges and warned them they were accountable to God for the standards they used to judge others. God didn't <u>require</u> perfection of Jehoshaphat, but he did want him to follow him very closely.

God is just and righteous. He recognizes the good we do along with the bad. The bad will burn up, the good done in God's power will be <u>acknowledged</u> in heaven. God doesn't require perfection of us, but he does want us to continually and continuously seek him for the ability to live in his power. He knows we are in a process of growing, and he is in <u>charge</u> of making that growth happen.

something to ponder

Jehoshaphat's experience reminds us that God holds us accountable for the authority we exercise, as shown in the following chart.

Accountability for Authority

You Are Commanded	You Must	Scripture
Be careful, you are judging on behalf of God.	Know the stakes	2 Chronicles 19:6
Be impartial and honest.	Know the rules	2 Chronicles 19:7
Be faithful.	Follow the rules	2 Chronicles 19:9
To fear God.	Know your boss	2 Chronicles 19:9

A Heart for God

the big picture

2 Chronicles 20:1–13

Judah's enemies came to make war against Jehoshaphat and he cried out to God for help. He prayed a very powerful prayer to God, asking for his help and deliverance.

This invasion was a great threat to the kingdom of Judah. Jehoshaphat called upon his people to fast and pray. They followed his directions, and his prayer modeled the heart of a man who honestly seeks God. In his prayer:

- He trusted God for the outcome and believed God could save the nation.

- He sought God's intervention because his people belonged to God.

- He acknowledged God's sovereignty.

- He praised God and took comfort in his promises.

- He professed complete dependence on God, not himself, for deliverance.

God is in charge of everything. That is called *sovereignty*. It means God is the blessed controller of all things and has the power to accomplish whatever he plans. King David said, "Yours, O LORD, is the greatness, the power and the glory, the victory and the majesty; for all that is in heaven and in earth is Yours; Yours is the kingdom, O LORD, and You are exalted as head over all" (1 Chronicles 29:11 NKJV).

To be God's kind of man today, we must follow Jehoshaphat's lead. We must depend on God's power rather than on our own. In

strengthen your family

our businesses and in our families, we can trust that God is in control and can ask for wisdom to respond to the challenges that face us. We also should praise and thank God ahead of time for what he will do.

Victory and Then Failure

the big picture

2 Chronicles 20:14-37

God sent his Spirit upon Jahaziel and he prophesied success for the army of Jehoshaphat and his army. Jehoshaphat, along with the people of Judah, worshiped God for his faithfulness in giving them confidence as they went into battle. They had success and rejoiced greatly. However, Jehoshaphat didn't do so well after joining Ahab's son, Ahaziah, in a business deal. As a result, God caused one of their ventures to go poorly. Later, after twenty-five years as king, Jehoshaphat died.

The alliance Jehoshaphat formed with Ahab came back to hurt him again. Once again, one man served the Lord and the other one served idols. A shipbuilding deal with Ahaziah failed, and both men lost all their ships. Jehoshaphat had experienced success in the past, but he didn't stay as faithful as he could have.

Success at one point doesn't guarantee success in all our ventures. We need to stay alert and watch for Satan's schemes to bring temptation—especially after a time of great success. God can cause things to go poorly if we disobey—even if we've been faithful in the past. Make partnerships only with those who love and serve God. Every Christian should examine his motives before entering into partnerships. Does the partner share the same goals? How much prayer was invested in this decision? Is this a quick fix or a long-term solution? Questions like these should be honestly answered before moving forward in partnership with anyone. Are you willing to settle for less potential success while at the same time pleasing God more? You may find that in the end you'll be more successful by following God.

apply it

Chapter Wrap-Up

- Noah and his family were the only people on earth whom God considered righteous. God chose Noah to build an ark and save himself, his family, and the animals of the earth for the coming flood. (Genesis 6:5–12)

- Following God's instructions, Noah faithfully built an ark for 120 years, even though the people around him criticized. When God sent the flood over all the earth, everyone and everything was destroyed, except the people and animals in the ark. (Genesis 6:13–7:24)

- After the flood receded, everyone left the ark. Noah again showed his faith in God by building an altar. God created the first-ever rainbow to symbolize his promise that he would never again destroy the earth by flood. (Genesis 8:1–9:19)

- Job was another righteous man who believed God couldn't do anything wrong. Even when Satan orchestrated the murder of Job's ten children and the destruction of everything he owned, Job still trusted God. (Job 1:1–22)

- When Satan saw that Job kept his allegiance to God, Satan broadened his attack (with God's permission) to include physical illness that took Job to the edge of death. Yet Job still didn't blame God for doing anything wrong. (Job 2:1–10)

- Four friends of Job tried to convince him he was suffering because he had sinned. Job maintained his innocence. At last, in answer to Job's cry, God responded by pointing to his own majestic sovereignty. Job was vindicated and richly rewarded for his steadfast faith. (Job 2:11–31:40)

- Aaron was the second in command alongside Moses, but he struggled with following God wholeheartedly. (Exodus 4–Deuteronomy 10)

- Enoch was a righteous man who walked closely with God; therefore, instead of dying, God caused him to vanish. (Genesis 5:23–24)

- Jehoshaphat was a king in Judah who wanted his people to seek God and so he removed the places of foreign and false god worship. (2 Chronicles 17:6)

Study Questions

1. What were the dimensions of the ark God instructed Noah to build?

2. After the Flood, what did God's creation of the rainbow represent?

3. How did God control what happened to Job?

4. How did Job keep from blaming God?

5. How did God use Aaron in the Israelites' history?

6. How is the end of Enoch's life described?

7. What is meant when "high places" are mentioned in Jehoshaphat's story?

Chapter 9: Men of Power—Lessons in Might and Missteps

Let's Get Started

Although many people in the Bible had God's power, there are three men in particular who showed God's strength in remarkable ways. Samson was physically powerful but spiritually weak. Elijah had great power, calling down fire from heaven in a tremendous display of God's glory; but a queen intimidated him. Elisha, whom Elijah mentored, performed even more miracles than Elijah did. All three of these men were people just like you and me. And just as God wanted to glorify himself through them, he wants to glorify himself through us. They weren't perfect and neither are we. If God can use them, he can use us. Let's see what we canlearn from them.

rules
Numbers 6:2–7

Samson—Man of Great Physical Power

JUDGES 13:24–25 *So the woman bore a son and called his name Samson; and the child grew, and the LORD blessed him. And the Spirit of the LORD began to move upon him at Mahaneh Dan between Zorah and Eshtaol. (NKJV)*

An angel foretold Samson's birth, and said to his parents, "No razor shall come upon his head, for the child shall be a Nazirite to God from the womb; and he shall begin to deliver Israel out of the hand of the Philistines" (Judges 13:5 NKJV).

A Nazirite had to follow these <u>rules</u>:

1. He had to abstain from wine and other fermented drink.

2. He could not drink vinegar made from wine or from other fermented drink.

3. He could not drink grape juice or eat grapes or raisins.

4. He could not eat anything that came from the grapevine, not even the seeds or skins.

5. No razor could be used on his head.

go to

ceremony
Numbers 6:19

fasting
Acts 14:23

Timnah
Genesis 38:12

judges
presiding officers
over Hebrew affairs

fasting
going without something desirable

6. He had to remain holy until the period of his separation to the Lord was over.

7. He could not go near a dead body, not even those of his parents or relatives.

Most people who made such vows went through a <u>ceremony</u> of sacrificing their hair to the Lord. But Samson was born for a special work.

Israel was entering the end of a historical time when **judges** ruled the land (see Illustration #14). The Hebrews were again under the thumb of the Philistines. Samson was one of the last judges and served Israel for twenty years. Unfortunately, Samson wasn't prepared for the crisis the Hebrews faced. He misused his gifts and the power the Holy Spirit gave him.

what others say

Michael Wilcock

The Nazirite would say a definite no to certain perfectly natural things in order to show how definite was . . . his dedication of himself to God.[1]

Although no one takes a Nazirite vow these days, we can do something with the same spiritual significance by **fasting** for a period of time from food or activity. The purpose is to develop spiritual muscles.

I Want What I Want

JUDGES 14:1–4 *Now Samson went down to <u>Timnah</u>, and saw a woman in Timnah of the daughters of the Philistines. So he went up and told his father and mother, saying, "I have seen a woman in Timnah of the daughters of the Philistines; now therefore, get her for me as a wife." Then his father and mother said to him, "Is there no woman among the daughters of your brethren, or among all my people, that you must go and get a wife from the uncircumcised Philistines?" And Samson said to his father, "Get her for me, for she pleases me well." But his father and mother did not know that it was of the LORD—that He was seeking an occasion to move against the Philistines. For at that time the Philistines had dominion over Israel. (NKJV)*

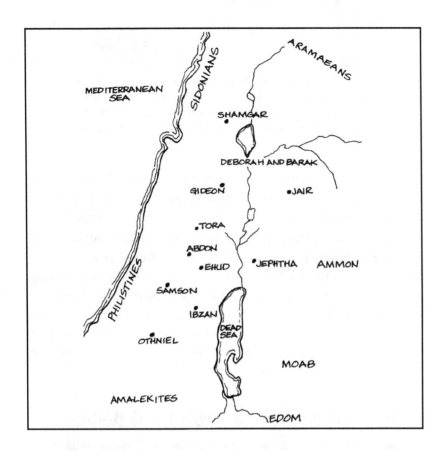

Illustration #14
Period of the Judges—The Israelites often suffered oppression from outside clans, such as the Philistines. The judges were unofficial leaders who stepped in to deliver various groups of Israelites from the foreign oppressors. Often, after the judge brought military victory, he or she would also rule. This map shows the seats of the judges and the enemies of Israel.

Samson's appetite for pleasure overcame his devotion to God. Imagine a Nazirite wanting to marry a Philistine woman who worshiped the god Dagon (see Illustration #15). Samson repeated this desire to compromise God's rules until he paid for his excesses with his life.

Illustration #15
Dagon—Known as the father of the god Baal, Dagon was associated with agriculture and the life-giving powers of water. He was the national god of the Philistines.

what others say

Dr. Tony Evans

Be clear on who you are. Present yourself as a slave of righteousness, not a slave of sin. You owe sin absolutely nothing. You are going to sin, but don't be a slave to sin. Don't let sin control you. Samson was a great man of God, but he became a slave to lust.[2]

Although God cannot be in the presence of evil, he uses it for his purposes. It seems that God allowed Samson to follow foolishness, intending to bring good from Samson's unrighteous conduct.

Since God doesn't want his children connected with unbelievers in marriage or business, we must teach our children that marrying or partnering with those who don't love and obey God will only bring great difficulty into their lives. "Do not be unequally yoked together with unbelievers. For what fellowship has righteousness with lawlessness? And what communion has light with darkness? And what accord has Christ with **Belial**? Or what part has a believer with an unbeliever?" (2 Corinthians 6:14–15 NKJV).

Remember? No Contact with Dead Bodies?

JUDGES 14:5–9 *So Samson went down to Timnah with his father and mother, and came to the vineyards of Timnah. Now to his surprise, a young lion came roaring against him. And the Spirit of the LORD came mightily upon him, and he tore the lion apart as one would have torn apart a young goat, though he had nothing in his hand. But he did not tell his father or his mother what he had done. Then he went down and talked with the woman; and she pleased Samson well. After some time, when he returned to get her, he turned aside to see the carcass of the lion. And behold, a swarm of bees and honey were in the carcass of the lion. He took some of it in his hands and went along, eating. When he came to his father and mother, he gave some to them, and they also ate. But he did not tell them that he had taken the honey out of the carcass of the lion. (NKJV)*

God showed Samson what he could do with the Spirit of the Lord empowering him. As a Nazirite, he wasn't supposed to touch any dead thing. He violated his vows by returning to the carcass and taking the honey.

Satan is also called a roaring lion in the Bible. "Your adversary the devil walks about like a roaring lion, seeking whom he may devour. Resist him, steadfast in the faith, knowing that the same sufferings are experienced by your brotherhood in the world" (1 Peter 5:8–9 NKJV). As Samson should have avoided the unclean lion carcass, we should avoid Satan's unclean influence in our hearts.

The Lord Jesus conquered Satan on the cross and <u>spiritual death</u> was eliminated. Like Samson, we can find sweetness in life from the victory of knowing Satan and his evil plans don't have to control us. But even though that fatal attraction is dead, we still must <u>choose</u> to live in God's power.

go to

spiritual death
1 Corinthians
15:55–57

choose
Romans 6:12

Can't You Keep a Secret?

the big picture

Judges 14:10–20

For Samson's wedding feast, he bet his companions they couldn't figure out his riddle in seven days. When they couldn't, they bullied Samson's new wife into getting them the answer. When they answered Samson's riddle, he realized how they had figured it out. Angered, he killed some Philistines and took their clothing to pay off the bet.

Samson's new wife deceived him because she favored her Philistine guests and also feared for her life. Samson killed those who turned his wife against him. Samson then abandoned his wife and ran to his parents' home.

This experience should have been a warning to Samson of his wrong choice in a wife, but he seemed oblivious to how he had brought this on himself. "The foolishness of a man twists his way, and his heart frets against the LORD" (Proverbs 19:3 NKJV). His anger may indicate that he felt guilty but wasn't willing to face his own poor choices.

Samson increased his exposure to deception by marrying an unbeliever. When we love someone, we don't want to truthfully face how that person is influencing us. Since his wife didn't care about spiritual things, she couldn't help his spiritual perspective.

Anger is a deceptive emotion that tries to make others seem like the cause of our problems. There is also a behavior called "displacement" where we blame something or someone for our anger, but the cause is really something else. Ask yourself, "What am I really angry about?" Then you can deal with the real issue.

strengthen your family

One of the advantages of marrying a Christian wife is to have her godly perspective to complement and add to your own. Two heads definitely are better than one, but that extra head should be based on the <u>mind of Christ</u>.

I'll Teach You a Lesson

the big picture

Judges 15:1–8

When Samson heard his father-in-law had given his wife to someone else in marriage, Samson took out his anger on all the Philistines by tying burning torches to foxes and sending them through the grain fields to burn the Philistine crops.

Setting the grain fields afire was a great threat to the Philistines because those fields provided the food for the next year. Ironically, instead of threatening Samson directly, the Philistines threatened Samson's wife, saying they would burn her and her father's house. She betrayed her husband again, and the very thing that she feared came upon her as she and her father's house were burned.

Samson's revenge didn't get his wife back. It just got him more troubles. We don't know why, but Samson had a hard time thinking clearly, which seems amazing considering he was a judge over Israel for twenty years. We don't hear about any of the good things that he did as a judge—if he did anything good. Evidently, God wants us to learn from the wrong choices Samson made.

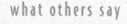
what others say

go to

mind of Christ
1 Corinthians 2:16

Charles R. Swindoll

You'll find out what Samson discovered—focusing on the sensual side of life will bring one anxiety, one heartache, after another. . . . The revenge he took against the Philistines incited them to an intense hatred in return.[3]

Revenge is never God's plan for us. He wants us to turn the other cheek if slapped. He is the one who is in charge of giving punishments and revenge.

We aren't even supposed to fret about the deeds or activities of the unrighteous. "Do not fret because of evildoers, nor be envious of the workers of iniquity. For they shall soon be cut down like the grass, and wither as the green herb" (Psalm 37:1–2 NKJV). However, God does want us to fight the influence of evil by doing good.

go to

revenge
Romans 12:19

good
Romans 12:21

I Did It My Way

the big picture

Judges 15:9–20

The Philistines took revenge on Samson by advancing on the men of Judah. Outnumbered and frightened, the men of Judah talked Samson into surrendering himself to the angry Philistines. As Samson was about to be handed over, God's power came upon him and he broke free and killed one thousand men.

Samson killed one thousand men with a club made of bone. The battle wasn't won because of the weapon or the man swinging it. It was because the Spirit of God moved the arm. Unfortunately, the man at the end of the arm took the credit. Then Samson said, "With the jawbone of a donkey, heaps upon heaps, with the jawbone of a donkey, I have slain a thousand men!" (Judges 15:16 NKJV).

Samson believed his own press. Only later did he credit the Lord's help. The theme of his life seems to be found in Judges 15:11: "As they did to me, so I have done to them" (NKJV).

what others say

Michael Wilcock

For the first time, he found himself in a situation he could not cope with. He asked for God's help instead of taking it for granted, and had a prayer answered. These remarkable events registered even with simple Samson.[4]

Samson is mentioned in the Hall of Faith in Hebrews 11:32. Only the grace of God can explain how a man of such strength could be overshadowed by his moral weakness and then be included in a list of godly men and women.

something to ponder

go to

glory
1 Corinthians 1:31

crowns
2 Timothy 4:8

cast
Revelation 4:10

nagging
Proverbs 27:15–16

We must be very careful to not take credit or <u>glory</u> for that which God does. One day we will receive <u>crowns</u> in heaven with gems marking the things we did for God. But we won't keep them. We'll <u>cast</u> them in honor before God's throne—because he was the source of them.

Another Nagging Woman Breaks Him!

the big picture

Judges 16:1–22

Samson lusted again, this time for Delilah. The Philistines paid her to find out the secret of his strength. After <u>nagging</u> him for a long while, Delilah finally got the truth: the source was his long hair. The Philistines attacked him, cut his hair, and were able to take him into bondage because he no longer had God's power.

Samson's lust for women led him to Gaza so he could visit a prostitute. During this visit he escaped from some Philistines who had plotted to kill him. His third encounter with a Philistine woman would be different. Unrestrained lust poisoned all his judgment as he surrendered to Delilah. Samson's desire for "strange" women blinded him. When his seven braids were cut, he betrayed his sacred vow to Jehovah God.

what others say

John Jewell

When the Philistines cut Samson's hair they took him, bound him, blinded him, danced around him, and made scorn and games of him. We are like Samson. The strength of our hair is the knowledge of the will of God. It is contained in our heads, the highest and principal part of us. If it is shorn off, if we are kept from hearing, reading, and understanding the Bible, then we will succumb to superstition.[5]

Nagging goes all the way back in history. Samson's first wife nagged him and so did Delilah. "She pestered him daily with her words and pressed him, so that his soul was vexed to death" (Judges 16:16 NKJV). Obviously, Satan knew the chink in Samson's armor, and he worked at it persistently through the ungodly women Samson chose. If Samson had picked more wisely, maybe he wouldn't have had to deal with so much destructive nagging.

Lust is like a whirlpool. The excitement of the forbidden spins you faster, filling your emotions with excitement. But the faster you spin, the deeper you plunge. When that whirlwind spits you out, there is no escape from the shame, loss of reputation, and suffering. The anguish is always greater than the <u>pleasures</u> of the sin.

Satan knows the chink in your armor. That's why you should always wear the <u>armor</u> of God. It gives us all the protection and power we need to fight against evil forces.

If your wife tends to nag you, could it be because you don't respond? Women often feel helpless in trying to get their husbands to meet their needs. As a result, anger feeds their relentless asking. You can turn that around by being responsive to her requests and desires.

go to

pleasures
Titus 3:3

armor
Ephesians 6:11

for your marriage

From Judge to Prisoner

the big picture

Judges 16:23-31

While Samson was in the custody of the Philistines, they gouged out his eyes. But eventually, his hair grew back and his strength increased. When given the opportunity, in his last moments, he called upon God for help. He caused the death of three thousand Philistines, but it cost his own life, too.

As a prisoner Samson was strapped into a harness like an ox, grinding wheat in a Philistine mill. After his eyes were gouged out, the darkness deepened his relationship with God. But his earlier choices had ended his chance to deliver Israel from the Philistines. The strongest man in the world ended up one of the most pitiful weaklings in biblical history. He was the laughingstock of his enemies and a warning to all of us.

what others say

Oswald Chambers

The spirit of obedience gives more joy to God than anything else on earth. By our obedience, we show that we love Him. The best measure of a spiritual life is not its ecstasies, but its obedience.[6]

Most troubling was Samson's final prayer. Instead of seeking power to avenge the name of God, he asked God for strength so that he could take revenge for the loss of his eyes. Samson missed God's best for him and the Israelites.

apply it

Do you sense God has a claim on your life? Does this claim have some goal? Or, are you tuning out God's plan and flirting around the edges of some whirlpool that threatens to pull you in? All of us who know God are called to obey him and serve him. Our choices can fill our lives with regret or fill our lives with fulfilling service. Which do you choose?

Elijah—Loner to Mentor

1 KINGS 17:1 *And Elijah the Tishbite, of the inhabitants of Gilead, said to Ahab, "As the LORD God of Israel lives, before whom I stand, there shall not be dew nor rain these years, except at my word."* (NKJV)

After the reigns of Saul, David, and Solomon, the ten northern tribes of Israel <u>rebelled</u> against the reign of David's throne. Jeroboam, the first king of the northern tribes, posted two calf images near the borders for his people to worship. After he died, six more kings came to power over the course of forty years. None of them did anything to return the people to the Lord.

King Ahab then came to power. Ahab married a woman from a nearby kingdom. Her name was Jezebel and she was a committed worshiper of Baal, the foreign god (see Illustration #17). Once she felt secure in her position as queen, it became clear she was the real power behind the throne. She influenced Ahab to set up an altar for Baal in Samaria, the capital of Israel. Then she began killing the prophets of Jehovah to rid the land of any godly influences. It was time for an extraordinary man to enter the picture. His name was Elijah.

go to

Gilead
Genesis 31:21

rebelled
1 Kings 12:19

what others say

J. Sidlow Baxter

Here is the man who bearded the beast in its very lair, the man who strode into the king's audience-chamber and denounced the king to his face, in the name of Jehovah. Here is the Martin Luther of old-time Israel.[7]

Imagine walking into the palace and uttering God's judgment to the king. The likelihood of surviving such an event was remote. Through his act, Elijah revealed his enormous <u>courage</u>. Courage is always rooted in three things: **purpose**, **justice**, and **duty**. Elijah possessed all three:

go to

courage
Deuteronomy 31:6

purpose
Ephesians 2:10

justice
Leviticus 19:15

idolatry
1 Kings 14:9

1. *Purpose:* As God's prophet, Elijah possessed focused purpose. Just like a police officer, fireman, or soldier is motivated by his calling, Elijah moved toward trouble with confidence. His **authority** came from his relationship with God, and his calling compelled him to act.

2. *Justice:* Elijah also possessed a divine sense of justice. As one who knew God and his commands, it was clear to Elijah that the kingdom of Israel's <u>idolatry</u> was breaking God's heart. Elijah's initial statement demonstrated how deeply rooted he was in the Law.

3. *Duty:* Elijah acted from duty. He was a prophet of God! It was his role and job to stand for God's righteousness. He hurled a challenge in Ahab's face because God sent him there. In a sense, Elijah was just doing his job.

purpose
reason for living

justice
fairness

duty
obligation

authority
command

It is God's Word, the Bible, that strengthens us and gives us the same kind of courage that Elijah possessed. God told Joshua, "This Book of the Law shall not depart from your mouth, but you shall meditate in it day and night, that you may observe to do according to all that is written in it. For then you will make your way prosperous, and then you will have good success" (Joshua 1:8 NKJV). The more we study the Bible, the more our spiritual inner life is strengthened. God's Scriptures teach us to recoil at injustice.

On-the-Job Training

the big picture

1 Kings 17:2–18

After Elijah made his powerful pronouncement to Ahab, the Lord told Elijah to leave Samaria. Elijah obeyed and stayed in a cave where ravens brought bread and meat for him to eat every morning and evening. Elijah drank water from a nearby brook. When the brook dried up, God sent him to a widow's house where God miraculously reproduced food for their provision.

After Elijah delivered God's judgment to Ahab in Beersheba, God told Elijah to flee to the Kerith Ravine, east of the Jordan River, which is a wilderness (see Illustration #16). The Lord added, "You shall drink from the brook, and I have commanded the ravens to feed you there" (1 Kings 17:4 NKJV). But the brook slowed to a trickle as the **drought** impacted the countryside. God was protecting Elijah from Ahab and teaching the prophet to depend on his Lord.

Illustration #16
The Life of Elijah—This map shows where major events occurred in Elijah's life. The events are numbered chronologically.

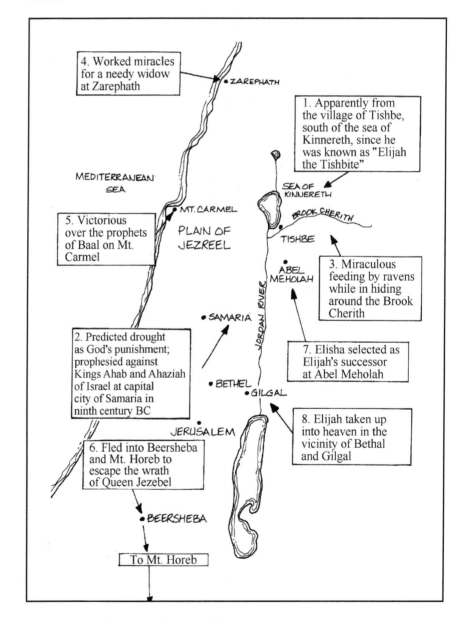

4. Worked miracles for a needy widow at Zarephath

1. Apparently from the village of Tishbe, south of the sea of Kinnereth, since he was known as "Elijah the Tishbite"

MEDITERRANEAN SEA

SEA OF KINNERETH

BROOK CHERITH

5. Victorious over the prophets of Baal on Mt. Carmel

MT. CARMEL

PLAIN OF JEZREEL

TISHBE

ABEL MEHOLAH

3. Miraculous feeding by ravens while in hiding around the Brook Cherith

SAMARIA

JORDAN RIVER

2. Predicted drought as God's punishment; prophesied against Kings Ahab and Ahaziah of Israel at capital city of Samaria in ninth century BC

7. Elisha selected as Elijah's successor at Abel Meholah

BETHEL

GILGAL

JERUSALEM

8. Elijah taken up into heaven in the vicinity of Bethal and Gilgal

6. Fled into Beersheba and Mt. Horeb to escape the wrath of Queen Jezebel

BEERSHEBA

To Mt. Horeb

When the brook dried up, God told Elijah to go eighty miles to the west coast, to a town called Zarephath (see Illustration #16). There he would meet a widow who would provide for him. Just as God had said, Elijah found her, a Gentile believer who was about to die from starvation. She responded to Elijah's command to feed him, by wondering out loud how she could provide enough for Elijah, herself, and her son. Elijah told her to trust God. She obeyed Elijah's request for food and served him first. God honored her faith and obedience. From that day on, there was always enough food to feed them.

depend on God
Psalm 62:7

Illustration #17
Baal—Baal was a weather god associated with thunderstorms and fertility. The Israelites fell into and out of Baal worship throughout their history because Baal's influence was strong in foreign tribes.

If you are faced with a bitter life situation that seems to chase your spirit the way Ahab chased Elijah, you need to look closely at Elijah's life. God wants you to give up your self-dependency and <u>depend</u> upon him. If you are thirsty for relief and the only brook you have clung to is now slowing to a trickle, it is time to tap into a new river of life.

The Showdown

the big picture

1 Kings 18:1–39
The Lord directed Elijah to meet with Ahab on Mount Carmel and propose a test between Baal (see Illustration #17) and Israel's one true God, Jehovah. Ahab and his "team," the 450 priests of Baal, tried to cajole their impotent god to burn up their sacrifice. They couldn't make it happen.

go to

twelve stones
Exodus 28:21

slain
killed

After three years of drought, God arranged for a showdown between Ahab's deity and Elijah's. The confrontation took place on Mount Carmel (see Illustration #16), which was regarded as Baal's sacred place, where Ahab assembled 450 false prophets against Yahweh's lone prophet. Thousands of Israelites showed up for this contest like some sports event. Elijah challenged them to make up their minds: "How long will you falter between two opinions? If the LORD is God, follow Him; but if Baal, follow him" (1 Kings 18:21 NKJV). Elijah challenged the prophets of Baal to place a bull on their altar and call on the name of their god. Elijah would then do likewise. The god who answered by sending fire would prove he is the one true God.

The crowd really enjoyed watching what would happen. Elijah may have been part showman and worked the crowd. The priests called on Baal for six hours, and during that time Elijah trashtalked them with helpful suggestions, such as "Shout louder! Your god can't hear you. Gosh, maybe it's his nap time!" The prophets cut themselves in an effort to force Baal to answer their prayers. But nothing happened.

Then Elijah took his turn. He called the people to gather around. They closely watched as he set up <u>twelve stones</u> representing the twelve tribes of Israel, then dug a trench around this altar. After the bull was **slain** and laid on the wood, Elijah asked the crowd to drench the entire altar with water from four large containers. Once completed, Elijah told them to repeat the soaking two more times. The water ran down the altar and even filled the trench. The stage was set!

This kingdom had been worshiping both God and Baal for some time. Whenever our loyalties are split, there is a sense of uncertainty. The masses may have been ready for a change.

something to ponder

Sometimes as we try to overcome a sin in our lives, we need to risk like Elijah did. Risking for us might mean telling someone about our struggle and asking him to pray for us. God will honor that vulnerability. God says, "Confess your trespasses to one another, and pray for one another, that you may be healed. The effective, fervent prayer of a righteous man avails much" (James 5:16 NKJV).

Elijah Prays

go to

grace
Romans 3:24

redeemed
Galatians 3:13

free gift
Ephesians 2:8–9

deserve
Titus 3:5

> 1 KINGS 18:36–37 *And it came to pass, at the **time** of the offering of the evening sacrifice, that Elijah the prophet came near and said, "LORD God of Abraham, Isaac, and Israel, let it be known this day that You are God in Israel and I am Your servant, and that I have done all these things at Your word. Hear me, O LORD, hear me, that this people may know that You are the LORD God, and that You have turned their hearts back to You again." (NKJV)*

time
3:00 p.m.

grace
undeserved favor

redeemed
bought back

The crowds must have hushed as they waited. How could one man compete against 450 priests? After the priest's six-hour prayer marathon, many of those present were probably bewildered when Elijah merely prayed two sentences and stopped. What a contrast!

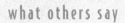
what others say

W. Phillip Keller

Just as the whole of the sacrifice, the wood, the altar, the soil upon which he now stood had been soaked, saturated, and literally submerged in water, so your own soul, spirit, and body have been submerged and saturated and soaked in the Word of the Lord. All was within the will of Jehovah God.[8]

The major difference between other world religions and Christianity is the focus upon the source of effort. With world religions, man must earn his relationship with the god he worships. But Christianity and a relationship with Jehovah are focused upon God's **grace**, which provided a way to be **redeemed** through Jesus's sacrificial death. Elijah didn't use his own efforts to make anything happen. Instead he prayed and depended on God's power.

Elijah's prayer served two purposes: to establish himself in the eyes of others as an obedient servant of God and to get the Israelites to turn their hearts back to Jehovah God.

When we see that God offers salvation as a <u>free gift</u>, not as something to be earned, we are encouraged. We know we can't ever be "good enough" to <u>deserve</u> God's love, therefore we can accept it as he offers it: unconditionally. Whereas people in other religions must always wonder whether they've performed well enough, Christians can know for sure.

key point

Watch Out! Success Is a Trap!

fear
Job 4:14

immobilize
make motionless

go to

the big picture

1 Kings 18:38–19:8

Elijah victoriously called fire down from heaven on Mount Carmel and called for the killing of the prophets of Baal. The predicted rain arrived and ended the drought. Queen Jezebel threatened Elijah, and he fled to escape her wrath. He grew depressed and prayed for death.

After Elijah prayed, fire fell from heaven and consumed the sacrifice, the wood, the stones, the soil, and the water in the trench. The people cried out, "The LORD, He is God!" (1 Kings 18:39 NKJV). At Elijah's request, the crowd seized the prophets of Baal and killed them. When Jezebel heard of this, she was furious. She sent word to Elijah that he would die before the next day because of what he had done. Elijah, filled with fear, fled to Judea.

what others say

Oswald Chambers

An average view of the Christian life is that it means deliverance from trouble. It is deliverance *in* trouble, which is very different.[9]

Elijah's depression shows that he was a man like us. It also revealed how fear can powerfully **immobilize** any of us, even when we serve God successfully. How could a threat from Jezebel have overwhelmed him after those mountaintop experiences? For three and one-half years, Elijah had trusted God completely for his very existence. Elijah even exhorted the widow, "Do not fear" (1 Kings 17:13 NKJV). What was the difference this time? We are all more vulnerable after a great victory. It is so easy to become self-confident and self-assured after an experience like this.

In the middle of the Negev Desert, Elijah stopped and prayed, "It is enough! Now, LORD, take my life, for I am no better than my fathers!" (1 Kings 19:4 NKJV). It was apparent Elijah was severely depressed. Mercifully, the Lord did not answer his prayer. At the end of his rope, Elijah fell asleep under a tree.

Satan watches for the times when we're successful and then uses our new confidence to make us proud. That pride makes us depend upon ourselves and sometimes even credit ourselves for what God did. After success, we must be careful to keep our eyes on God and acknowledge that he made it possible.

Some commentators believe Elijah was depressed because he had failed to end the worship of Baal. But others suggest it was caused by a sense of personal failure in his lack of trust in God when Jezebel threatened him. He might have mentally put himself down for his failure to believe God could deliver him. Although Elijah left Mount Carmel in victory, he never witnessed what God might have accomplished if he had stayed in Jezreel and faced Jezebel's threat head-on.

Elijah caved in to the darkest paralyzing aspect of fear. It caused him to flee from his work and did not allow God to supernaturally intervene as he had in the past. Fear diminishes our ability to focus on what God has done through us as leaders and as believers in the past. Fear also clouds our concentration on God's power and causes us to focus on our own inability. The solution is to keep <u>focused</u> on God's powerful <u>abilities</u>.

go to

focused
Hebrews 12:2

abilities
Jude 24

Mount Horeb
Exodus 3:1

zealous
enthusiastic

Solution for Depression

the big picture

1 Kings 19:9–21

God met with Elijah and gently allowed him to express his feelings of depression. Afterward God met his physical needs with rest and nourishment and directed him to anoint two new kings and Elisha as his successor. Elijah obeyed and his depression lifted.

God directed Elijah to <u>Mount Horeb</u> (see Illustration #16), the same place he revealed himself many years earlier to Moses. There Elijah complained to God that he had been **zealous** for him and his kingdom. He rehearsed how the Israelites had rejected God's covenant and killed his prophets. He whined that he was the only one left, and his life was at risk.

God answered his complaints by showing him powerful winds, earthquakes, and fire. Then God spoke to Elijah in a gentle whisper. Elijah again rehearsed how he had been zealous for God and his

go to

mentored
1 Peter 5:5

compassionate
Psalm 103:13–14

relationships
Proverbs 12:15

mentored
taught by an adviser

kingdom. God graciously listened and then gave him three tasks: anoint two different kings and select Elisha as his successor. Then, God gently revealed that there were actually seven thousand faithful believers in Israel.

Elijah left the mountain and found Elisha in a field. He placed the prophet's robe around Elisha's shoulders. Elisha left his family and for ten years was **mentored** by Elijah.

God wants to address our pity parties in the same way he did Elijah's. If we'll listen to his <u>compassionate</u> whisper, we'll be able to hear that we are not alone and that he wants to help us. The help may come as he gives us new tasks; or sometimes we need to get our attention off ourselves, so the help comes when God gives us someone to mentor or help.

The gentle whisper Elijah heard can symbolize the quiet inner guidance God uses to direct us. In this example, Elijah learned how to pass both God's authority and his own ministry to successors.

When a man is in leadership, he may think he should be a loner. He may think that separating himself emotionally from others distinguishes him as a strong leader. But that may only open him to the possibility of depression and moral failure—or at the least, isolation. Mentoring others and developing healthy <u>relationships</u> with them can diminish the possibility of those destructive tendencies.

When Elijah was depressed, God allowed him to express his feelings and work through his grief and disappointment. When you and I are depressed, we may think God will put us down for our feelings. Just as God dealt gently with this man who called fire down from heaven, he will deal gently with you and me. Elijah's story is an incredible picture of God's grace reaching out to a wounded man. In the same way, he desires to reach out to us when we are hurting.

God's solutions for depression:

- Trust God.
- Seek new purpose.
- Help others.
- Nourish the body.
- Express feelings candidly.

Last Steps for Elijah

go to

James
James 5:17

respects
Daniel 9:17

protégé
disciple or student

the big picture

1 Kings 20:13–2 Kings 2:11

Ahab died and his son Ahaziah became king. Because Baal worship continued in the kingdom, Elijah prophesied the new king's death. Arrogantly, Ahaziah sent fifty soldiers to seize Elijah, but they were killed by fire falling from heaven. The king sent another fifty. They also were killed. The king sent fifty more soldiers, but this time their leader had the sense to plead for their lives. Elijah agreed to return with them. He once again told the king, "You will die." In time, Elijah was taken up into heaven without actually dying physically.

During Elijah's sunset years we get a glimpse of a changed man. Once independent and a loner in the wilderness, Elijah became a man who embraced his fellow prophets and developed a deep friendship with Elisha. In his last years of life, Elijah touched the lives of many. He and his **protégé**, Elisha, visited the prophet training centers in the region. Just before Elijah was taken up by God, he parted the waters of the Jordan River and he and Elisha walked across. Soon after, Elijah was taken to heaven in a flaming chariot, leaving his position and ministry to Elisha.

what others say

Howard Hendricks

Elijah must have come to the end of his life with a profound sense of significance. It was not just that he had accomplished great things. He had, but more than that, he was leaving a legacy—the legacy of a man into whose life he had poured his own.[10]

In the New Testament Elijah is mentioned by <u>James</u>, the brother of Jesus, as an example of a man who believed in and practiced prayer. James refers to him as a man who is just like us. Considering the tremendous works that Elijah did, God evidently must want us to work similar works of faith. In a sense, we each can be just like Elijah because God <u>respects</u> any man's prayers of faith.

Although some may think that operating alone marks the strength of a man, Elijah learned that God wants men to interact with others and even mentor those who will continue God's work. Some would argue the time he spent with Elisha was Elijah's most important work. Who better to prepare the next prophet of God? God wants us to invest in the lives of others.

The best mentoring that a man can do is to invest in the lives of his family. Although a career may seem very important and take much time, only the investment of love and attention to the members of a man's family will bring the same kind of success that Elijah had. God even wants a man to be willing to <u>give</u> his life for his family.

Elisha—Miracle Man

1 KINGS 19:19–21 *So he departed from there, and found Elisha the son of <u>Shaphat</u>, who was plowing with twelve yoke of oxen before him, and he was with the twelfth. Then Elijah passed by him and threw his mantle on him. And he left the oxen and ran after Elijah, and said, "Please let me kiss my father and my mother, and then I will follow you." And he said to him, "Go back again, for what have I done to you?" So Elisha turned back from him, and took a yoke of oxen and slaughtered them and boiled their flesh, using the oxen's equipment, and gave it to the people, and they ate. Then he arose and followed Elijah, and became his servant. (NKJV)*

Elijah was known throughout the land as a mighty prophet of power. When challenged by Elijah to join in service to the Lord, Elisha jumped at the chance. He demonstrated total commitment by sacrificing his oxen—obviously, he didn't plan to resume plowing any day soon. There was nothing for him to return home to. For ten years, he walked with Elijah as a friend. Years spent as a servant, encourager, and companion prepared him for his new role as successor to the prophet Elijah.

give
Ephesians 5:25

Shaphat
Numbers 13:5

what others say

Bruce H. Wilkinson and Larry Libby

Elisha's first ministry was simply to become Elijah's friend. To be a listening ear; to offer words of counsel. To just be there. He poured the refreshing water of encouragement over Elijah's heart as a close companion.[11]

We don't know what it meant for Elisha to have the prophet's mantle placed on his shoulder. It could have been a common action that prophets frequently used. Regardless, it's obvious that Elisha knew immediately what it meant. We also don't know if Elijah and Elisha had previous contact. We do know that Elijah had earlier been <u>instructed</u> by God to go and commission Elisha as his successor, but whether Elijah knew him previously, we don't know.

It might not be clear today that Elijah gave permission to Elisha to go and do the things he asked. But based on the language of that day, when Elijah said, "What have I done to you?" that was the same as saying, "Do as you please" or "What have I done to stop you?"

From the fact that Elisha was leading twelve yoke (pairs) of oxen, we know that he was a well-to-do farmer and had a lot to give up. Just as Elisha destroyed everything that could draw him back from serving God, so must we. Jesus warned that "no one, having put his hand to the plow, and looking back, is fit for the kingdom of God" (Luke 9:62 NKJV).

The only way to grow spiritually is to be <u>convinced</u> that Jesus is God, and that he died for your sins. In addition, we must surrender to God's control and be committed to growing in his power. Although we won't do all these things perfectly, a half-hearted consideration of Jesus's claims will prevent us from becoming committed. We must count the <u>cost</u> and then surrender.

instructed
1 Kings 19:16

convinced
Romans 4:24

cost
Luke 14:28–33

I Know You're Going to Leave Me!

2 KINGS 2:1–6 *And it came to pass, when the LORD was about to take up Elijah into heaven by a whirlwind, that Elijah went with Elisha from Gilgal [see Illustration #16]. Then Elijah said to Elisha, "Stay here, please, for the LORD has sent me on to Bethel." But Elisha said, "As the LORD lives, and as your soul lives, I will not leave you!" So they went down to Bethel. Now the sons of the prophets who were at Bethel came out to Elisha, and said to him, "Do you know that the LORD will take away your master from over you today?" And he said, "Yes, I know; keep silent!"*

Then Elijah said to him, "Elisha, stay here, please, for the LORD has sent me on to Jericho." But he said, "As the LORD lives, and as your soul lives, I will not leave you!" So they came to Jericho. Now the sons of the prophets who were at Jericho came to

Enoch
Genesis 5:24

Elisha and said to him, "Do you know that the LORD will take away your master from over you today?" So he answered, "Yes, I know; keep silent!" Then Elijah said to him, "Stay here, please, for the LORD has sent me on to the Jordan." But he said, "As the LORD lives, and as your soul lives, I will not leave you!" So the two of them went on. (NKJV)

Elijah and Elisha both sensed that God would be taking Elijah up into heaven without experiencing death. We don't know how, but maybe God had communicated that to Elijah and then he had told others. When the other local prophets mentioned it to Elisha, he told them to be quiet. Maybe it was too painful for him to discuss.

what others say

Steve Farrar

If you . . . travel into the future, what would your legacy look like? Would there be a chain linking generation to generation with godly men who in turn produce more godly men?[12]

Elijah gave Elisha a challenge. He could choose to stay or he could choose to come with him and experience what God had in mind.

Only two people in the Bible never experienced death. One was Enoch and the other was Elijah. Even Jesus died, but then later was raised from the earth in his resurrected body. Obviously, this practice of taking people off the earth without their dying was not something God did often.

Just as Elisha had to choose whether to continue traveling on in discomfort in order to receive the blessing and power of Elijah, we must choose to be inconvenienced in order to live a godly life. For some it will mean service in a foreign country. For others, it may be a financial sacrifice, or it could mean standing alone in a family to represent Christ. Being a Christian isn't always comfortable, but it does bring eternal benefits and blessings.

Give Me a Double Portion of Power

2 KINGS 2:7–10 And fifty men of the sons of the prophets went and stood facing them at a distance, while the two of them stood by the Jordan. Now Elijah took his mantle, rolled it up, and struck the water; and it was divided this way and that, so that the two of them crossed over on dry ground.

And so it was, when they had crossed over, that Elijah said to Elisha, "Ask! What may I do for you, before I am taken away from you?" Elisha said, "Please let a double portion of your spirit be upon me." So he said, "You have asked a hard thing. Nevertheless, if you see me when I am taken from you, it shall be so for you; but if not, it shall not be so." (NKJV)

go to

Solomon
1 Kings 3:9

loves
Psalm 146:8

wise
Romans 16:27

knows
1 John 3:20

Everyone was waiting to see this incredible sight. They lined up along the Jordan River like spectators at a soccer game. Elijah did one last miracle, showing again the power of his cloak—which Elisha could inherit if he watched at the right time. Ten years earlier, Elisha had given up everything to follow Elijah. At the end, the only thing he asked was Elijah's blessing, like the blessing a father would give a son.

Elisha was passionate about becoming a prophet of God. When he asked for a double portion, Elijah responded that his request was "a hard thing." Elijah must have known that only God could give a double portion.

Solomon, a past king of Israel, had an opportunity to ask God for anything he wanted. He chose wisdom. As a result, God also gave him riches and victory. Like Solomon, Elisha could have asked Elijah for something material, but he chose something spiritual.

Every Christian should have a passionate desire for spiritual things. When we know how much God loves us, we will want to read his loving words in the Bible. When we recognize how wise God is, we will want to pray to find out his perspective. When we concentrate on how he knows the best thing for us to do, we'll want to obey.

There are many good reasons why we should be passionate about spiritual things. Not counted among them is the idea that following God will also bring us earthly gain. The apostle Paul wrote, "Yet indeed I also count all things loss for the excellence of the knowledge of Christ Jesus my Lord, for whom I have suffered the loss of all things, and count them as rubbish, that I may gain Christ" (Philippians 3:8 NKJV).

something to ponder

Wow—Whirlwind and Fire

2 KINGS 2:11–14 *Then it happened, as they continued on and talked, that suddenly a chariot of fire appeared with horses of fire, and separated the two of them; and Elijah went up by a whirlwind into heaven.*

pillar
Exodus 13:21

clothing
Colossians 3:8

And Elisha saw it, and he cried out, "My father, my father, the chariot of Israel and its horsemen!" So he saw him no more. And he took hold of his own clothes and tore them into two pieces. He also took up the mantle of Elijah that had fallen from him, and went back and stood by the bank of the Jordan. Then he took the mantle of Elijah that had fallen from him, and struck the water, and said, "Where is the LORD God of Elijah?" And when he also had struck the water, it was divided this way and that; and Elisha crossed over. (NKJV)

The whirlwind that Elisha saw was most likely the same kind of storm represented in the <u>pillar</u> of smoke and fire that accompanied the Israelites as they traveled through the wilderness. After Elijah was gone, Elisha picked up his cloak and called upon God to use him, like God had used Elijah.

Elisha called Elijah "father" and was so grieved by the loss of seeing Elijah transported into heaven that he ripped his own clothes. But it could also represent a shedding of his old life as a prophet-in-training. He was now a full-blown prophet and his new wardrobe was the prophet's mantle.

In a sense, we each "rip off" our old sinful <u>clothing</u> when we accept Christ as Savior and surrender to his lordship. Just as the stripping of Elisha's clothes could mean final surrender of everything that would prevent him from assuming the mantle and authority of Elijah, you must also give up everything that prevents you from experiencing your full authority as Christians. Give up sin and selfishness, and instead, "put on tender mercies, kindness, humility, meekness, longsuffering" (Colossians 3:12 NKJV).

Go Look If You Want To

2 KINGS 2:15–18 *Now when the sons of the prophets who were from Jericho saw him, they said, "The spirit of Elijah rests on Elisha." And they came to meet him, and bowed to the ground before him. Then they said to him, "Look now, there are fifty strong men with your servants. Please let them go and search for your master, lest perhaps the Spirit of the LORD has taken him up and cast him upon some mountain or into some valley." And he said, "You shall not send anyone." But when they urged him till he was ashamed, he said, "Send them!" Therefore they sent fifty men, and they searched for three days but did not find him. And* *when they came back to him, for he had stayed in Jericho, he said to them, "Did I not say to you, 'Do not go'?"* (NKJV)

go to

magnified
Philippians 1:20

magnified
made more
apparent

Elisha wasn't surprised at his own power, for God had been preparing him for this very moment. But evidently, the other prophets weren't so sure. Elisha tried to dissuade them from searching for Elijah, but finally gave in. It appears Elisha still had some learning to do about not letting other people influence him. But regardless, he already had their respect, for they bowed down to him.

As leaders, we must not be unduly influenced by the opinions of others. Although this is hard and something even Elisha had to learn, we will have more freedom to obey God and do the right thing when we aren't overly worried about what other people think.

The Double Portion Has Come True

the big picture

2 Kings 2:19–22; 4:1–6:13

God worked many miracles through Elisha. God's power became well known among the Israelites and his name spread throughout the world.

Elisha's passionate desire to glorify God and be used by him was rewarded. Even after he died, his bones did a miracle. When a dead person was thrown into Elisha's grave, the man came back to life.

what others say

Bruce H. Wilkinson and Larry Libby

Elisha never tried to imitate Elijah! It was not Elijah's mannerisms, style, or methods he had requested; it was Elijah's strength and spirit. Now, endowed with that strength, Elisha was free to utilize his own gifts—he was free to be himself.[13]

God never wants a person whom he uses to take credit for the things they do in God's power. In all things, God wants to be exalted and **magnified** in the eyes of others through the works we do for him.

It is a very serious offense in God's eyes for someone to take the glory that only God deserves. God is a jealous God and he is the source of everything good that happens on the earth. "I am the LORD,

go to

power
Psalm 68:35

rich
Matthew 19:23–26;
Mark 10:24–27;
Luke 18:24–27

Virgin
Luke 1:34–37

dead
Acts 2:24

that is My name; and My glory I will not give to another, nor My praise to carved images" (Isaiah 42:8 NKJV). If we attribute the good in our lives to something or someone other than God—even ourselves—then it becomes a "god." God cannot allow that to happen because only he deserves to be credited.

Nothing is too hard for God. His <u>power</u> makes everything that he desires possible. The disciples thought it was impossible for the <u>rich</u> to enter heaven, but Jesus said it was possible. The <u>Virgin</u> Mary thought it was impossible for her to become pregnant, but the Holy Spirit made it possible. Everyone thought it was impossible for Jesus to be raised from the <u>dead</u>, but God made it possible. When we begin to feel hopeless or helpless about our situation or problem, we can remember that with God, all things are possible.

Summary of Miracles of Elisha and Their Meaning

Miracle	Meaning	Scripture
Jordan divided	Demonstrated the transfer of power from Elijah to Elisha	2 Kings 2:14
Waters healed at Jericho	Demonstrated the Lord, not Baal, could heal the spiritual pollution of their souls	2 Kings 2:21
Mocking youths torn by bears	Demonstrated the consequences of open disrespect for the Lord	2 Kings 2:24
Water supplied	Deliverance from enemy	2 Kings 3:16
Widow's oil multiplied	Faith rewarded with abundance	2 Kings 4:5
Barren woman gave birth and her child raised from death	God's power was exhibited in answer to earnest prayer	2 Kings 4:35
Poisoned stew rendered harmless	Represented the poison of false gods and how God could make them unable to influence his people	2 Kings 4:41
Loaves multiplied	God could expand the resources dedicated to him	2 Kings 4:43
Naaman healed	Proof of God's power even over leprosy	2 Kings 5:10
Gehazi struck with leprosy	Gehazi had lied and God disciplined him	2 Kings 5:27
Iron ax head caused to float	God could supernaturally provide for his servant's needs	2 Kings 6:6
Syrians smitten	God protected his people	2 Kings 6:18
Resurrection of a man	If God could bring a dead man back to life, then he could give victory to Israel	2 Kings 13:21

Joab—Strength in Battle but Not Much Else

the big picture

2 Samuel 2:10-32

After King Saul's death, David was established as king over the house of Judah and Ishbosheth, Saul's son, was chosen as king in Israel. David chose his nephew, Joab, as the commander in chief of his army. His name means "Jahweh is father" and he was the son of David's half sister. Ishbosheth had as his commander a man named Abner. Joab and Abner arranged for twelve of their men to fight one another. All twenty-four men died. That touched off a battle that David's team won.

The usual concept of "winner takes all" doesn't apply in this situation because all the designated fighters died. Joab took that as a cue to attack. After losing the battle, Abner fled. Asahel, Joab's brother, along with Joab, ran after him. Abner stabbed Asahel, killing him. Joab was convinced to give up the chase only after Abner referred to all of them as brothers and threatened more bloodshed. Joab broke off the pursuit but intended revenge later.

This encounter began a long, personal war between David's followers and the troops loyal to Abner and Ishbosheth. The leaders of Israel and Judah had lost sight of God's plan of a united kingdom. Instead of being united in the Promised Land, which God had given them for their benefit, they negated his blessings by always fighting with each other.

what others say

Tony Evans

This is the crab-in-the-barrel syndrome. Crabs will pull each other down trying to climb over each other to get out of a barrel. The result is no one gets out and they all get cooked.[14]

When you face conflict, take a second and consider if you share more in common with your perceived "enemy" than that which divides you. Differences might be small when compared to your shared interests and values. When insisting on having it your way, alarm bells should be sounding deep in your heart. Pride, selfishness, or arrogance is usually the fertile soil in which these conflicts grow.

for your marriage

This is particularly applicable within marriage. Often, a wife can begin to be perceived as the enemy when we disagree or she doesn't go along with our desires the way we'd like. But she isn't the enemy. The enemy is Satan, who wants to divide our unity and bring disgrace on God's name. If we can look for the positives and forgive the negatives, Satan will be defeated and his war lost.

Revenge After All

2 SAMUEL 3:26–29 *And when Joab had gone from David's presence, he sent messengers after Abner, who brought him back from the well of Sirah. But David did not know it. Now when Abner had returned to Hebron, Joab took him aside in the gate to speak with him privately, and there stabbed him in the stomach, so that he died for the blood of Asahel his brother.*

Afterward, when David heard it, he said, "My kingdom and I are guiltless before the LORD forever of the blood of Abner the son of Ner. Let it rest on the head of Joab and on all his father's house; and let there never fail to be in the house of Joab one who has a discharge or is a leper, who leans on a staff or falls by the sword, or who lacks bread." (NKJV)

Joab was incensed that King David would allow Abner to change sides and welcome him into David's camp. He even criticized David for this choice. But Joab quickly took action to end this reunion. What makes this murder more troubling was that Abner killed Joab's brother, Asahel, in war. Abner even <u>warned</u> Asahel twice to stop the pursuit. Abner didn't want to kill him. But Asahel charged toward his death. The concept of fair warning was obviously important to Abner, but Joab preferred deception.

Joab was fiercely independent. And David's management style helped Joab become even more bold in his independence. David didn't punish Joab because he feared the risk of mutiny with the army that Joab led. They were related through the same tribe, and David would not deal harshly with his own family, much less the powerful Joab. Joab was also the most skilled commander in the army. Knowing David's weaknesses allowed Joab to run without fear of punishment.

go to

warned
2 Samuel 2:21–23

Finding Support in a Brother

the big picture

2 Samuel 10:1–14

When David sent his servants to express their condolences to a new king after the old king died in a neighboring country, the servants were mistreated. David then sent Joab and his army to fight that kingdom. Joab and his brother, Abishai, divided up their forces to support each other and God gave them victory.

When faced with the enemy to the front and the rear, Joab divided his army and proceeded with the attack. In the face of great stress and conflict, Joab demonstrated careful thought and planning. With the prospect of two fronts to handle, he divided the responsibility with his brother.

Joab was a multifaceted man. Although he was fueled by anger and didn't mind killing someone at a moment's notice, he was a skilled military tactician. In spite of his lack of godly character, God used him to bring victory to his chosen people. How much better if Joab had been a great man in every area of his life.

what others say

Eugene H. Merrill

Nahash died and was succeeded by his son Hanun. Because Nahash had shown David some unspecified kindness, David sent an envoy to Ammon to express his sympathy to Hanun regarding his father. This, David no doubt hoped, would enable him to have a friendly ally on his eastern flank.[15]

When facing insurmountable obstacles, we need someone to help us. Men frequently try to go it alone. But the Bible says, "As iron sharpens iron, so a man sharpens the countenance of his friend" (Proverbs 27:17 NKJV). Be willing to bring someone alongside to help you.

key point

It Takes One to Know One

the big picture

2 Samuel 11:1–27

When King David wanted to cover up his adulterous affair with Bathsheba, he used Joab to bring Bathsheba's husband, Uriah,

go to

revenge
1 Kings 2:5

in from the battlefield. When that didn't work, David arranged with Joab to have Uriah placed in such a position that he was killed in battle.

David had sinned, and he needed someone whom he could trust to start the cover-up. David reached out for the one man who he knew would get the job done. Joab had already proved that murder was an acceptable solution to problems. He was the perfect problem solver with no conscience.

Joab's willingness to arrange the death of one of his military leaders proved he was loyal only to himself and to whatever benefited himself. In this case, he was willing to sacrifice the life of a friend in order to stay in a good relationship with an adulterer. Although assertive in promoting himself, he wasn't assertive in seeking God's righteous living for others.

Joab might have been thinking that he was getting away with everything because he was ingratiating himself to the king, but there will come a time when David tells his son and the new king, Solomon, to take revenge on Joab. We always receive our just deserts.

what others say

Alan Redpath

I wonder what Joab thought when he received his king's command that amounted to murder. But Joab saw to it that Uriah died. In fact, he conducted the battle in a ridiculous fashion, going right up to the very walls of the city and asking for trouble![16]

Loyalty is very important to any leader and he knows it goes both ways—to his commander and to his subordinates. Supporting those who correctly implement directions will build loyal followers. But sacrificing the interests of followers to promote ourselves with our leaders will eventually self-destruct.

Lights! Camera! Action!

the big picture

2 Samuel 14:1-33

Joab was instrumental in restoring the relationship between David and his son Absalom after Absalom murdered his brother

approval
Galatians 1:10

Joab knew David's heart was tender toward his exiled son Absalom. He shrewdly hired an actor to manipulate Absalom's return. The woman was known as the "woman of Tekoa," and Joab told her to tell David that she had two sons who wouldn't agree. When David told her to let him bring peace between members of her warring family, she confronted him, saying he wasn't even doing the same thing in his own family. Joab must have looked on with gratification as he saw David understand and then give him permission to bring Absalom into his presence.

Joab might have been playing both sides of the fence. He would be courting David's favor and solving a heartache. At the same time, when David died, Absalom would be heir to the throne and in Absalom's favor also.

Righteousness calls for us to do the right thing regardless of whether it benefits or doesn't benefit us. If we can truly believe that God can bring whatever blessings he desires into our lives regardless of whether we "network" with the right people or whether we have other people's <u>approval</u>, we won't care about anything except obeying God.

I Answer to No One

the big picture

2 Samuel 18:1–23

Absalom set himself up as king in rebellion against his father, and David ran away along with his army and Joab. In time, Joab and the army fought Absalom and his army and Absalom lost. Even though David had told all his army to deal gently with Absalom, Joab killed Absalom. David greatly grieved.

Joab knew David wanted Absalom spared, but he killed him anyway. The revenge played out in this murder was overshadowed by the calculating actions of Joab. Once again his loyalty to David was violated with another murder. Joab must have felt untouchable.

judgment
Romans 14:10;
2 Corinthians 5:10

defend
Luke 9:26;
2 Peter 2:9

Joab made a special effort to kill Absalom, so he couldn't say that the opportunity quickly presented itself or that it happened accidentally. After the battle as Absalom rode away, his great mane of hair was caught in a tree, and he hung there. Someone saw him and reported it to Joab, who then went to that tree and thrust a spear into Absalom's helpless, living body. Joab even told the man that he would have given him ten pieces of silver and a belt if he had killed Absalom immediately.

what others say

Eugene H. Merrill

A soldier of David found him in this predicament but because David had ordered his men not to hurt Absalom, the soldier refused to harm him further. Bloodthirsty Joab was not so reluctant, however, and thrust Absalom in the heart with three javelins. Immediately 10 of his attendants struck Absalom to make sure he died.[17]

Joab could not say he didn't understand or hear David's orders. "Now the king had commanded Joab, Abishai, and Ittai, saying, 'Deal gently for my sake with the young man Absalom.' And all the people heard when the king gave all the captains orders concerning Absalom" (2 Samuel 18:5 NKJV). Joab didn't want to understand or listen.

There won't be any excuses we can give on <u>judgment</u> day as we stand before God's throne to defend ourselves. If we haven't asked Jesus to forgive and cleanse us, nothing will save us from an eternity in hell separated from God's presence. If we have Jesus as our Savior, we won't need any excuses. Jesus will himself <u>defend</u> us.

Joab Gives a Pep Talk to the King

the big picture

2 Samuel 19:1–8, 13

When Joab heard that David grieved Absalom's death even though they had won a great battle, Joab rebuked David for letting his army down. Even though David changed his attitude, he also intended to replace Joab as his commander in chief.

When Joab and the army returned from the victory that saved David's throne, they were shocked that he would not meet with them and acknowledge their contribution. Instead, David was shedding tears for his son, Absalom, and turning his back on those valiant men. Joab recognized the great insult this was to the troops he led. He confronted the king and told him to snap out of it and do his duty as supreme commander. He told David that if this continued, another rebellion might erupt.

Except for his betrayal of Uriah, Joab seemed to be a great commander for defending his troops' morale and concerns. He was a fighter's fighter, and he fought for his men. Again, Joab shows us the multifaceted side of a man who, in this case, stood up for the right thing, but in his overall life was primarily interested in his own welfare.

Many times it is necessary to confront those in leadership above us. Joab used an excellent technique to persuade the listener. He explained the likely consequences in terms that were sure to impact the listener. If we share with others the good results of their needed behavior and the bad consequences for their lack of it, we may be more successful in getting them to see things our way.

Another Murder? Is There No End?

the big picture

2 Samuel 20:1–22

David assigned Amasa to handle another rebellion in the kingdom. He moved slowly in his assignment. Joab saw Amasa as a rival general and murdered him while seeking out an enemy named Sheba.

Joab probably justified this murder as a service for David because Amasa had been a general under Absalom. Along with that strike against him, Amasa delayed in rallying the troops to handle the rebellion. Justified in his own mind, Joab saw it as another opportunity to remove someone who was in his way.

go to

replace
2 Samuel 19:13

what others say

Tony Evans

Jealousy says, "If I can't get to the top, I'm not going to be at the bottom by myself." This is a hideous sin that keeps people from reaching their full potential because other people do all they can to pull them back down.[18]

At one point not too many months previously, David had determined that Amasa would replace Joab. The assignment that David gave Amasa may have been his first step in lifting up Amasa into a position over Joab. Joab knew this, of course, and wanted to prevent it. But of course, that doesn't justify his murderous actions.

Insightful Objections

the big picture

2 Samuel 24:1–9

David told Joab to take a census of the people but Joab believed it was the wrong thing to do. He mentioned his concerns but David told him to do it anyway. As a result, David and Israel suffered God's wrath.

Even Joab knew the idea of a census was wrong. It amounted to a draft for the army, and there was no need to enlist men at that point because peace ruled the land and David was solidly in power.

This is the only time we find Joab showing any consideration for God's point of view. He told David that God could expand his troops if it were needed and that the census was a bad idea. David ignored Joab even though this was the first time Joab had given valid spiritual advice.

strengthen your family

Maybe if David had praised any spiritual growth of Joab in the past, or even now at this late date, Joab might have been encouraged to seek God wholeheartedly. As fathers, we need to be alert for opportunities to encourage and praise the spiritual development within our children—even if it seems too little too late.

But It Seems Reasonable

go to

looks
1 Samual 16:7

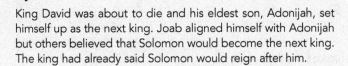

the big picture

1 Kings 1:1–9

King David was about to die and his eldest son, Adonijah, set himself up as the next king. Joab aligned himself with Adonijah but others believed that Solomon would become the next king. The king had already said Solomon would reign after him.

Since Adonijah was the eldest son at that time, it would seem from human reasoning that he should become the next king. After all, that was usually the way it worked. But God had other plans. He wanted Solomon to become king. Joab used his own human reasoning to choose whom he was going to support, but it turned out to not be a godly choice.

Adonijah was a very handsome man. Could it be that Joab was deceived by his good <u>looks</u> rather than paying attention to God's guidance? Joab most likely would have been part of hearing David choose Solomon as the next king, but for whatever reason, Joab chose to believe Adonijah would be king.

something to ponder

We need to look at life from God's perspective, not a human one, when we're trying to figure out how things should work. "Trust in the LORD with all your heart, and lean not on your own understanding; in all your ways acknowledge Him, and He shall direct your paths" (Proverbs 3:5–6 NKJV). What appears reasonable from a human perspective may not be God's viewpoint at all.

Get Rid of Joab

the big picture

1 Kings 2:1–6; 28–34

When David was instructing Solomon before his death, David told him to take revenge on Joab for killing Abner and Amasa. After David died and Adonijah failed in his bid to become king, Solomon commanded Joab to be killed.

David was on his deathbed. He instructed Solomon on kingly conduct. But when he gave advice on handling other people, Joab was the first name to pass his lips. He asked his son to give Joab the punishment he deserved. Knowing his end was near, Joab fled to the temple.

Joab knew death was at hand, but his desire to demonstrate strength and be in control appeared one last time when he refused to leave the temple. He likely thought forcing his death in the temple would put Solomon in a bad light with the people. He was wrong!

what others say

Thomas L. Constable

In mercy David had not executed the punishment that Joab's actions deserved, probably because Joab had shown David much loyalty and had served him well. But justice had to be done and Solomon had to do it.[19]

Joab had a hardened heart right to the end. He may have thought that he couldn't turn back from his previous method of operation, but God is always eager to receive a repentant sinner no matter when repentance happens. People who receive Christ on their deathbed will be saved just as much as someone who has walked with God all their lives. Their rewards in heaven will be different, but they both will enjoy heaven's delights. It's never too late.

Chapter Wrap-Up

- Samson was chosen by God to be a Nazirite but foolishly wanted a wife from the Philistine camp. Samson always seemed to want more, even more than God wanted for him. (Judges 14:1–4)

- Delilah eventually convinced Samson to tell her the secret source of his strength, and it caused him to be captured by the Philistines. Samson's divided loyalty brought an early death. (Judges 16:1–22)

- Elijah was a powerful prophet of God who defeated the priests of Baal by calling down fire from heaven. (1 Kings 18:1–39)

- After that successful display, Elijah was threatened by Queen Jezebel and he ran away, fearful and depressed. But God brought him the help he needed through Elisha and a new mission. (1 Kings 19:9–21)

188   **The Smart Guide to the Bible**

- Elisha was Elijah's fully committed assistant. When Elijah was about to go up into heaven, Elisha asked him for a double portion of power. (2 Kings 2:7–10)
- Elisha did even more miracles than Elijah and was a powerful representative for God among the people. (2 Kings 2:19–22; 4:1–6:13)
- Joab served the king David for a long time but his service was a mixed bag of loyalty and selfishness. (2 Samuel 2:13–1 Kings 2:34)

Study Questions

1. What did Samson force his parents to get for him even though they objected?

2. How did Delilah finally force Samson to tell her the secret of his great physical strength?

3. What did Elijah do on Mount Carmel that brought glory to God?

4. What kind of solutions did God give Elijah for his depression?

5. When Elijah was about to be carried up into heaven, what did Elisha ask for from Elijah?

6. How did Elisha know he had received the double portion of power that he asked for from Elijah?

7. Joab had a hardened heart. What actions of his showed it the most?

Chapter 10: Men of Wisdom—Lessons in Obeying God's Word

Let's Get Started

<u>Wisdom</u> is something we all want. But it can be elusive. We think we've finally gained some; then an unfamiliar situation arises, and we're clueless as to how to handle it. But God wants to give us wisdom—a wisdom that he defines as "first pure, then peaceable, gentle, willing to yield, full of mercy and good fruits, without partiality and without hypocrisy" (James 3:17 NKJV).

wisdom
James 1:5

Many men of the Bible had that kind of wisdom, but four men stand out. The first, Samuel, was a prophet, intercessor, priest, and judge, who was God's man at a turning point in Israel's history. As the last judge of Israel, Samuel oversaw their transition from a tribal people into a monarchy.

The second, Solomon, king of Israel, had supernatural wisdom, but that didn't always help him have a heart for God. The third and fourth, Ezra and Nehemiah, were both exiled Jews who called upon God and his Law to empower them to take courageous steps to build the people of Jerusalem.

Want wisdom? Me too. Let's see what rubs off when we hang out with wise guys.

Samuel—Prophet of Integrity

the big picture

I Samuel 1-3

Hannah was barren. She vowed that if she became pregnant, she would dedicate her child to serve in the temple. God answered her prayers, and she gave her son, Samuel, over to Eli, the temple priest, to be raised in the service of the Lord. As a youngster, Samuel learned to hear God's voice. God told him Eli's sons would be judged because they were wicked.

panoramic
high-level; overall

Are You Speaking to Me?

We only get a **panoramic** view of Samuel's life. His mother Hannah prayed for a child and, out of gratitude, she dedicated the child to serving the Lord. When Samuel turned three, Hannah took him to the tabernacle and gave him to Eli, the high priest. Eli proved a poor father with his own sons, but his father/mentor role with Samuel was successful.

When Samuel heard God's voice, he didn't know who was speaking. He thought it was Eli. Eli told Samuel to respond, "Speak, LORD, for Your servant hears" (1 Samuel 3:9 NKJV). When Samuel heard God's message of judgment for Eli and his family, he was afraid to tell Eli. Finally, at Eli's urging, he did.

what others say

Bruce H. Wilkinson and Larry Libby

When the Lord saw that Samuel could be trusted with even a heartbreaking task like this, he did not hesitate to place more and more authority into Samuel's hands. He began to use the young man as his spokesman to a whole generation.[1]

God's words to prophets or anyone during this point in Israel's history were very rare. No wonder both Eli and Samuel didn't recognize God's voice. For centuries, there hadn't been anyone God could trust with his message.

We should be careful about claiming that we hear God's voice. First Samuel 3:19 says, "Samuel grew, and the LORD was with him and let none of his words fall to the ground" (NKJV). In other words, everything he prophesied was fulfilled.

When we ask God to speak to us, we must be willing to obey. To ask God to speak to us with no intention of obeying is called "testing God," an arrogant and dangerous practice.

First Public Ministry

1 SAMUEL 7:3–6 *Then Samuel spoke to all the house of Israel, saying, "If you return to the LORD with all your hearts, then put away the foreign gods and the Ashtoreths from among you, and prepare your hearts for the LORD, and serve Him only; and He*

will deliver you from the hand of the Philistines." So the children of Israel put away the Baals and the Ashtoreths [see Illustration #17], and served the LORD only. And Samuel said, "Gather all Israel to Mizpah, and I will pray to the LORD for you." So they gathered together at Mizpah, drew water, and poured it out before the LORD. And they fasted that day and said there, "We have sinned against the LORD." And Samuel judged the children of Israel at Mizpah. (NKJV)

All of Israel was in sorrow because the Lord had seemingly abandoned them. But they had wandered away from God and were worshiping idols. In a large public meeting, Samuel challenged the country to destroy their Ashtoreth poles and commit themselves to the real God. During this time of prayer and sacrifice, many Israelis must have turned back to the Lord, since they asked Samuel to seek God's intervention.

what others say

F. B. Meyer

The power of Samuel's prayers was already known throughout the land, like those of John Knox in the days of Queen Mary. The people had come to believe in them. If only Samuel would pray, they might count on deliverance. They knew that he had prayed; they now entreated that he would not cease.[2]

Over and over again in the history of Israel, during times of prosperity they turned away from God. He would then allow them to be conquered by their enemies. This difficulty made them seek God's help. God would then rescue them. During times of peace and prosperity, they would turn away from God again. And so the cycle continued.

As leaders, we need to be sensitive to the spirit of the people we have responsibility over. If they are resistant, then we must be cautious about trying to lead them to new areas of growth or challenge. But if they are willing, we can jump forward with power.

Just as God responded every time the Israelites called for help, he will never fail to respond to our pleas in the midst of our struggles. Even if we have tried unsuccessfully over and over again to defeat a sin in our lives, he wants to help us.

go to

promised
Deuteronomy
17:14–20;
Genesis 17:6

It's Retirement Time, but He's Busy Choosing a King

the big picture

I Samuel 8–10

In his old age, Samuel retired and appointed his sons as judges in his place. But they didn't have a heart for God as Samuel did. The Israelites recognized that and complained. They wanted a king. After Samuel prayed about their request, he warned them about the disadvantages of having a king. Then, at God's direction, he anointed Saul as Israel's first king.

Samuel's sons actually used their leadership positions for their own financial advantage. They took bribes and ruled unfairly. When the people experienced injustice, they thought a king would make them happy. Samuel was grieved the nation wanted a king. After all, the Lord, who had delivered them from Egypt, was their real king.

Samuel never experienced a close relationship with his real father. Although Samuel grew in great stature, his sons, like Eli's sons, brought shame upon the nation when placed into leadership. Evidently, Samuel was unable to lead his sons into a close relationship with God like he had. Maybe that was because he didn't have a close relationship with his own father.

something to ponder

what others say

Steve Farrar

There is a balance between firmness and tenderness that good fathers constantly try to achieve. Most of us tend to err on one side or the other. But we must strive to maintain that balance for the sake of our children. Don't get discouraged in your attempts to find the balance. Hang in there. . . . We find balance by losing it.[3]

The request for a king by the Israelites was not improper. God had <u>promised</u> them such a leader, but they refused to wait for God's perfect timing. They wanted to be ruled by kings like the rest of the world.

The Israelites would suffer from having a king, but they wanted what they wanted! We suffer, too, when we demand something that God doesn't want to give us or we grab it before the proper timing.

Sometimes he allows us to have what we demand and then we're sorry. Experiencing the consequence of our hastiness makes us more willing to wait for God the next time.

Just as Israel wanted to be like the nations around them who had kings, we can fall into the wrong idea that what others have will bring us contentment and satisfaction. But whatever it is you want, unless God wants it for you, it will never satisfy.

A Little Pep Talk

the big picture

1 Samuel 12:1–25
Samuel gave a challenge and a sermon to the people of Israel. He reminded them of his own integrity and of their sin in asking for a king. They responded by asking for forgiveness, and he assured them God would not abandon them.

Samuel gave a parting shot in this speech as he confirmed Saul as the new and first Israelite king. He:

1. Asked them to come up with any example of how he had been dishonest or ungodly (verses 1–3).

2. Reviewed God's faithfulness in the past throughout the history of Israel (verses 6–12).

3. Confirmed Saul as king and commanded both him and them to follow God's commandments (verses 13–14).

4. Told them that if they followed God's commands, they would experience success, but if not they would be judged (verses 15–16).

5. Called thunder and rain down upon everyone because they had sinned in seeking a king before God's time (verses 17–18).

what others say

F. B. Meyer
It was a great opportunity to show them where they had gone wrong, and a man whose own hands are clean is permitted to be the sincere critic of others' misdoing. See to it that your

mote
Matthew 7:4

pray
1 Thessalonians 1:2

Hall of Faith
Hebrews 11:32

essay
make effort

mote
speck

own eye is single, and that the beam is extracted from it before you **essay** to remove the **mote** from your brother's eye.[4]

The forcefulness of his words and the sudden thunderstorm got everyone's attention. They confessed their sins, asking Samuel to pray that they wouldn't die. He did and then encouraged them to serve and fear God. Samuel had been effective!

Samuel said, "As for me, far be it from me that I should sin against the LORD in ceasing to pray for you; but I will teach you the good and the right way" (1 Samuel 12:23 NKJV). If we are leading people, especially in an area of ministry, then it is sin for us to not <u>pray</u> for them.

I Told You So!

the big picture

1 Samuel 13; 15–16

Samuel continued to be a courageous judge by confronting Saul's sin of offering a sacrifice he wasn't authorized to present. Then Saul disobeyed a second command of God and rationalized his behavior. Even when Saul asked for forgiveness, Samuel told him God had removed his kingly position from him. Saul's removal grieved Samuel deeply. God sent Samuel to anoint the future king, a young shepherd named David. Samuel died and everyone mourned for him.

Samuel must have felt like saying to the Israelites, "I told you this king idea wouldn't work!" Saul's disobedience grieved him and it took a lot of courage to confront Saul.

When Samuel anointed David as the king who would replace Saul, he must have been relieved and thrilled to know that God had chosen a man after God's own heart. Samuel is listed in the <u>Hall of Faith</u>.

Samuel's courage is more than we might think because a king had the power to kill anyone, even a favored prophet of the people. Also, Saul had proven himself mentally and emotionally unstable by throwing spears at people who made him unhappy.

Samuel demonstrated his heart for God by being grieved about the same things that grieved God. He was deeply saddened that the king of Israel didn't make righteous choices. There will be times when we will be grieved over someone's sin and we must confront them. Just as God gave Samuel the <u>courage</u> he needed, he will give us the courage to do the right thing.

Solomon—Wise Mind, Empty Heart

go to

courage
Acts 23:11

mercy
Jude 1:22–23

coup
rebellion to overthrow a head of state or government

> **the big picture**
>
> **1 Kings 1**
>
> Twenty-year-old Solomon had a rocky start to his reign as king over all of Israel and Judah. As his father, David, was about to die, Solomon's half brother, Adonijah, set himself up as king, even though David had previously determined that Solomon would take the throne. Solomon's mother, Bathsheba, and Nathan the prophet intervened and pressed David to publicly declare Solomon the king.

King David was near death when his son Adonijah declared himself king, made sacrifices, and started a big celebration. He enlisted the support of Joab, David's ruthless army commander, and Abiathar the high priest. Surprisingly, the destined king, Solomon, was absent from this drama.

Adonijah's bid for the throne was dangerous for Solomon. If David delayed in declaring Solomon king and Adonijah was successful, Solomon and all his friends would be treated as traitors and most likely be killed. This was the common practice of all new kings, so that no one would rise up and threaten their position and authority.

But David made it clear that Solomon was to be appointed king, and the near **coup** by Adonijah was stopped. Later, when Solomon held his rightful position as the king, he handled these acts of rebellion decisively.

When the coup was halted, Adonijah knew his life was in danger, so he pleaded for mercy from Solomon. Solomon gave it to him, promising that he wouldn't kill him. This first act of mercy in his reign would become a common practice of Solomon's.

Solomon's mercy is a trait that we all need to develop. <u>Mercy</u> is that response that recognizes someone doesn't deserve love but we choose to give it anyway. It's very similar to grace. Mercy and grace are the opposites of bitterness and resentment. Mercy and grace are healthy responses. Bitterness and resentment only poison and destroy our contentment and joy.

Revenge: A Horrible but Necessary Way to Start

the big picture

1 Kings 2

Before David died, he instructed Solomon to execute all of his enemies. Adonijah, his half brother, asked Bathsheba to intercede on his behalf so he could marry Abishag, a concubine of David. Solomon rightly saw this action as laying a foundation for a future attempt to take the throne. Since Adonijah had responded to mercy by making another attempt to usurp the throne, Solomon had him executed. Two others were killed and Abiathar the priest was fired from his position.

Although David was the warrior and Solomon a man of peace, he began his reign by:

1. Executing Adonijah for covertly seeking the throne.

2. Deposing Abiathar from the high priesthood for siding with Adonijah.

3. Executing Joab for treason and murder.

4. Imprisoning then executing Shimei for cursing David and transgressing house arrest.

what others say

Thomas L. Constable

In all Solomon's dealings with his political enemies—men who conspired against the will of God during David's reign—the young king's mercy and wisdom stand out. Because of his wise handling of these threats to the throne the kingdom was then firmly established in Solomon's hands.[5]

Solomon needed to establish his kingdom with authority. David's reluctance to hold others accountable worked for him, but threatened the stability of Solomon's reign. Solomon paid the consequences of his father's weaknesses and had to execute a lot of people to solidify his authority.

Solomon had said he wouldn't kill Adonijah, but that promise was based on Adonijah's commitment to not threaten his throne. Adonijah blew that commitment when he asked Bathsheba to intervene with Solomon so that he could marry one of David's concubines, for marrying one of the king's wives or concubines was essentially a claim to the throne. The people would feel justified in supporting Adonijah, who, as an older son of David, should have the first rights to the throne. Solomon recognized Adonijah's clever ruse and nipped it in the bud.

Just as Solomon needed to put his kingdom in order, as Christians we need to put to death all those things that could damage or diminish the reign of Christ in our hearts. These can be things like worry, fear, anger, distrust, or believing wrong ideas about God.

A Noteworthy Request

the big picture

1 Kings 3

Solomon began his reign by marrying a daughter of Pharaoh, and, although he loved God, he sacrificed and burned incense to the local gods. Then God revealed himself in a dream, and asked what Solomon wanted. Solomon requested wisdom to reign. Because Solomon asked for such a selfless thing, God promised him wisdom along with riches and honor. His newly given wisdom was quickly revealed when he wisely solved the problem of two women who claimed the same baby.

Too bad Solomon didn't ask for wisdom before he married the pharaoh's daughter. This was a political marriage and secured his southwest border. She would be the first of many women who would introduce idolatry to his realm.

what others say

James I. Packer

What makes life worthwhile is having a big enough objective, something which catches our imagination and lays hold of our allegiance; and this the Christian has, in a way that no other man has. For what higher, more exalted, and more compelling goal can there be than to know God?[6]

Solomon pleased the Lord when he asked for wisdom. He was twenty years old when he became king and he knew he was in over his head. Under Solomon's reign, Israel prospered more than at any other time.

However, a bad seed was imbedded in Solomon's request for wisdom. His prayer looked good but it was self-centered. He wanted wisdom to rule men. If David had been given the same choice, he likely would have asked for the ability to serve God more completely. David's cry would have been, "More of you, God." Solomon's cry was, "More wisdom for me." Look at Psalm 72, which was written by Solomon. The focus and attention were clearly toward the king.

Solomon should have requested better knowledge of God. You would think wisdom would lead us to get to know God better. But if our motives are rooted in feeding our egos and needs, there is little room left for godly wisdom. We should model our requests after the petition of Paul, who asked "that the God of our Lord Jesus Christ, the Father of glory, may give to you the spirit of wisdom and revelation in the knowledge of Him" (Ephesians 1:17 NKJV).

No End to the Riches

the big picture

I Kings 4

Solomon's wisdom also was revealed in his administration skills. He was a capable delegator, pulling together a talented group of managers to help him rule. Although his kingdom was vast, it enjoyed prosperity and joy [see Illustration #18].

To illustrate the scope of Solomon's riches and wisdom, the biblical record listed many facts about Solomon's reign.

His Land

- The people in his land were numerous and enjoyed great prosperity (1 Kings 4:20).

- The property stretched from the Euphrates River to the land of the Philistines and to the border of Egypt (1 Kings 4:21).
- The kingdoms within those areas paid taxes to support Solomon's grand kingdom (1 Kings 4:21).
- There was no fighting within his borders (1 Kings 4:24).
- Every person felt safe (1 Kings 4:25).

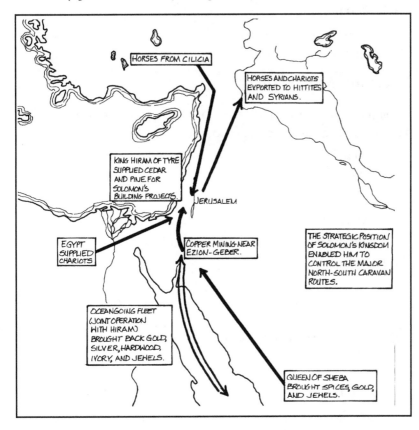

HORSES FROM CILICIA

HORSES AND CHARIOTS EXPORTED TO HITTITES AND SYRIANS.

KING HIRAM OF TYRE SUPPLIED CEDAR AND PINE FOR SOLOMON'S BUILDING PROJECTS.

JERUSALEM

EGYPT SUPPLIED CHARIOTS

COPPER MINING NEAR EZION-GEBER.

THE STRATEGIC POSITION OF SOLOMON'S KINGDOM ENABLED HIM TO CONTROL THE MAJOR NORTH-SOUTH CARAVAN ROUTES.

OCEANGOING FLEET (JOINT OPERATION WITH HIRAM) BROUGHT BACK GOLD, SILVER, HARDWOOD, IVORY, AND JEWELS.

QUEEN OF SHEBA BROUGHT SPICES, GOLD, AND JEWELS.

Illustration #18
King Solomon's Trade—The central location of Solomon's kingdom allowed him to control the trade routes throughout the region. His wisdom and wealth brought great prosperity to Israel.

His Palace

In one day, Solomon's household and visitors consumed:
- 185 bushels of fine flour
- 375 bushes of meal
- 10 fatted oxen
- 20 pasture-fed oxen
- 100 sheep

• Numerous deer, gazelles, roebucks, and fatted fowl (1 Kings 4:22–23)

His Support Staff

At Solomon's disposal were:

• 40,000 stalls of horses for his chariots

• 12,000 horsemen

• Numerous helpers to provide for King Solomon, his guests, the banquet tables, and the **livery**

Solomon's Accomplishments

Solomon was considered wiser than any person born up to that day. From his great mind, he produced:

• 3,000 proverbs (most of which are recorded in the biblical book of Proverbs)

• 1,005 songs (of which one is Psalm 72)

• Knowledge about a variety of trees, animals, insects, and fish

• A new system of government that worked

• The temple

• Peace and prosperity (1 Kings 4:20)

Two Incredible Building Projects

the big picture

1 Kings 5–7

Solomon used the best possible materials to build the temple, a house for God [see Illustration #19]. He sent far away for the building materials and then put the most talented craftsmen in charge of building it. It was dedicated seven years after it was begun. He also built his own home after that. Both the temple and his home were elaborately furnished.

The skilled craftsmen needed to complete this task were allowed two months off for every month of work. With three shifts rotating, it took seven years to build the temple. Some commentators believe this work schedule demonstrated Solomon's concern for these employees and their family lives.

But the focus on opulence and wealth foreshadowed the nation's decline. Style became more important than substance. Solomon began to depend upon the things around him rather than a vibrant relationship with the Lord.

Here are some basic facts about these buildings:

- The temple was 2,700 square feet.
- The temple was built of white limestone, cedar, and a gold exterior.
- The cedars used from the mountains of Lebanon were very old trees with hard, beautiful wood. They resisted decay and insect infestation.
- Solomon's house was 11,250 square feet and took thirteen years to build.

go to

allow
2 Samuel 7:13

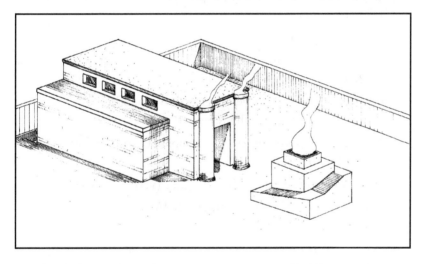

Illustration #19
Solomon's Temple—Solomon lavished tons of gold on the magnificent temple he built to honor God. At today's prices, it would be worth more than five billion dollars.

King David had wanted to build the temple for his God, but God wouldn't <u>allow</u> him to do it because he was a man of war. Instead, God told him through the prophet Nathan that his son would do it.

Just as Solomon made sure that the very best materials were used to build the house of God, we should give our very best to God. He gave us his very best: his sinless Son, Jesus Christ, for the sins of the world.

something to ponder

Opening Day

go to

women
1 Kings 11:1–4

the big picture

I Kings 8

To celebrate the finishing of the temple and to invite God to reside there, Solomon arranged for the ark of the covenant, along with the other items from the Lord's tent, to be installed. God's presence filled the temple and Solomon gave a sermon and a prayer. All the Israelites attending rejoiced.

In Solomon's sermon to the Israelites, he:

- Blessed the Israelites.

- Blessed God.

- Credited God for fulfilling his promise that David's son would build the temple.

In Solomon's prayer, he:

- Praised God for his faithfulness and loving-kindness (verses 23–26).

- Stressed that God can't be contained by a building but that God had chosen to reside in the temple (verses 27–30).

- Revealed the purposes of the temple for gaining forgiveness (verses 31–40).

- Responded to the call of the foreigner (verses 41–43).

- Sought victory in battle (verses 44–45) and deliverance from captivity (verses 46–53).

Solomon's blessing of the people certainly gives us a glimpse of a man who sought God. He said, "That He may incline our hearts to Himself, to walk in all His ways, and to keep His commandments and His statutes and His judgments, which He commanded our fathers. . . . Let your heart therefore be loyal to the LORD our God, to walk in His statutes and keep His commandments, as at this day" (1 Kings 8:58, 61 NKJV). It seems as if the many women he married from heathen backgrounds gradually turned his heart away from God.

For fourteen days, all the people rejoiced. They had concentrated on God's goodness and that fueled their joy.

God wants us to have times of celebration and to have a time of rest on the Sabbath. We need rest and rejoicing to combat the stress of living.

the big picture

Proverbs 1–31

During Solomon's reign, he was a prolific writer and wrote three thousand proverbs. Only eight hundred of them are compiled in the book of Proverbs. They cover many aspects of daily life. Their purpose is to help men develop wisdom that will honor God.

Solomon Spills His Wisdom

Topic	Selected Proverbs
Adultery	5:1–6 • 6:24–32 • 7:6–27 • 22:14 • 23:26–28 • 29:3 • 30:20
Alcohol	20:1 • 23:20–21, 29–35 • 31:4–7
Crime	6:30–31 • 10:9–16 • 13:11 • 15:6, 27 • 16:8, 19 • 17:15, 23
Discipline	3:11–12 • 5:12–14 • 9:7–10 • 13:18, 24 • 19:18 • 22:15 • 27:5
Friendship	12:26 • 13:20 • 16:28 • 17:17 • 18:1, 24 • 19:6 • 22:11
Gossip	11:13 • 16:28 • 18:8 • 20:19 • 26:22
Government	8:15–16 • 14:28, 34–35 • 16:12–15 • 21:1 • 24:24–25 • 25:5
Laziness	6:9–11 • 12:24–27 • 13:4 • 15:19 • 19:15 • 20:4, 13 • 24:30–34
Lies	6:16–17 • 12:17–19, 22 • 14:5, 25 • 17:4, 13 • 24:28–29 • 30:8
Love	10:12 • 15:17 • 16:13 • 17:9, 17 • 19:8 • 29:3
Neighbors	3:29–30 • 6:16–19 • 11:9 • 14:20–21 • 26:17–20 • 29:5
Parent/Child	6:20–23 • 10:1 • 15:20 • 17:6, 21, 25 • 22:6 • 23:13–14, 22, 24
The Poor	13:8, 18, 23 • 14:20, 31 • 17:5 • 19:1, 4, 7, 17, 22 • 30:11–14
Pride	6:16–17 • 8:13 • 11:2 • 15:25 • 16:5, 18 • 18:12 • 25:6–7
Temper	14:17, 29 • 15:1, 18 • 16:32 • 19:19 • 22:24–25 • 29:11, 22
Wealth	10:2, 4, 15, 22 • 11:4, 28 • 13:8, 21–22 • 14:24 • 20:21 • 23:4–8
Work	12:11, 14, 24, 27 • 14:23 • 16:26 • 18:9 • 22:29 • 27:18, 23–27

If everyone followed the wise advice of Solomon's proverbs, we would all be much happier and have more fulfilling relationships. He covers just about every possible topic and offers a balanced view of life with God's perspective in mind.

Great Knowledge, Little Responsibility

pride
Deuteronomy 17:20

best
Philippians 3:7–8

the big picture

1 Kings 9–11:8

God again appeared to Solomon and warned him to be careful to follow God's commandments. Unfortunately, shortly after, Solomon began a spiritual decline. He sold some Israelite cities, enslaved other nationalities, multiplied his wealth, gathered more horses, married foreign wives, and worshiped idols.

Solomon had no limit to his wisdom and no limit to his desire for pleasure and power. Administratively, his skills were the greatest in the world. But at times, he lacked character, especially in the realm of lust. Character does count. Solomon's control over his appetite for women was nonexistent. He allowed himself to experience just about anything he wanted. Because he was so rich, nothing was withheld from him.

what others say

Bruce H. Wilkinson and Larry Libby

God had said that the king of Israel was not to rule in such a way that his head would become lifted in <u>pride</u> over his countrymen. But Solomon fashioned for himself a gigantic throne of gold and ivory, adorned with twelve carved lions on its ascending steps.[7]

When God first gave the instructions for the future kings of Israel, he specifically said, "He shall not multiply horses for himself, nor cause the people to return to Egypt to multiply horses, for the LORD has said to you, 'You shall not return that way again.' Neither shall he multiply wives for himself, lest his heart turn away; nor shall he greatly multiply silver and gold for himself" (Deuteronomy 17:16–17 NKJV). Solomon broke all those rules. No wonder his heart turned away—God said it would.

We may think that God is being mean when he withholds certain things from us, especially things that we think will benefit us, but he knows what will draw our hearts away from him. He knows that being close to him is the <u>best</u> thing that could possibly happen to us. Nothing should draw us away from that.

It Is All Worthless

the big picture

Ecclesiastes 1–12

In the ebb of Solomon's life, he penned a book of the Bible that revealed his deep disillusionment about life. In these writings, he philosophically examined the fruitlessness and futility of what most people think will bring them happiness and contentment: wisdom, pleasure, accomplishments, and work. He concluded after living almost sixty years that none of those things can satisfy. Only God can.

Wisdom filled Solomon's life as a gift from God in answer to prayer. Songs flowed from his heart. His government worked like a clock. Everything about his kingdom and throne seemed in order. But in Ecclesiastes, Solomon said everything he had done was meaningless. His life ended in vanity, idolatry, sensuality, emptiness, and despair. He came to believe that "all his days are sorrowful, and his work burdensome; even in the night his heart takes no rest. This also is vanity. Nothing is better for a man than that he should eat and drink, and that his soul should enjoy good in his labor" (Ecclesiastes 2:23–24 NKJV). Nothing satisfies in this world, except God.

what others say

Ray Stedman

Here is the true message of this book. Enjoyment is a gift of God. There is nothing in possession, in material goods, in money, there is nothing in man himself that can enable him to keep enjoying the things he does. But it is possible to have enjoyment all your life if you take it from the hand of God. It is given to those who please God.[8]

Contrast David's experience: "I cried to the LORD with my voice, and He heard me from His holy hill. I lay down and slept; I awoke, for the LORD sustained me" (Psalm 3:4–5 NKJV). Both men experienced power, wealth, many wives, and great failures. One had a heart for God and the other had a heart that broke from emptiness.

The world says get more and be more, go for the gusto, do your own thing, and do it your way. But none of that will bring lasting satisfaction. Only a heart obeying God and seeking rewards in

go to

contentment
1 Timothy 6:6

heaven will have the <u>contentment</u> that God desires for us. Wisdom keeps us doing things right, but passion for God makes sure we do the right things.

The Ladder of Success Was Against the Wrong Wall

the big picture

1 Kings 11:9–43

Because Solomon had turned away from God's commandments, God rebuked him. He declared that the kingdom would be removed from Solomon's descendants. In the last years of his reign, enemies attacked Israel from the outside and Israelites rebelled against him. Even though Solomon tried to fight these dissensions, he couldn't prevent God's prediction from coming true. Solomon died after reigning forty years.

Though he was the famous builder of a grandiose temple and palace, and the richest man in the world, Solomon alienated his own people because he burdened them with excessive taxes and work. Leaders of other countries admired his wealth and wisdom, but all this pride was poison to his own people. He turned his back on a living relationship with God and sought everything this world could give. Unspeakable riches, seven hundred wives, three hundred concubines, and one prideful heart destined his reign for failure. There was never enough.

what others say

Patrick M. Morley

The culture we live in values possession and accomplishment higher than people and relationships. . . . Instead of encouraging and nurturing family and relationship values, our culture suggests professional achievement and financial success are the measure of a man.[9]

This world's search for information and knowledge will lead to the same emptiness Solomon found, unless it is guided by a heart filled with a passion for God. Unless this is the foundation, wisdom and knowledge become empty distractions.

Solomon had little spiritual power because he didn't practice what he preached. He sought platitudes and shortcuts to success. His generation became idolaters and lived in immorality.

Solomon's short sermons, called proverbs, offered practical instruction on life, money, marriage, children, and on how to be blessed and behave. But his life demonstrated a spiritual weakness. Seek wisdom for your mind, but apply it to your heart.

Ezra—Man of the Law

the big picture

Ezra 7

Way back when God made his covenant with the Israelites through Moses, he explained to them the blessings that they would receive if they obeyed the law, and the curses they would experience if they disobeyed. They disobeyed, early, long, and often. One of the covenant curses was that God would allow the Jews to return to captivity, and the curse was fulfilled during the prophet Jeremiah's lifetime. When the Israelites had been captives in Babylon for seventy years, God felt they had learned their lesson. He began allowing them to return to Judea.

The second Jewish group to return to Jerusalem was led by Ezra in 457 BC. Previously, Zerubbabel had taken a group of exiled Israelites back to Jerusalem eighty years earlier (538–515 BC). That is what was chronicled in the first six chapters of the book of Ezra. The Persian king Cyrus sent that first group. Ezra was allowed to return with his group by King Artaxerxes of the Persian Empire (see Illustration #20).

The king gave Ezra power to return to Jerusalem through a decree that supported any Jew's decision to return to Jerusalem. Artaxerxes even gave Ezra the utensils that had been stolen previously from Solomon's temple, and money for his return. This was a tremendous boost to the Jews' desire to rebuild the flattened temple (see Illustration #21). Nothing stops God from what he wants to do.

what others say

F. Charles Fensham

It seems as if Ezra was sent to an inspection to see if the law of God was still being kept. For the Persian king . . . it was a necessity that peace should prevail in Judah.[10]

Illustration #20
Persian Empire—The
Persian Empire
dominated the
ancient world at the
time of Ezra.

During the era that Ezra wrote about, other religious leaders in the world were living: Buddha in India, Confucius in China, and Socrates in Greece. Those men didn't seek the Jewish Jehovah God. But for any who would seek him, the Hebrew God revealed himself through the fulfillment of a prophecy made by Isaiah. Isaiah had predicted two hundred years before it happened that a king would allow the exiled Jews to return to their homeland. He named the king specifically: Cyrus. Only a real God could have made such a stunning prediction and controlled the circumstances to make it happen.

This king, Artaxerxes, is not the same king mentioned in the biblical book of Esther. It was his son. The name, Artaxerxes or Xerxes, was not only a formal name but a title meaning "king."

Isaiah
Isaiah 44:28–45:1

kings
Proverbs 21:1

God gave Ezra favor with the king because God wanted Ezra to fulfill his mission. "The king granted him all his request, according to the hand of the LORD his God upon him" (Ezra 7:6 NKJV). Whenever God wants something done, it will get done. God has the power to create and control. He influences even kings and nations. If God wants you to do something, don't worry; he can make it happen.

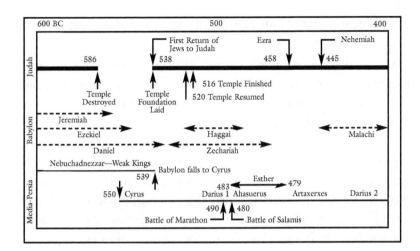

Illustration #21
Time Line—The captivity and return of the Jews.

Ezra was a **scribe** and the king recognized the wisdom that God had given him. When we apply what we learn in the Bible to our lives, then others will see the impact that God has on us. The Bible is a source of teaching, **reproof**, correction, and instruction in righteousness.

A Smaller Group That's Missing Someone

the big picture

Ezra 8

Ezra listed the names of the people who signed up to go back to Jerusalem. With women and children, the group most likely numbered four to five thousand. This group was much smaller than the group that had returned with Zerubbabel, who took back nearly fifty thousand.

As Ezra assembled the returnees, he recognized that no one from the tribe of Levi was there. The Levites were the priests and were responsible to teach the Law and serve in the temple. Ezra sent some of the leaders to go recruit Levites with a specially prepared message. It worked. Thirty-eight Levites joined them, along with 220 temple servants.

Then Ezra proclaimed a fast, asking for God's help and protection, especially since he had turned down military protection from the

go to

scribe
Ezra 7:10

wisdom
Ezra 7:25

source
2 Timothy 3:16

teach
Nehemiah 8:9

serve
Numbers 1:53

scribe
a highly trained expert on the Scriptures

reproof
encouragement to make a change

go to

Nehemiah
Nehemiah 2:9

thank
Daniel 2:23

pride
Proverbs 21:4

humility
Proverbs 22:4

mercy
Micah 7:18

against
Exodus 34:11–16;
Deuteronomy 7:1–4

government. After a four-month trip, Ezra and the group arrived safely in Jerusalem.

Maybe the Levites didn't volunteer because, back in Jerusalem, they would be responsible for the temple service, a demanding and disciplined assignment. Since there was no temple where they were in Persia, they didn't have to work.

Although Ezra didn't ask for military protection for his trip, Nehemiah would many years later as he took a third wave of exiles back to Jerusalem. This difference represents how God often leads different people in different ways. The one thing that never should change is specific Bible doctrine, but styles and methods can change and legitimately should reflect the wonderful diversity of God's people.

Ezra gave God the credit for recruiting the Levites. He said he was able to do it "by the good hand of our God upon us" (Ezra 8:18 NKJV). When we see God's hand in our lives, we must be sure to thank God for it. That way, we'll avoid pride and allow God to develop humility in our characters. Ezra also avoided pride when he called a fast so that everyone in the traveling party asked God for protection.

A Man of Passion and Intensity

the big picture

Ezra 9

When Ezra arrived in Jerusalem, he discovered that some of the Israelites had married non-Jews. Ezra was so distraught by this that he tore his clothes in grief and prayed to God on their behalf, asking for God's forgiveness and mercy.

Intermarriage was specifically against God's law for many reasons.

Ezra responded to this news in the customary mode of grief: he tore his garment and robe, and pulled out some of the hair from his head and beard. His righteous response had a profound effect on those around him, and they joined him in his grieving. Ezra kneeled down and stretched out his hands as he prayed. This was a position that showed his dependence on God and his mercy.

go to

servant
Isaiah 53:12

impelled
driven

what others say

Derek Kidner

Something of the devotion and insight of the man praying can be sensed in this confession . . . in the swift transition from "I," in the first sentence, to "our" and "we" for the rest of the prayer. Ezra could have protested his innocence, but like the servant in Isaiah he was **impelled** to reckon himself numbered with the transgressors.[11]

Ezra hadn't sinned himself by marrying outside their religion, yet he came to God with an attitude of repentance as if he had. He sought God's mercy on the people's behalf. That was a very loving thing to do and demonstrated a humble servant's heart. He may have also been motivated by a fear that their actions would again cause God to take them into captivity—since it was that kind of sin that had caused God to discipline them with captivity in the first place.

The sin of intermarrying with those outside the Jewish faith had nothing to do with a racial prejudice, for everyone involved was of the same Semitic race. But God had commanded his chosen people to not marry those who didn't love and follow Jehovah. When someone does, they are more tempted to fall away from worshiping and serving God. That is what happened to King Solomon years earlier and caused the people to turn away from the Lord.

A true leader needs to recognize the obstacles and dangers that will destroy the success of his mission. He must use his influence and energies to remain focused and stand against the challenge. Ezra was a man of great influence and action. This influence became magnetic to those he led because he was filled with passion, energy, and intensity. He was fully committed to his God Jehovah, and thus was devastated by the sin that surrounded him. "O my God, I am too ashamed and humiliated to lift up my face to You, my God; for our iniquities have risen higher than our heads, and our guilt has grown up to the heavens" (Ezra 9:6 NKJV). Giving God the credit will diminish pride in our lives.

As one man with deep remorse for sin, Ezra knew profound change was needed in these people's hearts. The complacent and easygoing remnant would soon be exposed to a man sold out to heavenly values. We can have that same kind of influence on those around us by taking sin seriously.

Weeping Pays Off

Nehemiah
Nehemiah 13:23

the big picture

Ezra 10

When others heard of Ezra's response to their sin, they gathered and wept along with him. Shechaniah confessed the people's sin to Ezra and suggested that the foreign women (and the children of those intermarriages) be put away. To present such a plan to everyone in all of Judah, all Israelites were told to come to Jerusalem. When they arrived, they were encouraged to separate themselves from their foreign wives and children.

Ezra's heart for God was infectious. His grief pricked the conscience of the people. Everyone was instructed to congregate in Jerusalem in three days to deal with the problem. If anyone refused, he would have to sacrifice everything he owned. At the meeting, leaders of each local area made a list of those who had indeed married foreign women. Only a few men opposed the plan. It took three months to institute it.

Although the plan to divorce their foreign wives and give up their children may seem extreme, some commentators believe it was necessary. Others have wondered, though, whether two wrongs make a right, and suggest that this plan was a wrong.

Regardless, it may be that the careful investigation and listing of those who had wrongly married was because Ezra's leaders needed to find out if any of the foreign women had converted to Judaism. If so, those women were acceptable and in those cases divorce was unnecessary.

Regardless of the depth or degree of sin, God always tells us there is hope. That's why Jesus came to die on the earth. His sacrificial death made it possible for us to be forgiven and have hope for the future—because every sin was included, no matter how wrong.

One by one others who shared his grief surrounded Ezra. Ezra never told them what to do but set a holy standard that others followed. His subordinates responded with the solution after watching the heart of one man burn for reconciliation with God.

Unfortunately, even after these steps were taken, the Israelites slipped back into their old habits later. Nehemiah will arrive a generation later to find that they had married foreign women again. We also can slip back into our old patterns of sin or spiritual laziness if we don't make a conscious effort to consider ourselves <u>dead</u> to sin and to <u>focus</u> constantly on God. It's a constant battle, but God wants us not to grow <u>weary</u>.

Just as the Israelites would suffer the consequences of losing everything they had if they didn't attend the meeting, we should give consequences to our children for their disobedience. That is the only way they will be motivated to change. God gives us that example as he also <u>disciplines</u> his own children. Sometimes, the bad things that happen to us are a result of our sin.

dead
Romans 6:11

focus
Hebrews 12:2

weary
Galatians 6:9

disciplines
Hebrews 12:6

Nehemiah—Building Walls, Building Bridges

the big picture

Nehemiah 1

Nehemiah was an exiled Jew living in a Persian palace in 445 BC. He served as the cupbearer to the Persian king. When Nehemiah learned that the walls of Jerusalem had not been rebuilt after the Jews were taken into exile in 586 BC, he became concerned. Without strong walls, Jerusalem was in danger of being attacked and conquered. He asked God for favor with the king so that he might be allowed to return to Jerusalem.

A Burdened Heart Seeks God

Nehemiah heard the news about Jerusalem's wall being broken down and the gates being destroyed by fire from his brother, Hanani, who had recently returned from a trip to Judah. Nehemiah was so upset that he wept, fasted, and prayed. As he prayed, God created a plan in his mind for seeking permission from the king to leave his duties and go to Jerusalem to rebuild the walls (see Illustration #22).

what others say

Max Lucado

We are tempted to wait to pray until we know how to pray. We've heard the prayers of the spiritually mature. We've read of the rigors of the disciplined. And we are convinced we've a long way to transverse.[12]

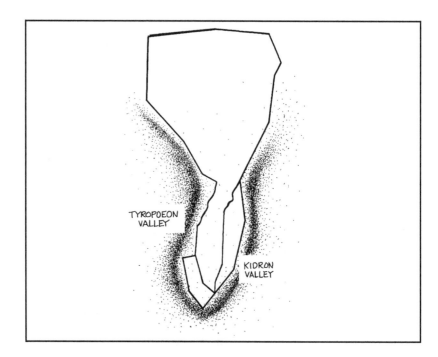

Illustration #22
The Walls of
Jerusalem—Ancient
Jerusalem, situated
on Palestine's moun-
tainous ridge, relied
on its walls to pro-
tect it from attackers
approaching from
the Tyropoeon and
Kidron valleys.

Nehemiah's prayer contained three elements:

1. Acknowledgment of God's greatness (verse 5)

2. Confession of Israel's sins (verses 6–7)

3. Request for God's help (verses 8–11)

key point

If we pray in this way, we will get God's attention.

A cupbearer had an important position in the king's court. Since he was
responsible for tasting the wine and passing it around, he was constantly at the
king's disposal. Plus, as the official taster, he would protect the king from any
poisoned wine. Being in the royal presence made him privy to confidential
information, and the king frequently talked things over with him. In the past,
a chief cupbearer had been responsible for calling attention to <u>Joseph</u>'s ability
to interpret dreams.

go to

Joseph
Genesis 41:15

Nehemiah's Sadness Shows

go to

patient
Romans 12:12

the big picture

Nehemiah 2–3

For four months, Nehemiah prayed about the situation. He tried to avoid being sad in the king's presence, but his heavy heart showed anyway. When the king noticed and asked about it, Nehemiah told him his concerns. The king asked what he wanted to do. Nehemiah told him he wanted to go to Jerusalem and rebuild the walls and gates. The king approved and sent him with military protection.

Once he arrived in Jerusalem, he secretly inspected the wall at night. The next day, he encouraged the people to rebuild. Although there was some opposition from those who were not Israelites, many people began working on rebuilding the wall.

Nehemiah answered the king's inquiry carefully. However, his prayers had paved the way. The king supported his idea and he was given permission to go to Jerusalem. When he arrived, he reviewed the walls of Jerusalem without telling anyone what he was doing.

This demonstrates what a careful planner Nehemiah was.

what others say

Bill Hybels

Be wary of insisting that you know better than God about when a prayer request should be granted. God's delays are not necessarily denials. He has reasons for his *not yets*.[13]

Nehemiah certainly was persistent and <u>patient</u> in prayer. Four months is a long time to be praying about something and seeking God's will without saying anything to anyone else. Yet somehow Nehemiah knew it wasn't the right timing to say anything. When the king inquired, Nehemiah quickly prayed in a method some call an "arrow" prayer—something quickly prayed on the spur of the moment. Previously he'd spent extended time in prayer, but in that moment came the opportunity to pray quickly before saying something to the king. Both kinds of prayer are appropriate and effective.

Nehemiah was afraid when the king noticed his sadness. Servants weren't supposed to show negative feelings. It could be interpreted by the king as disapproving of his actions or decisions and he might not like that. The servant's position or even his life could be in danger. No wonder Nehemiah prayed immediately.

Evidently, Nehemiah was a thoughtful and **prudent** leader. Although he took risks, he wasn't spontaneous or thoughtless. He planned his risks! And he made sure he was following God's plan. Leaders today need to do the same thing.

We All Have Opposition and Competition

the big picture

Nehemiah 4:1–6:14

Nehemiah encountered much opposition in the form of seven different destructive plans hatched by his enemies. In each case, Nehemiah proved himself a godly leader, a wise planner, and a spiritual person.

Nehemiah's enemies tried everything to stop the rebuilding of the walls. Sanballat, a Horonite; Tobiah the Ammonite; and Geshem the Arab may have had plans to take control of Jerusalem. When Nehemiah arrived to rebuild the walls, he threatened their plans. But as we'll see, sometimes the "enemy" was within Nehemiah's own camp.

This chart recaps the kinds of things that happened and how Nehemiah showed himself to be a man who trusted in God completely:

Examples of Times Nehemiah Prevailed over Opposition

Scripture	What Happened	What Nehemiah Did
Nehemiah 4:1–6	The opposition publicly mocked the Jews before the wealthy people and said the construction was faulty.	Nehemiah prayed that God would not forgive them. Everyone kept building, and the wall was reestablished to half its original height.
Nehemiah 4:7–9	The opposition threatened to attack the people while they were building.	Nehemiah and the Jews prayed and set up a guard day and night.
Nehemiah 4:10–23	The opposition used the threat of attack and rumors that the people were growing discouraged to make the people fearful and suspicious.	Nehemiah encouraged the people by reminding them that God would fight for them. He also positioned half of the workers with weapons.

Examples of Times Nehemiah Prevailed over Opposition (cont'd)

Scripture	What Happened	What Nehemiah Did
Nehemiah 5:1–19	The Jews faced a food shortage and many people didn't have enough money to pay their taxes. Therefore they were selling their children into slavery to one another. Also, their Jewish brothers were charging <u>usury</u>, which was forbidden by God's laws.	Nehemiah was angry at the injustices going on and confronted his fellow Jews. He told them to stop charging interest and to be generous with each other. Since he was appointed governor, he also provided food for many but didn't use the governor's food allowance. He also worked on the wall.
Nehemiah 6:1–4	Five times, the opposition invited Nehemiah to meet with them and find a compromise, which Nehemiah knew was a smoke screen to harm him.	Nehemiah refused their requests, saying he had too much good work to do.
Nehemiah 6:5–9	Sanballat sent a message for everyone to read that accused Nehemiah of planning a revolt against the rulers with the desire to set himself up as the king.	Nehemiah wasn't intimidated and sent a message saying that rumor wasn't true. He also prayed for God to strengthen him.
Nehemiah 6:10–14	A Jew, hired by Sanballat, tried to get Nehemiah to enter the temple to get protection from his enemies.	Nehemiah identified this as a **ruse** to make him enter the sanctuary of the temple, which was against God's rules. Only <u>Levites</u> were allowed to go into the inner temple. If he had done that, his credibility would have been destroyed. He refused the invitation.

usury
Exodus 22:25

Levites
Numbers 3:10

usury
high interest fees

ruse
trick

Examples of Nehemiah's Wise Words and Thoughts

Scripture	What Happened	What Nehemiah Did
Nehemiah 4:14	"Do not be afraid of them. Remember the Lord, great and awesome, and fight for your brethren, your sons, your daughters, your wives, and your houses" (NKJV).	He reminded people of how great God is.
Nehemiah 4:19–20	"The work is great and extensive, and we are separated far from one another on the wall. Wherever you hear the sound of the trumpet, rally to us there. Our God will fight for us" (NKJV).	He was great at rallying the people with wisdom and enthusiasm.

go to

anger
Ephesians 4:26

Examples of Nehemiah's Wise Words and Thoughts (cont'd)

Scripture	What Happened	What Nehemiah Did
Nehemiah 5:6, 9	"I became very angry when I heard their outcry and these words. . . . I said, 'What you are doing is not good. Should you not walk in the fear of our God because of the reproach of the nations, our enemies?'" (NKJV).	He wasn't afraid to confront those who were sinning.
Nehemiah 5:16	"Indeed, I also continued the work on this wall, and we did not buy any land. All my servants were gathered there for the work" (NKJV).	He was selfless and untiring; even involving his own employees.
Nehemiah 6:3	"I am doing a great work, so that I cannot come down. Why should the work cease while I leave it and go down to you?" (NKJV).	He knew his priorities and kept to them.
Nehemiah 6:12	"I perceived that God had not sent him at all, but that he pronounced this prophecy against me because Tobiah and Sanballat had hired him" (NKJV).	He wisely saw the motives behind the actions of people.

Nehemiah got angry at the injustices of his fellow Jews, but he didn't sin. The first flash of <u>anger</u> isn't wrong, but what we do with our emotions through actions or attitudes can be. God doesn't want us to harbor anger because then it becomes bitterness and resentment.

Nehemiah gives us a process for dealing with anger. He:

- Recognized he was angry and didn't deny it (5:6).
- Gave "serious thought" to the situation until he found the real cause of his anger (5:7).
- Confronted those who were sinning (5:7).
- Called a meeting to bring the issue to the attention of everyone involved (5:7).
- Suggested a solution (5:11).

apply it

Anger is something many of us struggle with. At times, we feel justified in our anger and rationalize that if the person who caused our anger would just act differently, we would too. But the truth is, we are responsible for our own reactions. No one else causes our anger. It is our reaction to the way we perceive the situation.

key point

What the Bible Says About Anger

Scripture Reference	What the Bible Says
Psalm 37:8	"Cease from anger" (NKJV).
Proverbs 14:17	Being quick-tempered shows a person is foolish.
Proverbs 15:1	Speaking gently turns away anger.
Proverbs 16:32	Being slow to anger shows strength.
Proverbs 19:3	When we don't take responsibility for our actions, we get angry at God.
Proverbs 19:11	A discrete person is slow to anger.
Proverbs 19:19	We should allow angry people to suffer consequences for their choices.
Proverbs 22:24–25	Don't associate with angry people lest they influence you.

The Walls Went Tumbling Up

NEHEMIAH 6:15–16 *So the wall was finished on the **twenty-fifth day of Elul**, in fifty-two days. And it happened, when all our enemies heard of it, and all the nations around us saw these things, that they were very disheartened in their own eyes; for they perceived that this work was done by our God. (NKJV)*

God did an amazing thing in empowering Nehemiah and his fellow builders to quickly complete the project. They completed it so quickly that even the enemies of Israel attributed the feat to God's enabling. Not only were they impressed, those opposing the project were less motivated to criticize and work against the Israelites.

what others say

Charles R. Swindoll

That has to be the most thrilling experience in the world—to watch God come to the rescue when you have been helpless. In the middle of the incessant assault of the enemy, in spite of the endless verbal barrage, the wall was built. While the enemy blasts, God builds.[14]

go to

glory
Galatians 1:3–5

jealous
Exodus 34:14

vessels
2 Corinthians 4:7

use
1 Corinthians 3:9

twenty-fifth day of Elul
about September 20

God loves to do amazing things so that he can get the glory. But he is a jealous God who wants to make sure only he receives the credit—because only he deserves it. He is the source and we are his vessels. He doesn't need us, but he chooses to use us as his co-laborers. What a mighty privilege that is.

If you are trying to do good things out of your own power, you won't receive any credit for it in heaven. And quite often, your

go to

listened
John 10:3

acknowledged
Hosea 6:3

obey
Deuteronomy 5:27

speak
Job 33:31

festival
Leviticus 23:42

wrong motives will be revealed and people will notice your pride. "Pride goes before destruction, and a haughty spirit before a fall" (Proverbs 16:18 NKJV).

The Amazing Things God Puts on a Heart

NEHEMIAH 7:5 *Then my God put it into my heart to gather the nobles, the rulers, and the people, that they might be registered by genealogy. And I found a register of the genealogy of those who had come up in the first return. (NKJV)*

The purpose of the census was to repopulate Jerusalem with people of pure Jewish descent. Few people were residing there at that time because it had been a dangerous place to live. When the walls were crumbling, residents were defenseless. But now that the walls were again strong, Jerusalem would be a safer place to live.

Nehemiah was a godly man who constantly listened to God's voice. He acknowledged God for the ideas he came up with. But even more important, when God led him, he obeyed.

We want to be like Nehemiah, always having our "spiritual antennae" out, aware of how God might be leading or speaking. But if we are not willing to obey, then God may not speak. He knows our hearts and responds to those who are eager to do what he says.

the big picture

Nehemiah 8-10

Nehemiah called everyone together at the Water Gate, one of the gates of Jerusalem, and Ezra, the priest, read from the Law. As he read, the people began weeping because they were convicted about their sin and their former negligence in following the Law. But Nehemiah, along with Ezra and the Levites, encouraged them not to grieve but to rejoice. They celebrated for seven days in a festival called the Feast of Tabernacles. Then after one day of rest, they assembled for a time of confession and reviewing God's works from the past. Finally, they renewed their covenant with God.

Let's Party!

Commentators estimate that there were thirty to fifty thousand people gathered for the reading of the Law. We don't know how everyone heard Ezra in such a large crowd. It may be that portions were read and then the Levites circulated among smaller groups, giving an explanation and answering questions. But regardless, the people were emotionally and spiritually touched. Ezra, who wrote the book of Ezra and is also credited by many for writing the book of Nehemiah, was a Jew who lived in the time of Nehemiah. He had returned with a group of exiled Jews to Jerusalem fourteen years before Nehemiah brought his group.

go to

instructed
Romans 10:17

hide
Psalm 119:11

prostrate
stretched out
facedown

The people responded to the reading of the Law by first standing up in respect and then bowing. "Ezra blessed the LORD, the great God. Then all the people answered, 'Amen, Amen!' while lifting up their hands. And they bowed their heads and worshiped the LORD with their faces to the ground" (Nehemiah 8:6 NKJV). Later they wept and mourned so intensely that Nehemiah had to encourage them to stop grieving and start celebrating.

The Law is the collection of rules that God gave Moses back in the days when the Israelites wandered through the wilderness. Israelites constantly went through cycles where they would follow the Law closely, then slide into ignoring it. During Nehemiah's time, he made sure they knew the Law and followed it.

Just like the Israelites, we should worship God with our minds and our bodies. Different people worship God in different ways, but every position, whether standing, bowing, raising our hands, shouting, or lying **prostrate** on the ground, is acceptable to God if done with a pure heart of worship.

The people took the Law to heart and it changed their behavior. Our "Law" as Christians is the Bible, and it should make a difference in our lives. As we read it, we are <u>instructed</u> in how God wants us to act and what to believe. Although it doesn't address every issue we might face, it gives principles that can be applied to every situation and challenge. If we <u>hide</u> it in our hearts, we will be able to use it when it is needed, moment by moment.

apply it

the big picture

Nehemiah 13:4–31

Nehemiah served as governor of Judah for twelve years and then returned to serve King Artaxerxes. We don't know for how long, but some commentators suggest two years. Then Nehemiah returned to Jerusalem and was shocked at the disappointing changes that had occurred since he left.

opposed
Nehemiah 2:19

just
Revelation 16:7

unpleasant
2 Thessalonians 1:6

reward
Psalm 62:12

A Shocking Return

When Nehemiah returned to Jerusalem after fulfilling his obligations to King Artaxerxes, he found several disappointing or sinful things occurring. He took measures to prevent them from continuing. Following is a chart of the problems and his response.

Nehemiah's Response to Sin

Scripture	Offense to God	Nehemiah's Response
Nehemiah 13:4–9	Tobiah, a Gentile, was given a room in the temple. This was wrong because he wasn't a Jew and because he had previously opposed the rebuilding.	Threw out Tobiah's things and had the room purified.
Nehemiah 13:10–14	Discovered the Levites hadn't been given their portions of the sacrifices; therefore they had abandoned their positions.	Reprimanded the officials and restored the Levites' positions. He reinstituted the tithe and appointed reliable men to distribute the tithe money.
Nehemiah 13:15–22	Jews were working on the Sabbath.	Rebuked the nobles of Judah and made sure the gates were closed during the Sabbath. The merchants weren't allowed into Jerusalem on the Sabbath.
Nehemiah 13:23–29	Jews had married foreign women and their children weren't able to speak the language of Judah.	He forcefully contended with those men and convinced them to not give their daughters to foreign men or let their sons marry foreign women.

Four different times, Nehemiah prayed something like, "Remember me, O my God, concerning this, and do not wipe out my good deeds that I have done for the house of my God, and for its services!" (Nehemiah 13:14 NKJV). Nehemiah wasn't afraid to ask for God's help and his blessings. He knew he was serving God faithfully and he trusted that God would reward him.

Nehemiah didn't merely scold people for their sin or negligence. He always had a solution that included action to correct the problem. He wasn't a man of solely negative words; he was also a man of positive action.

Because God is a just God, he will give unpleasant consequences to those who disobey and reward the right choices of those who obey. We may not see those factors always played out here on earth, but for sure we'll see them in heaven. God is faithful and just. He rewards those who have <u>faith</u> in him and who follow him. Like Nehemiah, we can ask to be remembered and rewarded.

faith
Hebrews 11:6

Chapter Wrap-Up

- Samuel began serving God as a child and faithfully served until he was the last judge of Israel. He obeyed God's voice and anointed the first two kings of Israel, Saul and David. (1 Samuel 1–16)

- Solomon was the third king of Israel and God gave him incredible wisdom, although he didn't always use it to make wise moral choices. He wrote many proverbs, ruled in grand style, and built God a magnificent temple. (1 Kings 1–11)

- Ezra led the second group of exiled Jews back to Jerusalem. Because of the high value he placed on God's Scriptures, he reinstated the study and obedience to God's Law. (Ezra 7–10)

- Nehemiah led the third group of exiled Jews back to Jerusalem, where he motivated the Jews to rebuild the walls of Jerusalem despite much opposition. (Nehemiah 1–13)

Study Questions

1. What indicated that Samuel was a true prophet of God?

2. How was Solomon's great wisdom demonstrated shortly after he asked for it?

3. Ezra was a scribe. What does that mean?

4. When Nehemiah called the people together to hear the reading of the Law, how did they respond?

Chapter 11: Men of Courage–Lessons in Strength and Bravery

Let's Get Started

In this chapter Caleb, Joshua, Gideon, and Jonathan demonstrate a trait many of us wish we had—courage, even in the face of death. You and I may not face death, but sometimes it's the more common dangers of life that bother us. Let's see how we can apply what these four men of the Bible teach us.

Caleb—Man of Courage and Faith

NUMBERS 13:30–33 *Then Caleb quieted the people before Moses, and said, "Let us go up at once and take possession, for we are well able to overcome it." But the men who had gone up with him said, "We are not able to go up against the people, for they are stronger than we." And they gave the children of Israel a bad report of the land which they had spied out, saying, "The land through which we have gone as spies is a land that devours its inhabitants, and all the people whom we saw in it are men of great stature. There we saw the giants (the descendants of Anak came from the giants); and we were like grasshoppers in our own sight, and so we were in their sight." (NKJV)*

Moses sent twelve brave and confident spies into the Promised Land. When they returned forty days later, ten of these men told everyone the land was everything they hoped for, except it was filled with giants who would kill them all. Fear swept through the crowd but Caleb jumped up and encouraged everyone to believe God's promises.

what others say

W. Phillip Keller

These are the sounds of a spirit attuned to God's Spirit. These are the sure trumpet notes of trust in the Almighty. These are the bugle blasts of the believer who sees with the pure perspective of faith in God and confidence in Christ.[1]

Caleb spoke with confidence because he knew that God had promised victory. But the crowd envisioned only loss and death.

Caleb's ability to trust God in the face of obstacles was based on:

- Focusing on God rather than the obstacles.
- Finding support in Joshua.
- Remembering God's faithfulness in the past.

God's promises are his fuel for faith. He has "given to us exceedingly great and precious promises, that through these you may be partakers of the divine nature, having escaped the corruption that is in the world through lust" (2 Peter 1:4 NKJV). Caleb was able to resist the evil desire of fear, even though the giants were in the Promised Land. We can resist distrust in God when we remember that he has promised to provide everything we need to live the way he wants us to.

Don't Focus on the Giants

NUMBERS 14:6–10 *But Joshua the son of Nun and Caleb the son of Jephunneh, who were among those who had spied out the land, tore their clothes; and they spoke to all the congregation of the children of Israel, saying: "The land we passed through to spy out is an exceedingly good land. If the LORD delights in us, then He will bring us into this land and give it to us, 'a land which flows with milk and honey.' Only do not rebel against the LORD, nor fear the people of the land, for they are our bread; their protection has departed from them, and the LORD is with us. Do not fear them." And all the congregation said to stone them with stones. Now the glory of the LORD appeared in the tabernacle of meeting before all the children of Israel. (NKJV)*

Joshua and Caleb tore their clothes to demonstrate their passion and to persuade the others to take the land God had promised. They pointed out the fortresses were no defense against God, who was with them.

As the Israelites marched through the desert they experienced a daily intimate relationship with God. They witnessed miracle after miracle and still they refused to capture the Promised Land.

What about the giants we face in our lives? Is fear keeping us from confronting them? Let Caleb's words of confidence seep into your soul. You don't have a <u>pillar of fire</u> to direct you by night, but the Bible is a source of guidance. Read it!

pillar of fire
Exodus 13:21

"Has a Different Spirit"

the big picture

Numbers 14:22–24, 36–38

Because the Israelites embraced the negative report of the ten spies so readily and utterly disbelieved the two positive spies, God said he would not allow the disbelieving generation into the Promised Land. "But My servant Caleb, because he has a different spirit in him and has followed Me fully, I will bring into the land where he went, and his descendants shall inherit it" (14:24 NKJV). The negative spies were struck down by a plague. Only Joshua and Caleb, the believing scouts, survived.

The Israelites were run over by their fear. Caleb saw the same fortresses, he walked next to the same giants, and he was exposed to the same intimidation. Yet he resisted the majority perception.

what others say

Oswald Chambers

The forward look is the look that sees everything in God's perspective. . . . Caleb had the perspective of God; the men who went up with him saw only the inhabitants of the land as giants and themselves as grasshoppers. Learn to take the long view and you will breathe the benediction of God among the squalid things that surround you.[2]

What kept the fear from overwhelming his senses? Caleb knew his purpose in life. He knew God's direction. They were to obey the Lord and possess the land. A simple message from God had brought them this far and Caleb was confident God would lead them all the way. Caleb's different spirit came from knowing obedience would bring victory. Purpose and priorities empower us to have courage.

Knowing your purpose in life and your priorities will help you stay true to God when doubt overwhelms you. If you know God has called you to a certain role or position, then he'll equip you for the task. If you are convinced God loves you, then the rejection of others won't bother you as much. If you know God is in control of your life, then fear won't paralyze you.

Faithful and Strong to the End

go to

patience
Luke 21:19

the big picture

Numbers 34:18–19; Joshua 14:6–14

Caleb was assigned to help apportion the land of Canaan when the Israelites conquered it (see Illustration #23). And when that happened, Caleb was given the land that was later called Hebron. He and Joshua were the only ones from the original group of Israelites who were allowed to go into the Promised Land.

Caleb had a different spirit that was evident to everyone. He believed God's promises and was rewarded for his courage, "because he wholly followed the LORD God of Israel" (Joshua 14:14 NKJV).

what others say

Charles R. Swindoll

Remember your old friend Caleb? He was 85 and still growing when he gripped an uncertain future and put the torch to the bridges behind him. At a time when the ease and comfort of retirement seemed predictable, he fearlessly faced the invincible giants of the mountain. There was no dust on that fella. Every new sunrise introduced another reminder that his body and rocking chair weren't made for each other. While his peers were yawning, Caleb was yearning.[3]

When we are struggling with conquering a sin or resisting temptation, we may fear that God has abandoned us. But just as Caleb stayed true to the end, so can we.

Patience and persistence will pay off.

Joshua—Mentored into Leadership

EXODUS 17:8–10 *Now Amalek came and fought with Israel in Rephidim. And Moses said to Joshua, "Choose us some men and go out, fight with Amalek. Tomorrow I will stand on the top of the hill with the rod of God in my hand." So Joshua did as Moses said to him, and fought with Amalek. And Moses, Aaron, and Hur went up to the top of the hill. (NKJV)*

Instant Commander in Chief

go to

historian
Exodus 17:14

accompanied
Exodus 24:13

serve
Matthew 20:28

alacrity
eagerness

At a young age, Joshua was chosen by Moses to be commander of the army. He had to have the wisdom to choose men who would be good fighters. This was a big leap: from brickmaker to military commander with no training. Moses merely told him to prepare for war. Joshua didn't whine about being untrained. He just went into battle expecting victory.

what others say

W. Phillip Keller

Yet the amazing thing was Joshua's prompt response. He did not delay! He did not offer up excuses for not going into action. He did not plead inexperience or lack of military training. Instead he simply set out to do this impossible assignment with **alacrity**.[4]

Joshua became the historian for the Israelites, and so he accompanied Moses to the base of the mountain as Moses met with God. Joshua must have been the first person to see Moses after he came down the mountain. Therefore, he may have gotten more information than anyone else.

Joshua may have been confident to fight because of the staff that Moses had used. Joshua had already seen the victories that had come from it. With it, Moses had divided the Red Sea and then made it close so that the Egyptian army was destroyed. What a history to call upon!

Joshua was called Moses's "assistant" (Exodus 24:13 NKJV). That's where future leadership starts. By being an assistant or servant in the beginning, we never forget what that felt like, and as a result, we motivate men better. Even Jesus said he came to serve.

We build our spiritual strength as we remember what God has done in the past. We may not have a staff to depend upon, but we have other valuable spiritual resources: the Bible, answered prayers, and fellowship with other believers.

something to ponder

A Man Jealous for Righteous Living

NUMBERS 11:26–29 *But two men had remained in the camp: the name of one was Eldad, and the name of the other Medad.*

faithful
Matthew 24:45–47

And the Spirit rested upon them. Now they were among those listed, but who had not gone out to the tabernacle; yet they prophesied in the camp. And a young man ran and told Moses, and said, "Eldad and Medad are prophesying in the camp." So Joshua the son of Nun, Moses' assistant, one of his choice men, answered and said, "Moses my lord, forbid them!" Then Moses said to him, "Are you zealous for my sake? Oh, that all the LORD's people were prophets and that the LORD would put His Spirit upon them!" (NKJV)

Because Moses's burden of leading the Israelites was too much, God shared his spirit with others. Joshua was an aid to Moses and in this passage shows his loyalty to his leader by objecting to two prophets that he felt were not qualified.

Maybe Joshua hadn't been at the meeting to know what was going on, but regardless, he interpreted what had happened as a threat to Moses's leadership. Joshua showed his loyal spirit right from the start. God often prepares us for leadership by easing us into our role. He gives us smaller problems at first. If we prove faithful with little, he will give us opportunities to be <u>faithful</u> with much.

Forty More Years

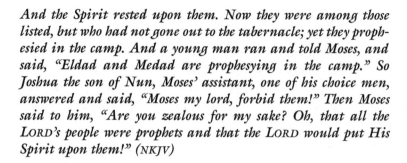

the big picture

Numbers 27:15–23

When Moses inquired of God who would continue to lead the Israelites into the Promised Land after his death, God chose Joshua. Then Moses commissioned him before the priests, and he was given a portion of Moses's spirit.

Joshua spent an additional forty years in leadership training as the Israelites marched through the wilderness because they had wanted to return to Egypt. During that time, his trust, faith, and patience were strengthened. Joshua's skill as a military man was unquestioned.

Obey and There Will Be Success

the big picture

Joshua 1:1–18

After Moses died, God spoke to Joshua and assured him that he would help guide the Israelites successfully into the land that he had promised them. He commanded Joshua to follow his commands and then Joshua would have courage and success. Joshua then began planning a strategy for attacking the people of Canaan (see Illustration #23).

Joshua had taken Leadership 101 and learned a simple lesson for success. "Only be strong and very courageous, that you may observe to do according to all the law which Moses My servant commanded you; do not turn from it to the right hand or to the left, that you may prosper wherever you go. This Book of the Law shall not depart from your mouth, but you shall meditate in it day and night, that you may observe to do according to all that is written in it. For then you will make your way prosperous, and then you will have good success. Have I not commanded you? Be strong and of good courage; do not be afraid, nor be dismayed, for the LORD your God is with you wherever you go" (Joshua 1:7–9 NKJV). Joshua knew he would have success if he made decisions courageously, obeyed God's Law, and studied the Book of the Law—God's Word.

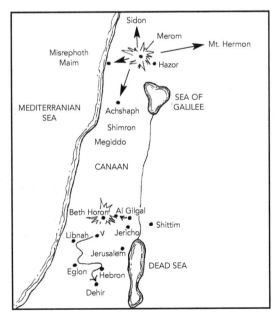

Illustration #23
Map of Conquest—Canaan was not a united nation when the Israelites invaded. It had been settled by a number of ethnic groups, each of which lived in small fortified city-states. When the Israelites arrived, the kings of these city-states united against them. Joshua's first thrust into Canaan cut the country in two, and the Israelites defeated first the southern and then the northern coalitions.

go to

Captain
Joshua 5:14–15

Gibeonites
Exodus 23:32

what others say

Alan Redpath

It was not a question of what resources or equipment Joshua had, or the numerical strength of his people. The situation was under the control of the <u>Captain</u> of the invisible host, who could defeat any strategy of the enemy.[5]

Over the many years that Joshua led the children of Israel into conquering the Promised Land, he modeled the characteristics and strengths of a courageous leader.

Joshua's Key Leadership Moments

Scripture	Event	Joshua's Motives, Desires, and Choices
Joshua 3:1–17	Commanded the ark to accompany them; waters of Jordan parted for the crossing.	Desired God to be glorified.
Joshua 4:1–24	Set up twelve stones in middle of Jordan where Israelites crossed; God exalted Joshua, and the people revered him like Moses.	Set up a memorial for everyone to remember what God had done for them; pointed their attention to God and away from himself.
Joshua 5:1–15	Practiced rites of circumcision and the Passover; God appeared, and Joshua worshiped Him.	Called himself a "servant."
Joshua 6:1–27	Marched around Jericho to conquer it.	Was willing to follow a bizarre command from the Lord.
Joshua 7:1–26	Israelites defeated at Ai because there was sin among them.	Underestimated the strength of the enemy and didn't initially take care of sin in the camp.
Joshua 8:1–35	Conquered Ai and completely destroyed it and its people.	Didn't let previous defeat prevent him from persevering.
Joshua 9:1–27	<u>Gibeonites</u> tricked the Israelites into making a treaty with them even though the Gibeonites were a people that Israel wasn't supposed to make peace with.	Didn't seek counsel of the Lord and was deceived.
Joshua 10:1–43	Defeated the Amorites in the Promised Land.	Joshua fought courageously because God said they would be victorious. Joshua believed him.
Joshua 11–17	Israelites waged war for at least five years, conquering main sections of the Promised Land.	Joshua faithfully persevered in the face of continuing battles.

Joshua's Key Leadership Moments (cont'd)

Scripture	Event	Joshua's Motives, Desires, and Choices
Joshua 18:1–10	Seven of the tribes had not taken possession of their land inheritance.	Joshua encouraged and motivated them to take the remaining steps necessary to take possession.
Joshua 23:1–16	Joshua called all the Israelites together to speak to them.	Joshua rehearsed God's faithfulness from the past and directed their attention to Him. He told them not to worship other gods.

Joshua was a great military commander, but after his death the importance of his spiritual leadership really became apparent. When he died there was no spiritual giant waiting in the wings. Israel had become dependent upon one leader to keep its spiritual focus. When he was gone, it became apparent the Israelites had no individual trust and hope in God. They began to wander spiritually, and Israel began to lose its firm grip on the land.

Although God wants us to be mentored by others and encouraged through their wise counsel, we shouldn't become too dependent upon one person. Our ultimate counselor is God himself. He doesn't want anyone to become more important than he is. Don't become too dependent on men.

Gideon—Man Who Grew in Spiritual Strength

JUDGES 6:11–13 *Now the Angel of the LORD came and sat under the terebinth tree which was in Ophrah [see Illustration #25], which belonged to Joash the Abiezrite, while his son Gideon threshed wheat in the winepress, in order to hide it from the Midianites. And the Angel of the LORD appeared to him, and said to him, "The LORD is with you, you mighty man of valor!" Gideon said to Him, "O my lord, if the LORD is with us, why then has all this happened to us? And where are all His miracles which our fathers told us about, saying, 'Did not the LORD bring us up from Egypt?' But now the LORD has forsaken us and delivered us into the hands of the Midianites." (NKJV)*

It had been two hundred years since the days of Joshua's leadership and God's mighty victories. Now Israel had been invaded

go to

threshing
Ruth 2:3

threshing
separating wheat
from chaff

numerous times and most recently by a nomadic mob called the Midianites. The Israelites were so oppressed that they hid underground and in caves.

When the angel visited Gideon, he was **threshing** wheat in a winepress, an unusual place to be harvesting. Normally it was done out in the open where the wind could blow away the chaff. Gideon was trying to work and hide at the same time.

what others say

Michael Wilcock

It is of the essence of the story that Gideon is not at the beginning a mighty man of valor, as is brought out, I think, by the way his courage grows so gradually; the angel is speaking prophetically about what God intends to make of him.[6]

The nation was defeated and demoralized and Gideon was hiding from the Midianites the day the angel of the Lord approached him and called him a valiant warrior. That must have sounded strange to Gideon. His father had told him stories of God's deliverance but they all seemed empty tales after seven years of Midian terror. He wanted to know why his nation was suffering and why he was hiding in that hole.

Isn't that a typical response? We always want to know the reason for our suffering and pain. His answer to the angel shows just how low Gideon and his countrymen had fallen. When you are that low any opportunity to climb up seems impossible. But God worked with Gideon and he will work with us to give us the courage we need.

Not Me, I'm the Youngest!

JUDGES 6:14–16 *Then the LORD turned to him and said, "Go in this might of yours, and you shall save Israel from the hand of the Midianites. Have I not sent you?" So he said to Him, "O my Lord, how can I save Israel? Indeed my clan is the weakest in Manasseh, and I am the least in my father's house." And the LORD said to him, "Surely I will be with you, and you shall defeat the Midianites as one man." (NKJV)*

Upon hearing this powerful challenge, Gideon whined some more. He tried to explain that considering his youth and the Midianite domination, he was the wrong guy for the job. The angel promised to see him through to victory. In effect, the angel said, "I see a warrior's heart in you even if you don't. Go and deliver Israel." As long as God is with us, we can't fail.

what others say

Jamie Buckingham

Gideon was a harassed and discouraged man. He bore the burdens of long defeat. He had not one to stand with him and no traditions to fall back on. He had no concept of the law of Moses and knew virtually nothing of the Bible of the day. . . . He was a very unlikely man to call to lead the nation. Yet God saw something in him that he didn't even see in himself.[7]

<u>Moses</u> tried to use the same excuse to refuse God's anointing of him as deliverer. Moses said he wasn't qualified. God gave him the same reason to obey as God gave Gideon: "I'll be with you."

When we are beaten down or depressed, it is difficult to see the positive qualities in our lives. It often takes an encouraging word to help push away those dark clouds that confuse and slow us down. As leaders, when we see others struggling, we must resist the temptation to fix the problem at first. Take the time to give an <u>encouraging</u> word. Recognize one of their strengths and tell them how you admire them for it.

<u>How About a Sign, Lord?</u>

the big picture

Judges 6:17–24

Gideon asked for a sign as a confirmation that God wanted to use him to defeat Midian. He brought an offering of a goat and bread and the Angel of God consumed the offering with a spontaneous burst of fire. Gideon then realized it truly was God.

For the first time in his life Gideon realized what was really possible—with God's help. Perhaps, just perhaps, he thought, the angel was correct. Those words, "The LORD is with you, you mighty man of valor!" (Judges 6:12 NKJV) must have hit a resonant chord in his heart because he asked for some confirmation. Afterward the frightened farmer stood straighter. He climbed from that winepress a different man and built an altar named "The-Lord-Is-Peace."

what others say

Kay Arthur

In the dark hours of Israel's history, God revealed Himself to Gideon as Jehovah-shalom, the Lord is peace.[8]

Clean Your Own House First

the big picture

Judges 6:25–32

God directed Gideon to tear down his father's altar of worship to Baal (see Illustration #17) in their city of Ophrah. Still afraid, he did it at night. When the people of the city found out, they wanted to kill Gideon. His father defended him, saying, "Would you plead for Baal? Would you save him? Let the one who would plead for him be put to death by morning! If he is a god, let him plead for himself, because his altar has been torn down!" (Judges 6:31 NKJV). As a result, Gideon got a new name: Jerubbaal, which means "Let Baal plead."

Before he could deliver Israel, God directed Gideon to take care of business at home. His father had an altar to Baal and an Asherah pole beside it. These were great offenses to God. Gideon gathered some help and did as the Lord instructed—but at night!

The man of valor didn't have the courage to move boldly during the day. But word leaked out about his activities and the next day many came to kill him. His father defended his action with logic, and the crowd accepted the challenge from the old man. Gideon had his first convert.

what others say

Bill Hybels

God wants us all to experience a deeper level of security. He wants emasculated men to become secure enough to confront timidity and fear, to take risks and make commitments. He wants macho men to become secure enough to crawl out from under the false pretensions and quit trying to impress people.[9]

Leaders should use this same principle for their philosophy. They can't be effective with others until they clean up their own lives. Hypocrisy was something Jesus identified readily in the people who opposed him. To say one thing and do another is a sin worthy of discipline in God's eyes.

Give Me Another Sign, Lord

hypocrisy
Luke 18:11

diffident
timid

fleece
a piece of lamb's wool

> ### the big picture
>
> ### Judges 6:33–40
>
> The Midianites and Amalekites attacked the Israelites. Gideon drew together the Israelites with a trumpet blast and sent messengers throughout the tribes. But Gideon still asked for another sign to make sure he was the chosen one to deliver the Israelites, so God showed him two miracles with wet and dry pieces of wool.

Courage was contagious. This farmer was now recruiting thousands and was proving to be a skilled and powerful deliverer. The Midianites formed an alliance with another warring tribe, so Israel was threatened again.

> ### what others say
>
> ### Michael Wilcock
>
> We ought not to blame Gideon for putting out his famous fleece. Here the Lord is coaxing along a reluctant leader who really is "**diffident**, modest, and shy," and who needs to have his confidence built up step by step by a patient, loving, but determined God.[10]

Gideon wanted assurance God was with him so he asked God for a demonstration to prove he was in God's will. If a **fleece** was wet and the ground dry when he woke up, he would know God's hand was on him.

God's most powerful guidance tool is his Word, the Bible. It provides every promise and every life-changing assurance we need. Read it because God said, "Meditate in it day and night, that you may observe to do according to all that is written in it. For then you will make your way prosperous, and then you will have good success" (Joshua 1:8 NKJV).

Moses
Exodus 3:12

encouraging
Proverbs 15:23

Demanding extra signs is an indication of unbelief. Fear often makes us wait for more confirmation when we should be taking action. Visible signs are unnecessary if they only confirm what we already know to be true.

Some Tactics!

the big picture

Judges 7:1–8

When Gideon gathered everyone together, there were thirty-two thousand men in the army. But God didn't want to use that many. So he instructed Gideon in two different encounters to decrease the number. Only three hundred ended up fighting for Israel.

From thirty-two thousand men to three hundred? That was an amazing step of faith for Gideon and for everyone else. But Gideon obeyed. First he allowed those who were afraid to leave. Twenty-two thousand left. Then God told Gideon that any man who knelt down to drink from the river was to be dismissed. But a man who lapped the water from his hands was retained. Only three hundred men lapped and God said he would defeat their enemies with those.

what others say

Jamie Buckingham

Gideon was a person just like us . . . when he obeyed God, miracles happened. . . . God can achieve great things with a few dedicated people who will give Him the Glory. God, who looks on the heart, is able to take a person who seems to be a coward and turn him or her into a hero—as long as that person is willing to do things God's way.[11]

God wanted to ensure this new leader and his loyal troops would know who gave them the victory. If there had been a lot of men fighting, then everyone could say that the victory came from their sheer numbers. But God wanted to bring glory to himself.

Letting the men go who were fearful is based on Deuteronomy 20:8: "The officers shall speak further to the people, and say, 'What man is there who is fearful and fainthearted? Let him go and return to his house, lest the heart of his brethren faint like his heart'"

(NKJV). We need to surround ourselves with those who are not faint-hearted. That way we'll be strengthened and not brought down spiritually and emotionally.

Do you want to receive the <u>glory</u> for what you do for the Lord? Whether you're in the ministry or in the secular world, God wants to make sure he receives the glory, and, believe it or not, sometimes our failures actually work toward that. When we admit failure or ask forgiveness, we show our humility and <u>dependence</u> upon God. Sometimes that's more glorifying to him than when our plans go perfectly.

glory
John 8:50

dependence
2 Corinthians 4:17

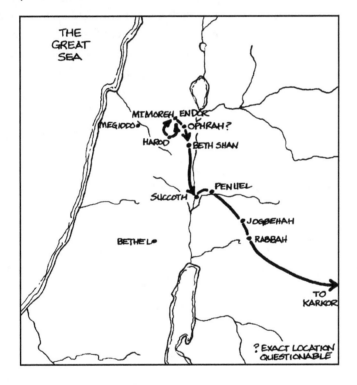

Illustration #24
Gideon's Campaign—Gideon's trust gave him courage to lead his small army against their enemies. Against all odds, Gideon's army defeated their rivals. The map shows the route Gideon traveled to gather his army and to pursue and defeat the enemy.

<u>Smash Those Pitchers</u>

the big picture

Judges 7:9-25

God provided a further assurance by telling Gideon to listen to the Midianites as they encamped nearby. When he did, he heard two men say they knew Gideon would defeat them. Bolstered, Gideon called the Israelites to attack and defeated the enemy in an unusual way (see Illustration #24).

go to

defeated
Romans 16:20

victorious
Revelation 15:2

melee
confused struggle

Shortly after 10:00 p.m. a new watch of guards in the Midian camp were shocked by the sound of smashing jars and hundreds of horns blaring. Gideon had instructed his people to make those noises so that they would sound like a much greater army than they were.

This collection of desert tribesmen never trusted each other and in the dark and confusion, they started fighting each other. The death and disarray caused the enemy to flee. It was a rout for Gideon's army and a victory for God.

Because of the recent change of guards, many more men were milling around than normal, which made the **melee** even more confusing. Gideon used the enemy's fear and confusion to make them kill each other while Gideon and his men watched from the sidelines.

Before the battle Gideon had sneaked into the enemy camp and overheard a soldier say the battle belonged to Gideon. Since God told him this would happen, he quickly returned. "Look at me and do likewise," he told them. "Watch, and when I come to the edge of the camp you shall do as I do" (Judges 7:17 NKJV). Gideon told them, "Don't do as I say, do as I do." There is no better way to demonstrate our resolve during threatening times than putting ourselves into the tough jobs.

Symbolically, we could listen in on Satan's conversations with his demons and hear the same kind of comments that the Midianites said. Satan knows he is a <u>defeated</u> foe, but he keeps hoping he'll win. God has already written the script. He will be <u>victorious</u> and his children will reign with him in glory.

Warrior Turned Diplomat

the big picture

Judges 8:1–21

The men of the tribe of Ephraim complained that they hadn't been called to the battle. Gideon dealt with them by complimenting them. Then he and his men asked for help from the men of Succoth, but they refused. God gave Gideon the victory and he took revenge on the men of Succoth.

The rout of the Midianites roared through the nation like a lightning bolt. Men from every tribe began chasing the invaders out of the land. The tribe of Ephraim joined the battle and helped capture two enemy generals. However, they complained they were not included in the initial battle plans. Gideon told them their brilliant move in capturing the generals outshone the early work of his army. This diplomatic answer <u>soothed</u> the hurt egos.

This was a masterful stroke. Gideon was on top of his world. He led a broken and defeated nation of twelve different tribes into a great victory. The tribe of Ephraim was known for their troublesome, arrogant attitude. Gideon could have brushed aside their complaints and inflamed tribal rivalries. After all, he was used by God to bring a mighty victory. Instead, in humbleness and wisdom, he paid tribute to their contribution.

As leaders we need to remember those we lead respond best to sincere compliments. They need to know their contribution was meaningful and appreciated. If we don't credit what they do, even if it's incomplete, they won't be encouraged to try the next time.

go to

soothed
Proverbs 15:1

ephod
Exodus 25:7

ephod
garment of a priest

Gold Keeps Turning into Gods

the big picture

Judges 8:22–32

Although the Israelites wanted Gideon to rule over them, he told them God should. But he did ask for the gold earrings the people had gotten from the defeated Midianites. He took that gold and made an **ephod**, which turned into a kind of god for the people and they worshiped it. Israel had forty years of peace under his leadership.

In just a few days Israel had gone from bondage to freedom. Drunk on that freedom, they focused their attention on the man who made it happen, not God. Gideon could have been the first monarch. The nation wanted him to rule, but wisely Gideon pointed them back to God.

go to

eldest
1 Samuel 14:49

what others say

W. Phillip Keller

In spite of the distraction caused by Gideon's golden ephod, he himself remained a remarkable force in Israel for the next forty years. It is indeed a measure of the man that without either pretense or ostentation his strong quiet presence among his people provided a base for peace. He had no need to take power into his hands nor assume undue authority over his contemporaries. Just being there was a guarantee of his great and godly influence in Israel.[12]

This farmer, whom God had used in a special way, did have a weak spot—gold. Gideon asked for an earring from each soldier's plunder. The gold from the rings alone weighed nearly forty-three pounds. With a portion of this gold he made a special tunic called an ephod. His intentions were probably to create a remembrance commemorating the victory, but the people began to worship the ephod as an idol.

As leaders we usually measure our behavior by our best intentions while others react to our actions alone. We need to think things through before acting. Good intentions will not help the consequences of a bad decision.

Jonathan—Faithful Friend

1 SAMUEL 13:2–4 *Saul chose for himself three thousand men of Israel. Two thousand were with Saul in Michmash and in the mountains of Bethel, and a thousand were with Jonathan in Gibeah of Benjamin. The rest of the people he sent away, every man to his tent. And Jonathan attacked the garrison of the Philistines that was in Geba, and the Philistines heard of it. Then Saul blew the trumpet throughout all the land, saying, "Let the Hebrews hear!" Now all Israel heard it said that Saul had attacked a garrison of the Philistines, and that Israel had also become an abomination to the Philistines. And the people were called together to Saul at Gilgal. (NKJV)*

Jonathan was the <u>eldest</u> son of Saul, the King of Israel. His name meant "Yahweh has given." Jonathan proved himself over and over as a gift from God. In this instance, he was a man of courage as he fought for the glory of Israel, leading his father's army. Jonathan attacked a Philistine outpost and obtained a great victory. He was building a solid reputation as a military leader.

go to
blacksmiths
1 Samuel 13:19–20

what others say

Bruce H. Wilkinson and Larry Libby

Saul's valiant son Jonathan had come to the firm opinion that it would be disastrous to allow the Philistine army to establish itself in the southern hill country of Judah. Not one to waste time on formalities, Jonathan leaped into action by leading a surprise attack on a Philistine garrison at Geba.[13]

Although it was common for a king to take credit for a military victory he had no part in, it was still wrong. It is still wrong today to take credit for a great accomplishment that belongs to a subordinate. It is just like stealing, and it will destroy your credibility.

Going Out on a Limb of Faith

the big picture

1 Samuel 14:1–23

Saul, Jonathan, and the army of Israel were being attacked by the Philistines. They were at a great disadvantage because the Philistines had removed all the blacksmiths. Therefore no one in the army had swords or spears except Saul and Jonathan. Jonathan secretly went behind the enemy lines to see what God would do for them. As a result, he killed many of the Philistines, and it caused the whole Philistine camp to become fearful. Then Israel had victory against them.

Jonathan said to his young armor bearer, "Come, let us go over to the garrison of these uncircumcised; it may be that the LORD will work for us" (1 Samuel 14:6 NKJV). What a statement! Faith and courage controlled Jonathan's life. Unknown to his father, he mounted an assault with two warriors—his armor bearer and himself. Jonathan used the words "it may be." He wasn't presumptuous by dictating to God what God should do. Instead, he felt a nudge to do something and was curious to find out how God would use it. It demonstrated his willingness to risk all for God.

John Hercus

The Philistines are one of the great world powers. They were the iron makers of the world; they were fighters to a man. You should talk about Philistines in the way you talk about the Egyptians, the Greeks, the Romans, the British. And Jonathan, the daring young spark, had been reckless enough to clean up one of their outpost garrisons. It is almost as though a band of American Indians had blown up West Point.[14]

key point

Jonathan had previously proven himself in battle, but now he would prove his faith in God as the foundation for his warrior's spirit. Jonathan wasn't empowered by his own power or ability, but by God, whom he trusted.

Wrongfully Accused

the big picture

1 Samuel 14:24–46

Saul foolishly forbade the men of his army to eat until he had complete victory over the Philistines. Jonathan hadn't heard about it and ate some honey. When Saul couldn't get God to give him direction for the battle, he knew something was wrong and vowed that whoever was the source of the problem would be killed. That person turned out to be Jonathan. Saul would have killed him if the Israelites hadn't intervened.

In great haste Saul had pronounced a death sentence for something ridiculous. Jonathan's actions were innocent, and thus he could not be charged with disobedience. However, his father backed it with a curse upon himself if he did not see the sentence executed. Faced with certain death, Jonathan told Saul, "I only tasted a little honey with the end of the rod that was in my hand. So now I must die!" (1 Samuel 14:43 NKJV).

what others say

Luis Palau

God chose Saul to reign. Saul chose to reign without God. In Saul's hand, the authority of the king became hard, brittle, arbitrary, and cruel. Saul held the scepter but the scepter held him. He issued commands simply to command.[15]

Talk about a man filled with peace. Jonathan didn't offer any excuses or make a passionate plea for mercy. He just stated the facts. The king's men recognized the injustice of it and saved Jonathan from this outrage.

Jonathan was the son of a mentally unstable father. It's amazing that Jonathan was such a stable individual himself with that kind of influence around him.

Souls Knit Together in Friendship

the big picture

1 Samuel 18:1–4

After David had finished talking with Saul, Jonathan became one in spirit with David, and he loved him as himself. From that day Saul kept David with him and did not let him return to his father's house. And Jonathan made a covenant with David because he loved him as himself. Jonathan took off the robe he was wearing and gave it to David, along with his tunic, and even his sword, his bow, and his belt.

Jonathan recognized David had the same faith and courage that was in his heart when he had attacked the Philistine army. That brought them together as friends, and "the soul of Jonathan was knit to the soul of David, and Jonathan loved him as his own soul" (1 Samuel 18:1 NKJV).

what others say

Gene A. Getz

The word *knit* literally means "chained"; that is, the soul of Jonathan was chained to the soul of David. They were bound to each other in an inseparable relationship and union. They were in a true sense "soul brothers."[16]

So strong were Jonathan and David's mutual feelings that they made a covenant with each other. Although Jonathan was heir to the throne, he would willingly lose the kingdom rather than his friendship with David.

Choices: Father or Friend

go to

doctrine
1 Timothy 4:16

the big picture

I Samuel 20:1–42

David returned from hiding and contacted Jonathan, who couldn't believe his father really intended to kill David. So they set up a test to see how Saul would react when David wasn't at his usual seat for dinner. When David was repeatedly gone from meals, Saul got angry and accused Jonathan of defending David. Saul even tried to kill Jonathan with a spear. This caused Jonathan to be depressed, and he communicated with David through their predetermined signal that David should flee the area completely.

Jonathan was such a loyal person that he couldn't believe his father harbored evil thoughts toward David, even though he'd seen evidence of it in the past. Although he loved David as a best friend, he was also loyal to his father. He wanted to think the best about his own father and king.

Jonathan's loyalty was certainly praiseworthy, but his naïveté almost got him killed. While it is good to be loyal and to think the best about people, we should also be discerning so that we don't walk into trouble.

God especially wants us to be discerning about false <u>doctrine</u>. There are many false teachers that could call themselves Christians. We must be careful to analyze whether they are truly teaching principles from the Bible. Otherwise, we'll be feeding our souls false information.

Jonathan's Encouraging Heart

1 SAMUEL 23:15–18 *So David saw that Saul had come out to seek his life. And David was in the Wilderness of Ziph in a forest. Then Jonathan, Saul's son, arose and went to David in the woods and strengthened his hand in God. And he said to him, "Do not fear, for the hand of Saul my father shall not find you. You shall be king over Israel, and I shall be next to you. Even my father Saul knows that." So the two of them made a covenant before the LORD. And David stayed in the woods, and Jonathan went to his own house. (NKJV)*

Even though Jonathan could rightfully claim the throne, he was convinced that God had <u>called</u> David to be king. Jonathan proved his friendship when he encouraged David even though Jonathan's own father was hunting him.

go to

called
2 Samuel 16:13

glorify
Philippians 2:9

subjugate
put under; deny

what others say

Alan Redpath

It is apparent that Jonathan showed greater faith in the promises of God than did David at this point. Jonathan asked him if he would remember him and his family, and show kindness to his house when the Lord had long since taken him to be with Himself.[17]

Jonathan laid aside his own potential to be king and believed that God knew best in choosing David as the next king. He had a loyal heart to David and to God. His faith was strong enough to **subjugate** his own desire for exaltation as king. Jesus had the same loyal and subservient heart to his Father, being willing to sacrifice his claim as God in heavenly glory to arrive on earth as a baby to fulfill his Father's gracious plan.

something to ponder

God did <u>glorify</u> Jesus—not because Jesus asked for it, but because he wanted his Son to be given the glory he deserved. If we can trust that God will provide everything we need—even praise—then we will be at peace.

Loyal to the End

the big picture

1 Samuel 31:1–13

Jonathan, Saul, and the Israelite army were fighting the Philistines when Jonathan was killed in battle, along with Saul and his two other sons. The Philistines found their bodies and mounted them on their temple wall. Some brave men of Jabesh Gilead rescued the bodies and burned them for burial.

All loyalty entails sacrifice. Jonathan's loyalty put him in harm's way and he was killed. His faith and courage provided the fertile ground from which his loyalty selflessly grew. When loyalty conflicts occurred between his father, David, and God, he let truth and love guide his decisions.

singing
2 Samuel 1:17

Mephibosheth
2 Samuel 9:7

Love is not just a feeling or an emotion. The best definition for love is making a choice for the highest good of the person loved. Jonathan made that choice often.

David was also loyal as a friend. Later, as the new king, David would honor his friendship with Jonathan by <u>singing</u> about his bravery and by providing for the needs of his crippled son, <u>Mephibosheth</u>.

As leaders, the loyalty conflicts that occur will drive us to examine the core values that direct our lives. The easy choice is quite often the wrong one. Integrity, honesty, and a desire for justice are inner motivations we get from God. They must be used as a plumb line to measure choices that seem right but aren't.

Chapter Wrap-Up

- Caleb was one of the spies sent into the Promised Land when the Israelites first arrived. Although others were afraid, he believed they could go in and take the land. Of the original group that left Egypt to go into the Promised Land, only Caleb and Joshua made it.
  (Numbers 13:30–33; Joshua 14:6–14)

- Joshua was Moses's assistant and after Moses died, he took over the leadership of the Israelites, leading them into the Promised Land in great dependence upon God.
  (Exodus 17:8–10; Joshua 23:1–16)

- Gideon started out being fearful, but God developed his courage and used him to defeat the Midianites. Gideon's diplomacy held the nation in unity and strength for forty years.
  (Judges 6:8)

- Jonathan was a mighty warrior, risking his life to go to the Philistine camp and test whether God wanted to give them victory. He also became best friends with David, and they made a covenant with each other to protect each other and one another's families. (1 Samuel 14:8–52; 18:1–4)

- Even though Jonathan's father was seeking to kill his friend, Jonathan affirmed that David would become king.
  (1 Samuel 23:15–18)

Study Questions

1. When the Israelites were afraid of the giants in the Promised Land, what did Caleb say to them?

2. What requirements did God give Joshua in order for him to have courage?

3. How did Gideon respond when God told him he would be Israel's deliverer?

4. How did Jonathan find out that the Philistines were afraid of the Israelite army?

5. How did Jonathan show his committed friendship with David?

6. How did Jonathan encourage David?

Chapter 12: The Prophets—Lessons in Speaking the Words of God

Chapter Highlights:
- Isaiah: Serving
- Jeremiah: Weeping
- Ezekiel: Watching
- Daniel: Discerning
- Jonah: Preaching

Let's Get Started

Have you ever been afraid to speak about your faith? How would you like to share Christ for twenty or forty years and have hardly anyone turn to him for salvation? A pretty discouraging thought, huh?

Well, that's exactly what the prophets of God encountered in the Old Testament times. Many of them saw very little results from their ministries. Most of the time they were laughed at and mocked. Yet, they faithfully believed the message they'd been given from God and proclaimed it anyway. That's consistency! Let's see what they did and how they can inspire us.

sons
Isaiah 7:3; 8:3

seraph
angel

Isaiah—Willing Servant

the big picture

Isaiah 6:1-13

Isaiah had a vision of God seated on his throne in great holiness and majesty, and the prophet recognized his unworthiness to stand before Jehovah. He thought he would die. But a **seraph** touched a burning coal to his mouth and said he was forgiven. When he heard God's voice wondering whom they—the Trinity—would send to speak on their behalf, he volunteered. Isaiah then got his marching orders to speak to the people of Judah, even though very few would respond.

Isaiah most likely started out as a scribe in the palace in Jerusalem but was called by God to be his prophet through a direct vision. He was called to give the Israelites both judgment and comfort. He was married to a prophetess and they had at least two <u>sons</u>. Also, he:

- Prophesied throughout the reigns of four kings (Uzziah, Jotham, Ahaz, and Hezekiah).
- Ministered for over forty years.
- Gave a lot of prophecies about the coming Messiah.

- Encountered little success in the response of the people.

- Had a way with words and wrote the book of Isaiah.

- Died by being sawed in two during the reign of Manasseh (Hezekiah's successor).

- Is quoted over fifty times in the New Testament.

His name means "salvation is of the Lord"—the theme of his prophetic ministry.

Isaiah knew right from the beginning that the people he was a prophet to would not respond to him. God told him, "Make the heart of this people dull, and their ears heavy, and shut their eyes; lest they see with their eyes, and hear with their ears, and understand with their heart, and return and be healed" (Isaiah 6:10 NKJV). God wasn't actually telling Isaiah that he should try to turn the people away, but that God knew they wouldn't respond well because God knew everything. But he still wanted Isaiah to tell of the Lord's love and judgment because a few would respond.

It's amazing to think that any of us would sign up for a job that we knew wasn't going to be successful. Isaiah had a deep faith and trust in God, and that gave him the power to persevere in the face of deep rejection.

Isaiah gave some of the most specific prophecies about the Messiah. The following chart shows a few:

Isaiah's Prophecies of a Coming Savior

prophecy

Scripture	Prophecy	Where Fulfilled
Isaiah 7:14	Born of a virgin	Matthew 1:22–23;
Isaiah 11:1, 10	A descendant of Jesse and King David	Luke 3:23–31
Isaiah 50:6	Voluntarily suffer	Matthew 26:67
Isaiah 53:4	Take the sins of the world upon himself	Matthew 8:16–17
Isaiah 53:9	Be buried in a rich man's grave	Matthew 27:57–60

The chances for even a few of the three hundred Old Testament prophecies about Christ to be fulfilled are astronomical. Isaiah contributed the most to that incredible collection of true prophecies.

go to

faithful
Revelation 14:12

Isaiah didn't volunteer for his position flippantly. He asked the Lord how long he would preach with no one responding. We shouldn't make ourselves available to God unless we're really willing to stay <u>faithful</u>, regardless of the response we get.

When Isaiah appeared before God's throne, he knew he was sinful. God provided his forgiveness. None of us are worthy to stand before God or to be used by him, but he provided for our sins to be forgiven through Jesus's death on the cross.

Jeremiah—Weeping Prophet

JEREMIAH 9:1–2
Oh, that my head were waters,
And my eyes a fountain of tears,
That I might weep day and night
For the slain of the daughter of my people!
Oh, that I had in the wilderness—
A lodging place for travelers;
That I might leave my people,
And go from them!
For they are all adulterers,
An assembly of treacherous men. (NKJV)

Whether or not we experience success in God's role for us, we can be faithful.

key point

Illustration #25
Cistern—Cisterns were bottle-shaped hollows in the ground where rainwater was collected. They served both individual households and entire communities, depending on their size. The Bible records that Jeremiah and Jacob's son Joseph were both held captive in cisterns.

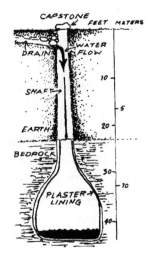

go to

adequate
Jeremiah 1:6–7

cistern
Jeremiah 38:9

wept
Jeremiah 13:17

horrible
Jeremiah 20:7

desire
Jeremiah 20:9

cistern
reservoir

Hope from a Broken Heart

Jeremiah was called to be a prophet at a young age and didn't feel <u>adequate</u> for the job. But he was willing to obey God and ended up preaching for forty years to the rebellious people of Judah.

Jeremiah:

- Was hated and treated harshly by the people, even dropped into an empty <u>cistern</u> (see Illustration #25) and left to die.

- Was not allowed to marry, as a visual aid of the coming judgment when many people would be without their spouses because of death.

- Was persecuted by a false prophet named Hananiah, but predicted his death.

- Was alive at the time when the prophets Zephaniah, Habakkuk, Daniel, and Ezekiel prophesied.

- Wrote the biblical book of Lamentations after Jerusalem's destruction at the beginning of the exile.

- Frequently <u>wept</u> because of his deep grief over the sins of the people (that's how he received the nickname "the Weeping Prophet").

His message to the Israelites of Judah was that if they would not repent, calamity would come. But he spoke without anger. He covered his prophecies with tears of compassion. Because the people did not repent, they were taken into captivity into Babylon.

what others say

Irving L. Jensen

Jeremiah was the gentle and compassionate type. . . . He knew that within a short time the proud, beautiful city of Jerusalem with its magnificent temple would be in ruins, and that his beloved people would be in captivity. . . . No wonder Jeremiah wept.[2]

As an intensely emotional person, Jeremiah wrote about his feelings a lot. He honestly expressed deep sadness over his people's rebellion against God. He even wrote of the <u>horrible</u> ways he was treated and his <u>desire</u> at times to quit. In his lifetime, Jeremiah endured being publicly humiliated, threatened, put in stocks, dropped in a cistern, running for his life, and being carried away from his home land against his will.

Commentators believe that Jeremiah's book is a collection of his sayings but they are not put in any particular order. Therefore, prophecies appear together that occurred years apart.

Like so many of the Israelite prophets, Jeremiah's job was to try to turn the people's hearts back toward God even though God knew it wouldn't happen. Yet Jeremiah persevered. If you are in a ministry or job where you feel like your actions aren't bearing much fruit, hang in there like Jeremiah. Your responsibility is not to make results happen, but to be faithful and obedient to God.

Ezekiel—Watchman

EZEKIEL 24:16–18; 33:7 *Son of man, behold, I take away from you the desire of your eyes with one stroke; yet you shall neither mourn nor weep, nor shall your tears run down. Sigh in silence, make no mourning for the dead; bind your turban on your head, and put your sandals on your feet; do not cover your lips, and do not eat man's bread of sorrow." So I spoke to the people in the morning, and at evening my wife died; and the next morning I did as I was commanded. . . . So you, son of man: I have made you a watchman for the house of Israel; therefore you shall hear a word from My mouth and warn them for Me.* (NKJV)

Ezekiel was chosen by God to be a prophet when he was thirty. Five years earlier, he had been among the Judeans, who were exiled from Jerusalem by the Babylonians. He was married and had two children. His wife was the delight of his eyes and a prophetess in his ministry. But God told him she would die. When Jerusalem fell once more, Ezekiel used his wife's death to drive home a message to the surviving exiles in Babylon.

Ezekiel's ministry overlapped the ministries of Jeremiah and Daniel, coming at the end of Jeremiah's and at the beginning of Daniel's. Ezekiel:

• Was a priest before he was a prophet.

go to

Shekinah
Ezekiel 3:23

vision
Ezekiel 8:2

linen
Ezekiel 16:10

eagles
Ezekiel 17:3

withered vine
Ezekiel 19:12

Shekinah
glory of God in
the temple

- Showed a concern for the priesthood, sacrifices, and the **Shekinah**.

- Saw God in a <u>vision</u> several times.

- Was instructed by God to use many different kinds of visual aids like a <u>linen</u> garment, two <u>eagles</u>, and a <u>withered vine</u>.

- Was likely killed by fellow exiles because he stood against their idolatry.

Ezekiel did many unusual things. They were supposed to be signs

what others say

H. A. Ironside

When his neighbors questioned Ezekiel as to his strange behavior he explained that his loss was but a small one compared with the sorrows and bereavements that were to come to the inhabitants of Jerusalem and all the people of Israel.[3]

to the people that God loved them and wanted them to draw closer to him. Like Ezekiel, we are watchmen looking for opportunities to tell others about Jesus.

Ezekiel's Actions Demonstrate God's Love

What Ezekiel Did	Scripture
Shut himself up inside his house	Ezekiel 3:24–27
Drew the city of Jerusalem on a clay tablet	Ezekiel 4:1
Lay on his left side for 390 days	Ezekiel 4:4–5
Lay on his right side for 40 days	Ezekiel 4:6
Baked bread over cow manure	Ezekiel 4:12–15
Shaved his head and beard	Ezekiel 5:1–4
Left home to represent exile	Ezekiel 12:3–7
Sang a song of mourning about the leaders	Ezekiel 19:1

God called Ezekiel a watchman on a watchtower. Such a job in those days was dangerous for the watchman and the city. If the watchman wasn't careful, the city could be overrun and destroyed. God was telling Ezekiel that he had a very important job to do—one which affected a lot of people. He faithfully preached to the people as a result.

As Christians, we are responsible to tell others about God's wonderful gift of grace through his Son, Jesus. Like a watchman, we are supposed to be faithful in looking for opportunities to speak of him.

Loneliness, isolation, and troubles frequently touch the life of a leader. Attacks come toward all who stand for something. When your feet are firmly planted in principle and pressure mounts to compromise, steel yourself with courage. God will fill your life with boldness when standing for him. When bold conflicts approach, it takes bold leaders to say no. As Ezekiel stood against his own people, God told him, "Behold, I have made your face strong against their faces, and your forehead strong against their foreheads. Like adamant stone, harder than flint, I have made your forehead; do not be afraid of them, nor be dismayed at their looks, though they are a rebellious house" (Ezekiel 3:8–9 NKJV). Be encouraged, God will help you. Deep, resounding confidence comes from an intimate relationship with him. The prophet Isaiah said, "The Lord GOD will help Me; therefore I will not be disgraced; therefore I have set My face like a flint, and I know that I will not be ashamed" (Isaiah 50:7 NKJV). The Lord can help us.

God considers us so important that he calls us his <u>ambassadors</u>. The responsibility of an ambassador is to represent his native country and to look out for its interests in a foreign land. As Christians, we are <u>foreigners</u> on this earth, watching for Jesus's return and representing him to the inhabitants of the earth. We are looking out for the best interests of our future country, heaven.

Daniel—Man of Integrity and Insight

DANIEL 1:8–9, 17 *But Daniel purposed in his heart that he would not defile himself with the portion of the king's delicacies, nor with the wine which he drank; therefore he requested of the chief of the eunuchs that he might not defile himself. Now God had brought Daniel into the favor and goodwill of the chief of the eunuchs. . . . As for these four young men, God gave them knowledge and skill in all literature and wisdom; and Daniel had understanding in all visions and dreams.* (NKJV)

Judah was raided by King Nebuchadnezzar, and Daniel was taken to Babylon. There Daniel studied the Babylonian culture and language in preparation for serving his captors. While being schooled

ambassadors
2 Corinthians 5:20

foreigners
Ephesians 2:19

End Times
when Jesus returns

and trained in Babylon, Daniel refused to eat anything from the king's table because he wanted to keep true to his Jewish laws for eating. Therefore, he lived on a vegetarian diet. He risked death by not eating from the king's offerings, yet God made sure his "strange" opinions and practices didn't offend the king—at this point. In fact, Daniel became a high official.

When Daniel was serving under his third king in Babylon, Darius, his power and influence had grown so that he was one of the highest ranking officials in the empire. The king liked Daniel so much that he intended to place him above his Babylonian peers. They were jealous and hunted for something to accuse Daniel of. Daniel always prayed three times a day. He would kneel in his home, open a window facing Jerusalem, and talk to God. Knowing this, his enemies talked the king into issuing a decree that prevented anyone from praying for thirty days. If Daniel prayed once more it would cost him his life. The choice was: conform or perish.

He chose to continue his daily prayers. As a result, the king was forced to give the predetermined consequence: the offender had to be thrown into the den of hungry lions (see Illustration #26). God miraculously intervened and closed the lions' mouths. Then the king caused Daniel's accusers to be thrown in, and they were promptly eaten. The king issued a decree which honored Daniel's God. Throughout his interaction in a foreign land, Daniel kept his integrity and prophesied many events that were to come true later. Some won't be fulfilled until the **End Times**.

Illustration #26
Lions' Den—Daniel trusted God for deliverance and the lions did not harm him.

go to

described
Daniel 1:4

blame
1 Corinthians 1:8

Steve Farrar

Prayer is to the soul what exercise is to the body. A spiritual self-starter is a man who is in good spiritual shape. That means he does two things: (1) He consistently eats the nutritious diet of the Scripture; and (2) he consistently spends time in aerobic kneeling. Prayer is the exercise of the man who is a spiritual self-starter.[4]

When Nebuchadnezzar plundered Israel, he had the most talented and skillful young people brought back to Babylon. Daniel was <u>described</u> as good-looking, intelligent, and knowledgeable. Daniel could have gone home each day, closed the windows to his house, and prayed in secret. But everyone knew his commitment to pray. Therefore it would be dishonest. His choices were to either stand fast or compromise.

The Four Kings Daniel Served

Name	Empire	Chapter	Events
Nebuchadnezzar	Babylonia	1–4	Daniel was rescued from a death sentence by interpreting a dream. Three faithful Jewish friends, thrown into the fiery furnace, were unharmed.
Belshazzar	Babylonia	5, 7, 8	Daniel read the writing on the wall, which signaled the end of the Babylonian Empire. He turned down any reward for this feat.
Darius	Medo-Persia	6	Daniel was thrown into a lions' den and emerged unharmed.
Cyrus	Medo-Persia	10–12	The exiles returned to their homeland in Judah, but Daniel stayed to serve the king.

When the world pressures you to conform, will you choose to compromise, or will you choose to stand firm in your faith? If we compromise, we can lose our ability to speak honestly about Jesus. Daniel was able to stand on his integrity and faith. There are three things you need to know before stepping into your own lions' den:

1. Daniel knew his heart was right with God. You need to know you are forgiven and all known sin is out of your life. Having no <u>blame</u> comes only from a right relationship with Jesus. "My God . . . shut the lions' mouths . . . because I was found innocent before Him" (Daniel 6:22 NKJV).

go to

conform
Romans 12:2

2. Daniel knew his heart was right with others. Duty and honor to others were more than words to Daniel. He treated everyone with respect, fairness, and an honest day's work. "And also, O king, I have done no wrong before you" (Daniel 6:22 NKJV).

3. Daniel trusted God for every part of his life. "No injury whatever was found on him, because he believed in his God" (Daniel 6:23 NKJV).

The world seeks to <u>conform</u> us. Our Christianity is fine with them if we keep it private. Daniel served four kings for over sixty-five years. The story of the lions' den is a classic story of one man's integrity and God's intervention. But when he first arrived he had three choices. One, give in to the culture and compromise his faith. Two, live like a hermit and isolate himself from all the sinners around him. Three, influence those he touched with his faith in God. You and I have the same choices. What will you choose?

Jonah—You Can Run, but You Can't Hide

> *JONAH 1:1–3 Now the word of the LORD came to Jonah the son of Amittai, saying, "Arise, go to Nineveh, that great city, and cry out against it; for their wickedness has come up before Me." But Jonah arose to flee to Tarshish from the presence of the LORD. He went down to Joppa, and found a ship going to Tarshish; so he paid the fare, and went down into it, to go with them to Tarshish from the presence of the LORD. (NKJV)*

Second Kings 14:25 mentions Jonah as a prophet who lived during the reign of Jeroboam II in the Northern Kingdom of Israel. Jonah predicted that a portion of the Syrian territory would be recaptured and returned to Jewish control. However, six hundred miles northeast of Israel was the Assyrian city of Nineveh. One hundred twenty thousand people filled its streets, and they were feared and hated by the Israelites. They presented a grave military threat to Israel.

God told Jonah to go there to give them a prophetic word. Instead of going to Nineveh, Jonah rebelled and ran. He booked passage on a ship headed for Tarshish, a city in Spain, about as far in the opposite direction as one could sail in those days. After boarding, he went down into the hold and fell asleep.

But God turned the sea stormy and got Jonah's attention by having a huge fish swallow him (the Bible never actually calls it a "whale"). As a result, Jonah repented, and stopped running from God. After he preached at Nineveh, the entire city repented. But Jonah was mad. Jonah's hatred for the Ninevites was so great, he resented God's merciful choices. He basically told God, "I just knew you would do this, but it's wrong to love and redeem my enemies."

God allowed a shade plant to grow and shade Jonah. Then it withered, exposing Jonah to fierce heat. Sullen and hot, Jonah asked to die. He wanted that silly plant to live but not the masses in Nineveh. God asked Jonah that if the prophet could care so deeply about a mere plant, why couldn't he believe the Creator would care for the people of Nineveh?

go to

paid
2 Corinthians 5:21

what others say

Charles R. Swindoll

Take Jonah. (No one else wanted to.) He was prejudiced, bigoted, stubborn, openly rebellious, and spiritually insensitive. Other prophets ran to the Lord. He ran from him. Others declared the promises of God with fervent zeal. Not Jonah. He was about as motivated as a six-hundred-pound grizzly in mid-January.[5]

D. Stuart Briscoe

As we look into the portrayal of God in this story, it is obvious to me that the aspect of God's character the writer is most concerned to project is his kindness.[6]

If you are running from God, you might know the darkness Jonah experienced. Condemnation and guilt bring powerful anxiety. Sleep brings the only relief. But when you wake up, the emotional struggle resumes, only more intense.

If this describes you, you can be sure God is designing a storm to get your attention. He loves you, and the blood of Christ paid for your sins. If you have booked passage on the same trip the backslider Jonah took, think twice. He cares for you too much to leave you alone. You may be tossed about while God battles for your heart. He tells us, "'Surely, as a wife treacherously departs from her husband, so have you dealt treacherously with Me, O house of Israel,' says the LORD. A voice was heard on the desolate heights, weeping and supplications of the children of Israel. For they have perverted their way;

forgiven
Ephesians 4:32

they have forgotten the LORD their God. 'Return, you backsliding children, and I will heal your backslidings.' 'Indeed we do come to You, for You are the LORD our God'" (Jeremiah 3:20–22 NKJV).

The sailors were awake and calling on their gods, but Jonah, a prophet of God, was asleep. Not for long, though. The captain of the ship came down to chasten him and ask why he wasn't praying. It wasn't until the ship's crew cast lots and the lot fell on Jonah that he finally admitted he was running from the God of heaven. At his insistence, the crew threw him into the ocean, where a great fish swallowed him. He expected to die, and he finally realized the miraculous fish was for his benefit. As a result, he prayed a thankful song to God.

Jesus taught, "Love your enemies . . . and pray for those who spitefully use you and persecute you" (Matthew 5:44 NKJV). How much of Jonah's bias is echoed in your heart? Do you find it difficult to pray for your enemies? Jesus's command is difficult, but it cannot be ignored.

If we don't choose to love our enemies, we'll be filled with bitterness. Bitterness is like a poison inside us. We may think our anger hurts others, but it's really only hurting us. The solution is to forgive and give up thinking we must make people pay for hurting or disappointing us. If we remember how much we've been <u>forgiven</u> by God, we may find it easier to forgive others.

Chapter Wrap-Up

- Isaiah began his ministry by seeing a vision of God's throne and volunteering to become a prophet. He served for forty years, yet had little success in making the people change. Regardless, he served faithfully. (Isaiah 6:1–13)

- Jeremiah was a prophet who saw his nation's unwillingness to repent and felt very sad about it. As a result, he cried often and was known as the weeping prophet. (Jeremiah 9:1–2)

- Ezekiel was known as God's watchman because he was assigned by God to watch the sins of Judah and warn them to change. (Ezekiel 33:7)

- Daniel set a strong example through his obedience to proper dietetic laws and by his great discernment. God prevented hungry lions from eating him when he was thrown into the lions' den. (Daniel 1:8–9:17)

- Jonah didn't want to preach to the people of Nineveh because he knew God would withhold judgment upon Israel's enemies if they repented. They did, and Jonah was angry. But God taught Jonah about grace and compassion. (Jonah 1:1–3)

Study Questions

1. How did Isaiah become cleansed so that he wouldn't die in God's presence?

2. What caused Jeremiah to be known as "the weeping prophet"?

3. What was the most difficult situation Ezekiel experienced as a prophet?

4. Why did Daniel not want to eat the royal food and wine?

5. Who did God want Jonah to preach to?

Part Two:
Men of the New Testament

Chapter 13: Jesus– Very God and Very Man

Chapter Highlights:
- Born of a Virgin
- Jesus's Deity
- Jesus's Humanity
- Jesus's Death
- Resurrection: Conquered Death

Let's Get Started

During the first century, a charismatic Jewish man from Galilee rose up. He proclaimed the need for transformation by returning to some of the laws and commandments of God. He gathered a following, but his ideas were too radical for the establishment. He was turned over to the Roman authorities and executed. His name was Judas of Galilee. The world has forgotten him.

Another man from Galilee rose up and once again proclaimed the need for transformation. He also attracted a following and was eventually handed over to the Romans and executed. His name was Jesus of Nazareth. His name will never be forgotten.

As we begin this section on the men of the New Testament, we must first direct our attention to the Man who was fully human and yet fully divine. He will be the only Man covered in this book—or who ever lived—who fits such a remarkable description. The purpose of Jesus's humanity is clearly demonstrated in the prophecies he fulfilled, his miraculous conception and birth, his life, his death and finally, his resurrection.

Judas of Galilee
Acts 5:37

what others say

Josh McDowell

The names of the past proud statesmen of Greece and Rome have come and gone. The names of the past scientists, philosophers, and theologians have come and gone; but the name of this Man abounds more and more. . . . Herod could not destroy Him, and the grave could not hold Him.[1]

Shock and Awe

MATTHEW 8:23–27 *Now when He got into a boat, His disciples followed Him. And suddenly a great tempest arose on the sea, so that the boat was covered with the waves. But He was asleep. Then His disciples came to Him and awoke Him, saying, "Lord, save us! We are perishing!" But He said to them, "Why are you fearful, O you of little faith?" Then He arose and rebuked the winds and the sea, and there was a great calm. So the men marveled, saying, "Who can this be, that even the winds and the sea obey Him?"* (NKJV)

"Who can this be?" the disciples asked. That question is still being asked today. Men still marvel at the answer. The struggle to answer this question is buried beneath questions men have asked throughout the ages: "Where did I come from?" "Who am I?" "Why all this evil?" "What can be done to fix it?"

Many religions, beliefs, and lifestyles have attempted to answer these questions over the centuries. All of them fail to provide a satisfactory answer because they fail the test in two ways. First, the answers they give do not satisfactorily answer the dilemma of the Creation, the Fall, and the redemption of mankind. Second, they do not work in practical daily living.

During the last 150 years, the new belief, or worldview, that has battled for the imaginations of mankind is materialistic naturalism. This philosophy teaches that life just happened and that we are in this world because we evolved to where we are today. Such a view has been embraced by many in the scientific and philosophical communities. These deceptive ideas impact every aspect of our lives today.

what others say

Phillip E. Johnson

The materialist story is the foundation of all education in all the departments at all the secular universities, but they do not spell it out. It is:

- In the beginning were the particles and the impersonal laws of physics.
- And the particles somehow became complex living stuff;
- And the stuff imagined God;
- But then discovered evolution.

That is the basic story of evolutionary naturalism, or scientific materialism. There was no "Word"—no intelligence or purpose—at the beginning. Only the laws and the particles existed, and these two things plus chance had to do all the creating. Without them nothing was made that has been made. God did not create man . . . primitive human beings relied on their uninformed imagination to create God.[2]

The Bible stands in contrast to worldviews like naturalism. The Bible answers those questions clearly through the life of One who came to earth more than two thousand years ago. Only the life and death of Jesus Christ answer the puzzling issues of the Creation, the Fall, and Redemption.

The Questions Asked from the Beginning

Event	Questions
Creation	Why am I here? What is my purpose? What is life? Why is there something instead of nothing?
Fall	Why is there evil? Why all this pain? Why do I do the things I do?
Redemption	How do I fix it? Is there any hope? What happens after death? What is the difference between right and wrong?

Prophecies Galore

JOHN 1:1–4 *In the beginning was the Word, and the Word was with God, and the Word was God. He was in the beginning with God. All things were made through Him, and without Him nothing was made that was made. In Him was life, and the life was the light of men. (NKJV)*

These verses are the basis for understanding who Jesus Christ is. Who was the Word? John answered in verse 1:14 when he wrote, "And the Word became flesh and dwelt among us, and we beheld His glory, the glory as of the only begotten of the Father, full of grace and truth" (NKJV). Jesus, who existed before time began, came to earth in the form of a man. Why? Because creation was broken by man's sin, and because the restoration of that brokenness will be handled by this incarnate Man.

what others say

Ray C. Stedman

John begins his gospel with an eighteen-verse introduction, the theme of which is the question: "Who is Jesus—really?" Where did he come from? What is represented in the remarkable manifestation that was the life of Jesus of Nazareth? This prologue contains a summary of John's most profound convictions about our Lord. It focuses on the central fact of Christian faith: Christianity is not a philosophy; it is about a Person, and that Person is central to all Christian faith. To take

Jesus out of Christianity would be like taking numbers out of mathematics, like taking doctors out of medicine, or like trying to think of daylight without the sun. Jesus is absolutely central to Christian faith. That is what constitutes Christianity as a unique religion. All the other great religions of earth center upon the teaching, the ideas, the philosophies that are represented in them, but not Christianity. It centers upon a marvelous, beautiful, remarkable, astonishing Person.[3]

Imagine you just picked up a cup of coffee in your local bookstore and started wandering through the book stacks. Your eyes jump when you see a book with your name on the spine. You pull it off the shelf and see that it is a compiled book written by many different authors over a 1,500-year period. Curiosity captures your interest. You pull the book from the shelf and open the pages. You are shocked to find that the authors died 400 to 1,100 years ago, and yet they knew a lot about you. In fact they predicted your birth, your life, and your death. They detailed how you look, described your personality, detailed the city of your birth, and described your mission in life. It also described the horrific and specific details of your torture and execution.

You would be shocked and confused at the revelation, but Jesus Christ wouldn't be. He knew all about it because he knew his purpose and the events to come, even from the very beginning of time.

Moses opened the Bible with the words *"In the beginning God created the heavens and the earth."* It is a fitting start to God's rescue letter to us. A letter written over the course of 1,500 years by 40 different authors documents how man was created, how man fell, the consequences of the Fall, and God's plan to rescue us from the Fall. The Creation, the Fall, and Redemption form the landscape that frames our faith and the answers about life issues.

The Bible answers these questions and points to one person. From Genesis to Revelation the problem is detailed, the solution is provided, and restoration is promised. Jesus Christ is the central character documented throughout the Bible. Jesus Christ plays the pivotal role in this divine plan.

One sage said, "The Old Testament is the New Testament concealed, and the New Testament is the Old Testament revealed." Prophecies, and what scholars call foreshadowing, both in the Old Testament, come true in the pages of the New Testament. These images and direct prophecies build trust in the validity of the Bible.

There are enough prophecies fulfilled by Jesus about his messiahship to fill a book (and there are books like that), but some of the highlights are in the following chart.

Prophecies Fulfilled by Jesus

How Fulfilled	Prophecy	New Testament Fulfillment
Jesus born to a woman	Genesis 3:15	Galatians 4:4
Born in Bethlehem	Micah 5:2	Luke 2:4–5, 7
Timing of birth	Daniel 9:25	Luke 2:1–2
Born of a virgin	Isaiah 7:14	Luke 1:26–27, 30–31
Slaughter of children at time of Jesus's birth	Jeremiah 31:15	Matthew 2:16–18
Flight to Egypt	Hosea 11:1	Matthew 2:14–15
A prophet (John the Baptist) prepares way	Isaiah 40:3–5	Luke 3:3–6
Declared Son of God	Psalm 2:7	Matthew 3:17
Ministry in Galilee	Isaiah 9:1–2	Matthew 4:13–16
Speaks in parables	Psalm 78:2–4	Matthew 13:34–35
Freedom for spiritual and physical "captives"	Isaiah 61:1–2	Luke 4:18–19
Rejected by Jews	Isaiah 53:3	John 1:11; Luke 23:18
Triumphal Entry	Zechariah 9:9	Mark 11:7, 9, 11
Betrayed for 30 pieces of silver	Zechariah 11:12	Matthew 26:14–15
Sacrifice for others' sins	Isaiah 53:5	Romans 5:6, 8
Pierced at crucifixion	Zechariah 12:10	John 19:34
Clothing gambled on	Psalm 22:17–18	Matthew 27:35–36
Forsaken by God	Psalm 22:1	Matthew 27:46
No broken bones	Psalm 34:20	John 19:32–33, 36
Buried with the rich	Isaiah 53:9	Matthew 27:57–60
Resurrection	Psalm 16:10	Mark 16:6–7
Ascension	Psalm 68:18	Mark 16:19

Who Do You Say That I Am?

MATTHEW 16:13–17 *When Jesus came into the region of Caesarea Philippi, He asked His disciples, saying, "Who do men say that I, the Son of Man, am?" So they said, "Some say John the Baptist, some Elijah, and others Jeremiah or one of the prophets." He said to them, "But who do you say that I am?"*

Simon Peter answered and said, "You are the Christ, the Son of the living God." Jesus answered and said to him, "Blessed are you, Simon Bar-Jonah, for flesh and blood has not revealed this to you, but My Father who is in heaven." (NKJV)

When you look at the men in the Bible, you see men who failed but who, through their faith, found restoration; men who failed and who wasted their lives; and finally, a few men who were flawed but who persevered in their faith.

But when we examine the life of Jesus a different portrait emerges. His life cannot be compared to any others. He lived a sinless life marked by service and sacrifice. He fulfilled his Father's plan to deliver to all creation a restoring plan of hope.

When God became a man, a unique character emerged. His human personality jumps off the pages when you read the Gospels. There is something winsome in his loving actions, unique in his relationships with others, and persuasive in the message of his life. These qualities are not possessed by a liar or a lunatic. He must be the one he claims to be.

what others say

Josh McDowell

In fact, the identity of Jesus is utterly crucial to understanding everything he had to say. All that Jesus said and did pointed to his identity as the Messiah, the Son of God, and to the purpose for which he came to earth. If he is not who he claimed to be then his teachings are either the ramblings of a lunatic who sincerely thought he was God (but wasn't) or the words of a liar who knew he wasn't God (but said he was). If his claims are true, however, then he is not a liar or a lunatic—he is Lord![4]

Born of a Virgin

ISAIAH 7:14 *Therefore the Lord Himself will give you a sign: Behold, the virgin shall conceive and bear a Son, and shall call His name Immanuel. (NKJV)*

A child will be born. This child will be fully man because he was born of a woman. Since man is the cause of the brokenness in the world, only a man can pay the ultimate price to redeem it. This male child will be called *Immanuel*, which literally means: "God with us."

His birth is also unique in all creation. He was born of a <u>virgin</u>. Jewish tradition said that the sin nature is passed through the father, and so the conception by the Spirit of God—without human male involvement—was necessary to ensure that Jesus didn't have a sin nature. Jesus is fully human because of his mother and fully God because he was conceived by the Holy Spirit.

virgin
Matthew 1:18–23

Note the two views of his birth. A child is born reflecting his humanity, and a Son is given reflecting his deity. There are two big differences between being born and being given. His birth reflects the new nature of human form that he freely received, and the gift of the Son reflects the love of God by One who could never be born. As the Son of God, Jesus has always existed.

what others say

Dan Hayden

Isaiah is very specific. What will save us is a special Person: a Child, a Son. Salvation will not come in the form of a great idea, nor will it be found in some new philosophy of government. Our only hope is in a Person—*that* is what Isaiah is saying in Isaiah 9:6.[5]

Ray Pritchard

In order for Christ to be our Savior, three conditions had to be met:

He must be a Man. An angel could not die for our sins.

He must be an infinite man. A mere mortal could not bear the infinite price that had to be paid for our sins.

He must be an innocent man. A sinner could not die for the sins of others

The virgin birth guarantees that our Lord fulfills all three conditions. Because he was born of Mary, he is fully human. Because he was conceived by the Holy Spirit, he is fully God. Because he was born holy, he is sinless in thought, word, and deed. Thus he is fully qualified to be our Savior.[6]

Saved from What?

EPHESIANS 2:1–3, 12 *And you He made alive, who were dead in trespasses and sins, in which you once walked according to the course of this world, according to the prince of the power of the air, the spirit who now works in the sons of disobedience, among whom also we all once conducted ourselves in the lusts of our flesh, fulfilling the desires of the flesh and of the mind, and were by nature children of wrath, just as the others . . . that at that* *time you were without Christ, being aliens from the common-wealth of Israel and strangers from the covenants of promise, having no hope and without God in the world. (NKJV)*

As a direct result of our sin, we are

- Dead in our sins.
- By our nature children of wrath in God's sight.
- Strangers from the promises of God.
- Without hope.

This is not a pretty picture. We are a rebellious creation. We inherited it from our first parents, and during the last countless centuries we have submitted to our own rule and reign rather submitted to the rule and reign of God. As a result of our sin, we need to be saved from the consequences of our sin. The consequence is death and a direct result of God's holy wrath. Think of it this way. God created us to have relationship with him. We rejected the Creator's offer and chose to do things our way. We deserve to spend eternity in hell. God, however, has other plans for us. Central to that plan is Jesus Christ.

Only a real man and the true God can deal with the problem of our sin. Sin is distinctly a human problem that can be solved only in a godly manner. Our sin comes between us and a holy God. This is not a mythical problem, an animal problem, or an angelic problem. Our sin qualifies us for judgment. Justice cries out, and only one thing can deliver us from the wrath of God—the sacrifice of his incarnate Son.

Jesus Became a Bondservant

PHILIPPIANS 2:5–8 *Let this mind be in you which was also in Christ Jesus, who, being in the form of God, did not consider it robbery to be equal with God, but made Himself of no reputa-*

tion, taking the form of a bondservant, and coming in the likeness of men. And being found in appearance as a man, He humbled Himself and became obedient to the point of death, even the death of the cross. (NKJV)

go to

bondservant
Exodus 21:2–6

servant
Mark 10:45

A Holy God loves his creation so much that he sends his Son to earth. Jesus willingly took on the form of a human. He gladly dwelt as a human among humans for thirty-three years.

Jesus came in the form of a <u>bondservant</u>! The concept of a bondservant was clearly understood by the believers in the early church. Once a slave had finished his service, he had the opportunity to continue being a slave to his master by voluntarily submitting to the relationship. In essence he would say, "I believe I will be better off under your rule and reign rather than under my own, so I submit to your leadership."

To memorialize the decision, the master would take the new volunteer to the wooden doorjamb of his home and plunge an awl through the servant's earlobe. The marks on the body and the blood on the wood would signify the agreement. The slave would now be called a bondservant. The image of the bondservant is representative of the method of crucifixion and Jesus's willing death on the cross. Jesus became a man for us in order to put into motion the Father's redemption plan.

what others say

C. S. Lewis

The Eternal Being who knows everything and who created the whole universe, became not only a man but (before that) a baby, and before that a (fetus) inside a Woman's body. If you want to get the hang of it, think how you would like to become a slug or a crab.[8]

Jesus called himself a <u>servant</u>, and all of his followers are challenged to be a servant also: selfless, concerned about others, surrendering their rights, and resisting bitterness. Every Christian's calling is to holiness and becoming more like Jesus.

something to ponder

He Lived for Thirty-three Years

Luke 4:16–30

For thirty years Jesus grew up just like any other child. As a young man he worked in the carpentry shop of his father. Then he became active in public ministry. After a year, he returned to His home town, Nazareth. The scene opens in the synagogue on Sabbath. Jesus stands up and reads a portion of Isaiah:

The Spirit of the LORD is upon Me,
Because He has anointed Me
To preach the gospel to the poor;
He has sent Me to heal the brokenhearted,
To proclaim liberty to the captives
And recovery of sight to the blind,
To set at liberty those who are oppressed;
To proclaim the acceptable year of the LORD.
Luke 4:18–19 (NKJV)

Jesus closed the book and said, "Today this Scripture is fulfilled in your hearing" (Luke 4:21 NKJV). The religious leaders were surprised at what Jesus said, so much so that they ultimately sought to kill him. But as they were going to push him off a cliff, he passed through their midst. This wasn't the first or the last time that Jesus's life would be threatened.

Qualities of the Perfect Man as Seen in Christ[9]

Attitudes	Actions	Scripture
Eternal Mind-Set	• Did the will and work of the Father (not working toward His own success/desires)	John 4:34; 5:30; 8:28–29
	• Was filled with the Spirit (Word) (not the world's wisdom/ways)	Luke 4:1, 14
	• Gave the Gospel to others (not temporary pleasures or relief)	Mark 1:14–15; John 3–4
	• Lived a holy, obedient life (not sinful)	Philippians 2:8; 1 Peter 2:22
Love/ Understanding	• Sought to meet needs of others (not uncaring/self-focused)	Matthew 4:23; Luke 4:18–21
	• Sacrificed self and own desires (not self-preserving/selfish)	Luke 22:42; Philippians 2:6–8
	• Was gentle whenever possible (not hard/demanding)	Matthew 11:29; John 21:15–19

Qualities of the Perfect Man as Seen in Christ⁹ (cont'd)

Attitudes	Actions	Scripture
Zeal/Courage/ Confidence (Because of God and his promises)	• Led the disciples and others (not a follower when He shouldn't be)	John 6:2
	• Showed initiative when He should have (not waiting for someone else)	Mark 6:34–44; Luke 6:12–16
	• Comforted when necessary (not a compromiser/man-pleaser)	Matthew 23:1–36; Mark 11:15–18
	• Was decisive according to God's revealed will (not wishy-washy or afraid)	Mark 4:1–11; Mark 8:31–38
Conscientiousness	• Fulfilled responsibilities (Not irresponsible)	John 17:4; 19:30
	• Was diligent (Not lazy or a quitter)	John 5:17; Hebrews 12:2–3
Humility	• Served and listened to others in His leadership (not proudly lording it over others)	John 6:5–10; 13:2–17
	• Glorified another (the Father) (not greedy for attention or recognition)	John 8:50, 54; 17:1, 4

Did you ever wonder why Jesus had a three-year ministry? He could have been sacrificed for our sins that day in Nazareth. We know he lived a sinless life in obedience to his heavenly Father. His death would have satisfied God's demand for justice, His blood would have washed us clean from sin, and his resurrection would have placed him at the right hand of the Father so that he could intercede on our behalf. The Bible tells us there are many miracles and sayings of Jesus that were not recorded for our benefit. So what's the purpose of his three-year ministry? There are three main reasons that Jesus needed to live for those three years: to fulfill prophecy, to reveal his deity, and to provide a model for Christians.

Need for Humanity

> **MATTHEW 5:17** *Do not think that I came to destroy the Law or the Prophets. I did not come to destroy but to fulfill.* (NKJV)

Jesus's humanity and three-year walk as a human fulfill prophecy. The Old Testament is filled with more than sixty prophecies and more than three hundred references about:

• His preexistence

not yet come
John 2:4;
John 7:6

- His ancestry

- His birth

- His character

- His ministry

- His dual nature

- His death

- His resurrection

- His ascension

- His second coming

All prophecies needed to be fulfilled within the life of Jesus. Many times in Scripture Jesus says that his time has <u>not yet come</u>. This reflects the perfect plan that the Father put together and the Son willingly accepted.

Jesus's Deity

> JOHN 7:16–18 *Jesus answered them and said, "My doctrine is not Mine, but His who sent Me. If anyone wants to do His will, he shall know concerning the doctrine, whether it is from God or whether I speak on My own authority. He who speaks from himself seeks his own glory; but He who seeks the glory of the One who sent Him is true, and no unrighteousness is in Him." (NKJV)*

The life of Jesus is documented in the four Gospels of Matthew, Mark, Luke, and John. Each book presents a different focus on Jesus. The book of Matthew shows Jesus as King. His authority as a teacher and healer reveals him as someone to trust and obey. The book of Mark reveals a suffering servant that profiles his willingness to sacrifice and his courage to act on our behalf. The book of Luke seems to be written to the everyday man featuring Jesus as Savior. It divulges more about what he did, the actions he took, and his impact on others. Finally the book of John describes Jesus as divine. Over and over, the apostle John records Jesus's direct statements about his divinity.

Throughout the four Gospels we see a Jesus who forgives sin, heals sickness, knows men's thoughts, and raises the dead. This overwhelming demonstration of perfect power, love, and wisdom sends an obvious message: Jesus Christ is the Son of God.

Jesus's Humanity

2 CORINTHIANS 3:18 *But we all, with unveiled face, beholding as in a mirror the glory of the Lord, are being transformed into the same image from glory to glory, just as by the Spirit of the Lord.* (NKJV)

Jesus lived in public ministry for three years to demonstrate the futility of our sinful choices. He first modeled the importance of a sacrificial life when he told us that the last would be first and the first would be last. He modeled the importance of a dependent life when he acknowledged that he did nothing apart from that which the Father told him. And finally he lived a holy life to demonstrate that he could empower us to live free from the bondage of persistent and habitual sin. "He who says he abides in Him ought himself also to walk just as He walked" (1 John 2:6 NKJV).

Jesus lived because we were trapped in the bondage of our own sinfulness. His life stands in sharp contrast to the lives we live today. The struggle for self-fulfillment, self- sufficiency, self-absorption, and self-security consumes our *self*. His life makes change possible. His life makes redemption possible. His life makes peace, a reality. Forever.

key point

Jesus's Death

ISAIAH 53:4–6 *Surely He has borne our griefs and carried our sorrows; yet we esteemed Him stricken, smitten by God, and afflicted. But He was wounded for our transgressions, He was bruised for our iniquities; the chastisement for our peace was upon Him, and by His stripes we are healed. All we like sheep have gone astray; we have turned, every one, to his own way; and the LORD has laid on Him the iniquity of us all.* (NKJV)

Isaiah 53 is one of the most striking messianic chapters in the Bible. Within its twelve verses we find a thorough explanation of what the death of Jesus Christ accomplished. This was written approximately seven hundred years before the time of Christ, yet it documents in precise detail how Christ's death satisfies God's righteous demand for judgment of our sin. It was no accident that this plan was executed with precision for our benefit.

go to

clothing
Genesis 3:21

These verses also detail the extreme separation that we experience from God because of our sin. Each of us, by choice and by association with our original parents, Adam and Eve, is alienated from God's holiness. Because he cannot connect with anything sinful, he must draw away from us. Yet because of his great love, he provided a way to be reunited with him through Jesus's death on our behalf.

All the Blessings We Receive from Our Association with Jesus

Jesus Was . . .	So We Receive . . .	Scripture
Punished	Forgiveness	Isaiah 53:4–5
Shamed	Glory	Psalm 69:7; Hebrews 12:2
Cursed	Blessings	Galatians 3:13–14
Rejected	Acceptance	Ephesians 1:3–4
Killed	Life	Romans 6:6–7; Galatians 2:20
Sin	Righteousness	2 Corinthians 5:21
Wounded	Healing	Isaiah 53:4–5; 61:1–3
Made Poor	His riches	2 Corinthians 8:9

something to ponder

All the sin, wrath, and punishment we deserve is placed upon the sinless, innocent Jesus at his death. That is impressive, but just as important is that all the good, beauty, and peace due Jesus is given to us. In reality we the guilty get the perks of the innocent Lamb, and Jesus got the punishment we deserved.

Sacrifice Called For

> 2 CORINTHIANS 5:20–21 *Now then, we are ambassadors for Christ, as though God were pleading through us: we implore you on Christ's behalf, be reconciled to God. For He made Him who knew no sin to be sin for us, that we might become the righteousness of God in Him. (NKJV)*

The ultimate sacrifice took the One who knew no sin to be sin for us. In fact, a pattern of sacrifice is detailed in a progressive manner in the Bible. First, one animal sacrifice per man; then, one sacrifice per family; next, one sacrifice per nation; finally, one sacrifice per world.

Sacrifice has stalked the sinful footsteps of men since the Fall. In Genesis, the first animal sacrifice took place when God provided <u>clothing</u> to cover Adam and Eve's shame. This set in motion and established a godly precedent that no one can escape. You cannot cover your sin with your own good works.

The concept was extended to one sacrifice for a family in the story of the Passover lamb. Each family was instructed to place the blood of a sacrificial lamb on the doorposts of their homes. "Now the blood shall be a sign for you on the houses where you are. And when I see the blood, I will pass over you; and the plague shall not be on you to destroy you when I strike the land of Egypt. So this day shall be to you a memorial; and you shall keep it as a feast to the LORD throughout your generations" (Exodus 12:13–14 NKJV). The significance of this bloodletting foreshadowed the shedding of Jesus's blood on the cross. Note the comment, "And when I see the blood, I will pass over you."

One sacrifice for the family was extended to one sacrifice for the nation during the Day of Atonement ritual. Once a year the high priest would enter the temple and sacrifice a lamb for the sins of the nation.

Jesus's death was more than a hideous murder of an innocent man. It was not a senseless act of angry people. This sacrificial system was finished when God set in motion one final <u>sacrifice</u> for the world. Once and for all God's redemptive plan was finished with the death and resurrection of Jesus.

It could be puzzling to consider the prophet Isaiah's words, "Yet it pleased the LORD to bruise Him; He has put Him to grief. When You make His soul an offering for sin, He shall see His seed, He shall prolong His days, and the pleasure of the LORD shall prosper in His hand" (Isaiah 53:10 NKJV). How could God be pleased to allow such darkness and pain for his own Son? God certainly didn't get some morbid satisfaction in seeing his Son suffer. But God the Father knew the passion, power, and perfection that would be released in the death and resurrection of his Son. In his gracious love for his creation, he was pleased with the plan because of the greater benefits it offered.

sacrifice
John 1:29;
Hebrews 10:1–14

Resurrection: Conquered Death

1 CORINTHIANS 15:12–19 *Now if Christ is preached that He has been raised from the dead, how do some among you say that there is no resurrection of the dead? But if there is no resurrec-*

go to

grief
1 Corinthians
15:54–55

tion of the dead, then Christ is not risen. And if Christ is not risen, then our preaching is empty and your faith is also empty. Yes, and we are found false witnesses of God, because we have testified of God that He raised up Christ, whom He did not raise up—if in fact the dead do not rise. For if the dead do not rise, then Christ is not risen. And if Christ is not risen, your faith is futile; you are still in your sins! Then also those who have fallen asleep in Christ have perished. If in this life only we have hope in Christ, we are of all men the most pitiable. (NKJV).

The resurrection of Jesus is crucial to his purpose in coming to earth. Without his resurrection, there is no hope of eternal life because we are still in our sins. When Jesus rose from the dead, he conquered death and made heaven accessible to those who received his substitutionary death. The Resurrection is essential to the foundation of Christianity.

Jesus himself claimed to be the resurrection and the life. He told this to Martha after her brother Lazarus died. "Jesus said to her, 'I am the resurrection and the life. He who believes in Me, though he may die, he shall live. And whoever lives and believes in Me shall never die. Do you believe this?'" (John 11:25–26 NKJV). He asks the same question of every believer.

what others say

Charles Swindoll

Pull out the Resurrection from the story of Christ, and the elements of our faith fall like dominoes. If Christ wasn't raised, then not only will we die, but we'll die in our sins.[10]

Jesus's resurrection is the only reason that Paul could write, "But I do not want you to be ignorant, brethren, concerning those who have fallen asleep, lest you sorrow as others who have no hope" (1 Thessalonians 4:13 NKJV). Although we still grieve at the loss of a loved one, we don't have the same kind of grief of those who have no hope. We know we'll see a Christian loved one again. That makes all the difference.

Chapter Wrap-Up

- Jesus amazed everyone he encountered, especially the disciples when he calmed the winds and sea. (Matthew 8:23–27)
- John knew Jesus well and respectfully identified him as the Word who made the world in the beginning. (John 1:1–4)
- Jesus had the most unique conception and birth of anyone on earth because he was born of a virgin and conceived by the Holy Spirit. (Isaiah 7:14)
- Even though he was God in human flesh, he still submitted himself to serve God's purposes as a bondservant. (Philippians 2:5–8)
- Jesus lived as a human for thirty-three years so that he could be a model for Christians to follow. (2 Corinthians 3:18)

Study Questions

1. What was the response of the disciples toward Jesus when Jesus calmed the winds and the sea?

2. What did the apostle John write about Jesus in his Gospel, and what did John call Jesus?

3. What amazing thing made Jesus's conception and birth different from every other person's on earth?

4. Even though Jesus was God in human flesh, what surprising thing did he allow himself to become?

5. Why did Jesus need to live for thirty-three years when he could have fulfilled the plan of redemption immediately after first revealing his deity?

Chapter 14: Paul—Passionate Writer for God

Chapter Highlights:
- Saul Meets the Lord
- Paul the Missionary
- Paul Is Persecuted
- Paul Takes the Gospel to the Gentiles

Let's Get Started

The work of Paul was a huge contribution to the cause of Christ in the first century. Paul started out as a Jewish Pharisee who hated those "new believers" of Jesus Christ. But God grabbed his heart in a unique fashion and turned it into a heart of love for himself and followers of Jesus.

Paul has had a powerful influence in the lives of Christians throughout the centuries. His story is told in the book of Acts and his heart is shown in his letters to groups of Christians, which we now use as books of the New Testament.

From his strong example of faithful living in spite of the most horrible conditions, you and I will learn to love and value God more. We'll also be inspired to regard our lives as only important for the wonderful task of representing Jesus to others. That was Paul's mission statement.

go to

stoning
Acts 7:54–60

consenting
Acts 8:1

blame
Acts 7:60

I'm Gonna Get Those Christians!

ACTS 8:3 *As for Saul, he made havoc of the church, entering every house, and dragging off men and women, committing them to prison. (NKJV)*

Saul hated Christians. He hunted them without mercy. He wasn't some hired thug; he was a highly trained Pharisee, a religious man, and he intended, with every ounce of his being, to rid his world of this heretical group of Christians. He saw them as a threat to the Jewish Law. He was single-minded in his hunt. He took care of people's coats who were <u>stoning</u> a young Christian preacher named Stephen. It was a bloody sight, yet Saul watched and was <u>consenting</u> to Stephen's death. Later, Saul would be called Paul. Saul is his Jewish name and Paul is his Roman name.

As Stephen faced death, he graciously asked the Lord not to <u>blame</u> the murderers. Stephen went into the Lord's presence in front of

Paul. Even in his bloody thirst, Paul had to wonder about the light and life in Stephen's heart, and may have compared it with the darkness and death that filled his own.

Light Brings a Changed Heart

ACTS 9:1–8 *Then Saul, still breathing threats and murder against the disciples of the Lord, went to the high priest and asked letters from him to the synagogues of Damascus, so that if he found any who were of the Way, whether men or women, he might bring them bound to Jerusalem. As he journeyed he came near Damascus, and suddenly a light shone around him from heaven. Then he fell to the ground, and heard a voice saying to him, "Saul, Saul, why are you persecuting Me?" And he said, "Who are You, Lord?" Then the Lord said, "I am Jesus, whom you are persecuting. It is hard for you to kick against the goads." So he, trembling and astonished, said, "Lord, what do You want me to do?" Then the Lord said to him, "Arise and go into the city, and you will be told what you must do." And the men who journeyed with him stood speechless, hearing a voice but seeing no one. Then Saul arose from the ground, and when his eyes were opened he saw no one. But they led him by the hand and brought him into Damascus. (NKJV)*

Stephen's death caused the Christians to flee in all directions. Saul knew Damascus would be one spot to find those refugees. Little did he know who was chasing whom. On the way there, Saul met Jesus on that dusty road. After encountering Jesus and being struck blind, Paul was led to a believer in Damascus. There he was filled with the Holy Spirit and baptized. His vision returned.

what others say

Oswald Chambers

But the humility Paul manifests was produced in him by the remembrance that Jesus, whom he had scorned and despised, whose followers he had persecuted, whose Church he had harried, not only had forgiven him, but made him His chief apostle.[1]

Paul later referred to his conversion experience by writing, "But I press on, that I may lay hold of that for which Christ Jesus has also laid hold of me" (Philippians 3:12 NKJV). Paul was saying that Jesus apprehended him. The one man who made a living apprehending those who loved Jesus was now apprehended by Jesus's love.

Paul immediately began telling about Jesus and his own conversion experience in the synagogue. Obviously he was a man who had been drastically changed. Just as he had thrown himself totally into wanting to kill Christians, now he was totally involved in speaking of his new Savior. With Paul, it was all or nothing.

I'll Send You Letters While I'm Away

ACTS 13:1–3 *Now in the church that was at Antioch there were certain prophets and teachers: Barnabas, Simeon who was called Niger, Lucius of Cyrene, Manaen who had been brought up with Herod the tetrarch, and Saul. As they ministered to the Lord and fasted, the Holy Spirit said, "Now separate to Me Barnabas and Saul for the work to which I have called them." Then, having fasted and prayed, and laid hands on them, they sent them away. (NKJV)*

Some personality traits don't change. Saul, whose name was changed to Paul, shifted his power and energy from pursuing Christians to spreading Christianity. He and Barnabas became the first Christian missionaries (see Appendix B—Paul's Missionary Journeys).

what others say

Warren W. Wiersbe

Until now, Jerusalem had been the center of ministry, and Peter had been the key apostle. But from this point on, Antioch in Syria would become the new center and Paul the new leader. The Gospel was on the move![2]

Significant Events on Paul's Journeys

Trip	Significant Event
FIRST (AD 46–48)	The people of Lycia wanted to make Paul and Barnabas gods. Of course, the missionaries refused (Acts 14:11–18).
SECOND (AD 49–52)	A Philippian jailer was converted after a big earthquake caused the chains of Paul, Silas, and the other prisoners to unfasten (Acts 16:25–34).
THIRD (AD 53–57)	God performed many miracles through Paul. Even handkerchiefs and aprons he had touched were powerful enough to heal and cast out evil spirits (Acts 19:11–12).
FOURTH (AD 59–60)	On the way to Rome where he would be imprisoned and tried in court, Paul was shipwrecked, but many were brought to salvation in Jesus. Some commentators do not actually call this a missionary journey; others do (Acts 27—28).

Paul didn't immediately become a missionary after his conversion. Commentators believe he spent some years in Tarsus (<u>Arabia</u>) before returning to become more involved with the early church fathers. At one point, he spent <u>fourteen</u> years learning more about what he should believe.

Winner of the Unpopularity Contest

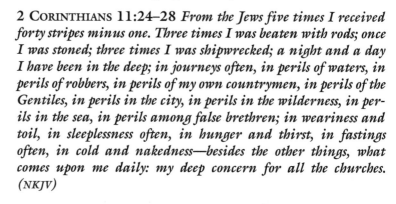

2 CORINTHIANS 11:24–28 *From the Jews five times I received forty stripes minus one. Three times I was beaten with rods; once I was stoned; three times I was shipwrecked; a night and a day I have been in the deep; in journeys often, in perils of waters, in perils of robbers, in perils of my own countrymen, in perils of the Gentiles, in perils in the city, in perils in the wilderness, in perils in the sea, in perils among false brethren; in weariness and toil, in sleeplessness often, in hunger and thirst, in fastings often, in cold and nakedness—besides the other things, what comes upon me daily: my deep concern for all the churches.* (NKJV)

go to

Arabia
Galatians 1:17

fourteen
Galatians 2:1

help
Hebrews 2:18

Jesus
John 16:33

vilified
hated

Talk about a changed man. Paul traded all the privileges of his birth and position for the gospel. That choice got him whipped, beaten, stoned, plotted against, and **vilified**. This man was truly transformed by his relationship with Christ.

what others say

Patrick M. Morley

To the same degree Paul persecuted the Christians, he was persecuted in return. It was not an easy-street life. For Paul, following Christ and God's purpose for his life was not an option, not a cushy desk job, but a mandate to exist and function in the way God directed, whatever the cost.[3]

Wherever Paul went, trouble was soon to follow. "When we came to Macedonia, our bodies had no rest, but we were troubled on every side. Outside were conflicts, inside were fears" (2 Corinthians 7:5 NKJV). Paul was no different from anyone else. He not only dealt with fear, he admits he had many fears! But his life was marked by victory over those fears.

apply it

Life always offers difficulties, even if a person isn't a Christian. But if you are a Christian, at least you have a purpose in hardship. And you have a great God who wants to <u>help</u> you. <u>Jesus</u> said we would have tribulation, <u>Peter</u> asked why we would be surprised at our tribulations, and Paul said that no one is exempt from suffering for the Lord. You're not alone. God wants you to be strengthened through it all. Difficulties transform us into the image of Christ.

Peter
1 Peter 4:12

vision
Acts 10:9–16

decided
Acts 15:28–30

vision
something seen
supernaturally

Gentiles Need Jesus Too

ACTS 15:12 *Then all the multitude kept silent and listened to Barnabas and Paul declaring how many miracles and wonders God had worked through them among the Gentiles. (NKJV)*

After Paul and Barnabas returned from their first missionary journey, a controversy began within the new Christian church about whether the gospel should be preached to those who weren't Jews.

The apostle Peter had brought it up after God, in a **vision**, told him to preach to the Gentiles. Some said that the Gentiles had to be circumcised in order to qualify for Christianity. A great discussion began among the leaders. Paul and Barnabas told them of how God had used them among the Gentiles. As a result, the leadership group <u>decided</u> to allow Gentiles to hear about Jesus, without being circumcised.

what others say

Warren W. Wiersbe

Their emphasis was on the miracles that God had enabled them to perform among the Gentiles. These miracles were proof that God was working with them and that they were God's chosen messengers.[4]

I Won't Let Him Flake Out on Us Again!

ACTS 15:36–41 *Then after some days Paul said to Barnabas, "Let us now go back and visit our brethren in every city where we have preached the word of the Lord, and see how they are doing." Now Barnabas was determined to take with them John called Mark. But Paul insisted that they should not take with them the one who had departed from them in Pamphylia, and had not gone with them to the work. Then the contention became so sharp that they parted from one another. And so Barnabas took Mark and sailed to Cyprus; but Paul chose Silas and departed, being commended by the brethren to the grace of God. And he went through Syria and Cilicia, strengthening the churches. (NKJV)*

There is a common saying in management circles: "You only can expect what you inspect." Paul was concerned for the growth of the new churches and wanted to revisit them. Barnabas, the encourager, wanted to give John Mark another chance. Paul flatly refused to take him. He probably believed the mission would be compromised. At this point, Paul may not have thought John Mark was trying hard enough, but later he would have more grace toward him.

what others say

John Pollock

Paul saw it as rank desertion. Mark's excuse has been variously guessed. Some think Paul had fallen ill of malaria, and made for the mountains to seek cooler air rather than from deliberate intent, and Mark was frightened. Whatever the cause, Mark's withdrawal left a wound in Paul which took years to heal.[5]

Paul focused exclusively on the task, while Barnabas saw only the man. Barnabas took John Mark on his own trip. Later in life Paul's thinking about John Mark turned around, because Paul asked for his help. "Only Luke is with me. Get Mark and bring him with you, for he is useful to me for ministry" (2 Timothy 4:11 NKJV). (John Mark later became known as Mark.) The hurt feelings were healed. Obviously, Paul learned a valuable lesson.

For many leaders it is so easy to focus on the task. Results count and the job needs to be done. That is a short-term view and never addresses our responsibility to develop those we are leading. Paul, in his perfectionism, didn't want to risk the success of "the mission" with a weak team member. Barnabas was able to see that developing "the man" would make "the mission" even stronger. Barnabas was right, the job got done, and the man was restored. When we allow a long-term viewpoint to influence our leadership skills we will become better leaders.

Other Attitudes Paul Expressed

Paul grew from a hateful, revenge-seeking Pharisee intent on fulfilling the Law, to a Christian who lived out the very fruit of the Spirit he wrote about to the Galatians. "But the fruit of the Spirit is love, joy, peace, longsuffering, kindness, goodness, faithfulness, gentleness, self-control. Against such there is no law" (Galatians 5:22–23 NKJV). Here are some of the qualities he revealed:

Paul's Godly Qualities

Scripture	Paul's Character Quality
Acts 20:19, 24	Humility
Philippians 2:3–5	Selflessness
2 Corinthians 7:4	Joy regardless of circumstances
2 Timothy 1:4	Deep love and concern for other believers
Philippians 1:19–21	Willingness to sacrifice himself for the cause of Christ

Paul gained those qualities the same way the rest of us do: he had problems that forced him to trust in Christ continually.

Books Paul Wrote

Paul was the most prolific writer of letters to the Christian churches. He cared about them so much that he wanted to keep in touch with them and instruct them in continued growth. Here are the letters he wrote and the main premise of each one. Most often, his message is one of stressing God's salvation through grace, and eliminating his readers' desires to be **legalistic** about faith.

go to

legalistic
Ephesians 2:8–9

legalistic
having to do it by
the rule book

exhorted
encouraged urgently

what others say

Max Lucado

All the world religions can be placed in one of two camps: legalism or grace. Humankind does it or God does it. Salvation as a wage based on deeds done—or salvation as a gift based on Christ's death.[6]

Books Paul Wrote

Biblical Book	Main Premise
Romans	Paul presented God's gift of salvation through Jesus Christ, rather than through good works.
1 & 2 Corinthians	Paul addressed problems going on within the church in Corinth.
Galatians	Paul encouraged Galatian believers not to go back into thinking their salvation was based on doing good things.
Ephesians	Paul inspired the Christians at the Ephesian church to know the power they have to live as Christians.
Philippians	Paul **exhorted** the Christians at Philippi to know how they can have unity and joy.

tradition
what people have
said through the
years

Books Paul Wrote (cont'd)

Biblical Book	Main Premise
Colossians	Paul instructed the Colossian church to have the right priorities of putting Christ first in their lives.
1 Thessalonians	Paul directed the believers at Thessalonica to grow in their new faith in Christ.
2 Thessalonians	Paul encouraged the believers in Thessalonica to remove the false teaching that some teachers had been putting in their minds.
1 & 2 Timothy	Paul wrote to the young pastor, Timothy, to encourage and instruct him in responsibilities at the Ephesian church.
Titus	Paul stressed to Titus, a young pastor on the island of Crete, how to run his church both administratively and as a counselor to spiritual problems.
Philemon	Paul subtly asked Philemon to accept back as a brother in Christ a runaway slave named Onesimus.

Paul's Death

ACTS 28:30–31 *Then Paul dwelt two whole years in his own rented house, and received all who came to him, preaching the kingdom of God and teaching the things which concern the Lord Jesus Christ with all confidence, no one forbidding him. (NKJV)*

Although the end of Paul's life was not chronicled in Scripture, **tradition** says that he was released after no charges were brought against him in Rome at his trial. After his release, he supposedly made another trip to the provinces of Macedonia, Achaia, Asia, and finally Spain. Tradition also alleges he was eventually beheaded by the Roman government.

what others say

John Pollock

Of Paul's final trial nothing is known beyond the tradition that he was condemned by resolution of the Senate on the charge of treason against the divine Emperor. How long Simon Peter and Paul were in prison together before being executed the same day, as an early and strong belief asserts, cannot be fixed: possibly as much as nine months.[7]

Paul was taken to Rome in order to be tried for treason against the Roman state because the Roman state said Caesar was god. The Jews who wanted to get rid of Paul claimed he was preaching against Rome's authority in Jerusalem and hoped the Roman officials would kill him for it. But they couldn't supply any specific evidence and no one who was accusing him showed up at his first Roman trial. Later at another Roman trial he was found guilty and executed.

Chapter Wrap-Up

- Paul had been trying to kill or stop Christians from preaching Jesus as the Messiah but when Jesus appeared to him in a bright light, Paul was converted and became a Christian himself. (Acts 9:18)

- After God's directions became known, the Christian leaders sent off Paul and Barnabas on their first missionary journey. They ended up making three more trips. (Acts 13:1–3)

- While Paul was on his missionary journeys, he had a lot of horrible things happen to him, including being beaten, stoned, shipwrecked, attacked, and falsely accused. He went without sleep, food, and drink. But he stayed faithful to God throughout everything. (2 Corinthians 11:24–28)

- When a controversy arose about whether Gentiles could also become Christians, Paul and Barnabas explained how much the Gentiles were responding to their preaching. As a result, the early Christian leaders saw the need to preach to Gentiles too without requiring them to become circumcised. (Acts 15:12)

- Paul and Barnabas had a big disagreement about whether John Mark should go on their next missionary journey, since he had left them prematurely on their previous trip. Paul and Barnabas went in separate directions as a result, but God used it to impact even more people. (Acts 15:36–41)

Study Questions

1. What brought about Paul's change of heart concerning Jesus and Christians?

2. How did the Christians know what God wanted Paul and Barnabas to do?

3. What are some of the things that happened to Paul while he was on his missionary journeys?

4. How did Paul participate in the controversy about whether Christians should preach to Gentiles?

5. What did Paul and Barnabas disagree about?

Chapter 15: Peter—Growing in Faith

Let's Get Started

Peter was the impulsive and expressive disciple of Jesus who said some silly things and did some impetuous stuff, but proved himself a faithful follower in the end. He is an example to many of us who are impulsive. Jesus saw Peter's potential and gave him a new name representing his future position in the church. We'll be focusing on only a few of the many verses that refer to Peter, but even those few will show us what kind of person he was and how he changed.

Ready, Fire, Aim!

MATTHEW 4:18–20 *And Jesus, walking by the Sea of Galilee [see Illustration #27], saw two brothers, Simon called Peter, and Andrew his brother, casting a net into the sea; for they were fishermen. Then He said to them, "Follow Me, and I will make you fishers of men." They immediately left their nets and followed Him.* (NKJV)

Peter immediately left his nets to follow Jesus. He was just that type of man. He was the first one in line, the first to raise his hand, and the first to move. Decisions came quickly to him. Inaction was intolerable and he avoided it at all costs. Peter was a natural go-getter.

what others say

Herschel H. Hobbs

No man should ever limit God by his own power or understanding. When faith is tested to the utmost, we should rest in God and leave the unknown to him. It is better to walk with God in the dark than to walk alone in the light. In his own time God will make all things plain.[1]

Peter was independent and confident, and our society admires and rewards men like him. He was a self-made man who got things done. Of course, he could come across as a little pushy now and then, but you couldn't help admiring a self-starter like Peter.

You may have many wonderful qualities, but are they controlled by the Holy Spirit or are you operating in your own power? God wants us to depend upon him, not our own <u>understanding</u>.

Illustration #27
The Life of Peter—
This map shows where major events occurred in Peter's life. The events are numbered chronologically.

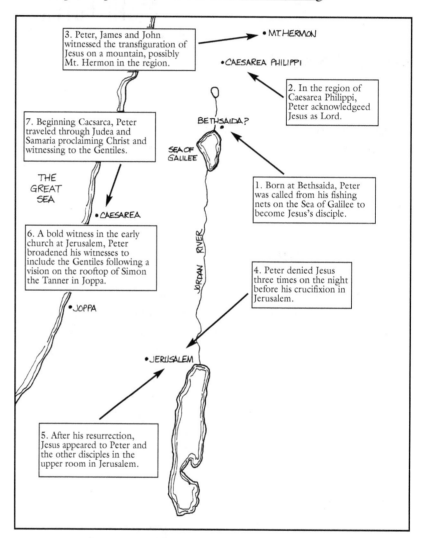

3. Peter, James and John witnessed the transfiguration of Jesus on a mountain, possibly Mt. Hermon in the region.

• MT. HERMON

• CAESAREA PHILIPPI

2. In the region of Caesarea Philippi, Peter acknowledgeed Jesus as Lord.

BETHSAIDA?

7. Beginning Cacsarca, Peter traveled through Judea and Samaria proclaiming Christ and witnessing to the Gentiles.

THE GREAT SEA

SEA OF GALILEE

1. Born at Bethsaida, Peter was called from his fishing nets on the Sea of Galilee to become Jesus's disciple.

• CAESAREA

6. A bold witness in the early church at Jerusalem, Peter broadened his witnesses to include the Gentiles following a vision on the rooftop of Simon the Tanner in Joppa.

JORDAN RIVER

4. Peter denied Jesus three times on the night before his crucifixion in Jerusalem.

• JOPPA

• JERUSALEM

5. After his resurrection, Jesus appeared to Peter and the other disciples in the upper room in Jerusalem.

Jump Now, Float Later

understanding
Proverbs 3:5–6

MATTHEW 14:22–32 *Immediately Jesus made His disciples get into the boat and go before Him to the other side, while He sent the multitudes away. And when He had sent the multitudes away, He went up on the mountain by Himself to pray. Now when evening came, He was alone there. But the boat was now in the middle of the sea, tossed by the waves, for the wind was contrary. Now in the fourth watch of the night Jesus went to them, walking on the sea. And when the disciples saw Him walking on the sea, they were troubled, saying, "It is a ghost!" And they cried out for fear. But immediately Jesus spoke to them, saying, "Be of good cheer! It is I; do not be afraid." And Peter answered Him and said, "Lord, if it is You, command me to come to You on the water." So He said, "Come." And when Peter had come down out of the boat, he walked on the water to go to Jesus. But when he saw that the wind was boisterous, he was afraid; and beginning to sink he cried out, saying, "Lord, save me!" And immediately Jesus stretched out His hand and caught him, and said to him, "O you of little faith, why did you doubt?" And when they got into the boat, the wind ceased. (NKJV)*

weary
Galatians 6:9

Look up the word *zest* in the dictionary and you might see Peter's likeness. Peter loved Christ with his whole heart and it showed. He would be the first one jumping out of a boat to meet Jesus on the shore. It comes as little surprise he would ask to meet Jesus on the water!

It also comes as no surprise to see Peter sink beneath the waves when he took his eyes off Jesus. He was quick to jump in, but lacked the staying power to follow through. You and I also sink into our difficult circumstances when we take our eyes off Jesus. "Looking unto Jesus, the author and finisher of our faith, who for the joy that was set before Him endured the cross, despising the shame, and has sat down at the right hand of the throne of God" (Hebrews 12:2 NKJV).

All of us have seen leaders like Peter jump quickly into situations without counting the cost. They try relying on their own skill to push through stormy times. Their resolve is strong, their courage is unquestioned, and they want to make a difference. Intentions are good, but the outcomes can be erratic. We need to remember that we should move fast with decisions that can be reversed, and slower with irreversible ones.

Peter was quick to sign up but often faltered in continuing strong. We should also be careful about staying faithful and not growing <u>weary</u>. The Christian life isn't a sprint, it's a marathon.

I Know Who You Are!

MATTHEW 16:13–20 *When Jesus came into the region of Caesarea Philippi, He asked His disciples, saying, "Who do men*

answer
Matthew 10:32

stone
John 8:59

say that I, the Son of Man, am?" So they said, "Some say John the Baptist, some Elijah, and others Jeremiah or one of the prophets." He said to them, "But who do you say that I am?" Simon Peter answered and said, "You are the Christ, the Son of the living God." Jesus answered and said to him, "Blessed are you, Simon Bar-Jonah, for flesh and blood has not revealed this to you, but My Father who is in heaven. And I also say to you that you are Peter, and on this rock I will build My church, and the gates of Hades shall not prevail against it. And I will give you the keys of the kingdom of heaven, and whatever you bind on earth will be bound in heaven, and whatever you loose on earth will be loosed in heaven." Then He commanded His disciples that they should tell no one that He was Jesus the Christ. (NKJV)

How come no one was surprised Peter answered the big question for everyone else? Peter knew where Jesus was leading the discussion. Like a bubble ready to burst, Peter was ready to jump when Jesus asked, "Who do you say that I am?" Peter was ready and answered on behalf of everyone, "You are the Christ, the Son of the living God" (verse 16 NKJV). His answer shot from his lips because it was the honest confession of his heart.

Every person in the world will some day <u>answer</u> that question and it will determine whether they are allowed into heaven or sent to eternity without God's presence. If we say Jesus is the Christ, we are acknowledging our need of a Savior and that he is actually God.

When Jesus said "I AM" he was calling himself God, for that's how God referred to himself in the Old Testament. That is why the religious leaders wanted to <u>stone</u> him.

Open Mouth, Insert Foot 1

MATTHEW 16:21–23 *From that time Jesus began to show to His disciples that He must go to Jerusalem, and suffer many things from the elders and chief priests and scribes, and be killed, and be raised the third day. Then Peter took Him aside and began to rebuke Him, saying, "Far be it from You, Lord; this shall not happen to You!" But He turned and said to Peter, "Get behind Me, Satan! You are an offense to Me, for you are not mindful of the things of God, but the things of men." (NKJV)*

Peter had it all figured out. Jesus was the Messiah, the Son of God. This returning King would deliver the Jews from their persecutors.

Peter loved Christ, but he wasn't ready to hear anything contrary to his own plans. He had it all worked out in his mind. No one was going to tell him anything different. Not even Jesus.

Open Mouth, Insert Foot 2

MATTHEW 17:1–8 *Now after six days Jesus took Peter, James, and John his brother, led them up on a high mountain by themselves; and He was transfigured before them. His face shone like the sun, and His clothes became as white as the light. And behold, Moses and Elijah appeared to them, talking with Him. Then Peter answered and said to Jesus, "Lord, it is good for us to be here; if You wish, let us make here three tabernacles: one for You, one for Moses, and one for Elijah." While he was still speaking, behold, a bright cloud overshadowed them; and suddenly a voice came out of the cloud, saying, "This is My beloved Son, in whom I am well pleased. Hear Him!" And when the disciples heard it, they fell on their faces and were greatly afraid. But Jesus came and touched them and said, "Arise, and do not be afraid." When they had lifted up their eyes, they saw no one but Jesus only. (NKJV)*

Shooting from the hip, Peter blurted out that they should build a memorial. How fitting that God interrupted the zealous Peter. In mid-sentence Peter got the message. His only response was to fall facedown to the ground before Jesus Christ and the presence of God.

What an appropriate response for Peter: to fall facedown in worship before God's presence. Instead of trying to make plans and do things, we should humble ourselves by being quiet. When we see Jesus in heaven, we're not going to talk; we'll bow.

Peter continued to reveal his impetuousness many times. When Jesus wanted to wash Peter's feet, he protested. "You shall never wash my feet!" Only when Jesus answered, "If I do not wash you, you have no part with Me," did Peter agree and say, "Lord, not my feet only, but also my hands and my head!" (see John 13:6–9 NKJV).

ear
John 18:7–11

When Jesus was arrested in the garden, Peter impulsively cut off the <u>ear</u> of the servant of the high priest. Peter was trying to make things turn out the way he wanted. To Peter's credit, whenever the truth was revealed, he quickly changed his thinking.

There is so much of Peter in all of us. We busy ourselves with activities that seemingly honor the Lord, when we need to take time to worship him. We worship when we focus on his graciousness, mercy, love, faithfulness, kindness, and goodness.

Pride Before the Downfall

MATTHEW 26:31–35 *Then Jesus said to them, "All of you will be made to stumble because of Me this night, for it is written: 'I will strike the Shepherd, and the sheep of the flock will be scattered.' But after I have been raised, I will go before you to Galilee." Peter answered and said to Him, "Even if all are made to stumble because of You, I will never be made to stumble." Jesus said to him, "Assuredly, I say to you that this night, before the rooster crows, you will deny Me three times." Peter said to Him, "Even if I have to die with You, I will not deny You!" And so said all the disciples.* (NKJV)

Peter was telling the Lord, "You have trained me. I love you. I am a changed man. I will never leave you." But Peter was unprepared for total commitment because too much of Peter stood in the way.

what others say

John MacArthur Jr.

Peter was a man of action—impulsive and eager. I call him the Apostle with the foot-shaped mouth because he was always sticking his foot in it. He was always blurting out, charging ahead in a mad hurry.[3]

Peter's great confidence was his greatest weakness. Peter loved the Lord, was forgiven, and desired to serve him forever. However, Peter was just hours away from catastrophic failure, even as he boasted his fidelity to the Lord.

It will take Peter's broken heart to allow that last drop of his pride to spill out. Then Peter will be ready to die for Christ. Pride always stands in the way of being able to see God's purposes and of knowing how to respond the way he wants us to.

Someone has said, "He who is disappointed in himself is he who first trusted in himself." We will avoid that kind of disappointment if we recognize that we can do anything good only through the Holy Spirit's power in our lives. Don't let self-confidence ruin your God-confidence.

suicide
Matthew 27:5

Peter and the Wail

MATTHEW 26:69–75 *Now Peter sat outside in the courtyard. And a servant girl came to him, saying, "You also were with Jesus of Galilee." But he denied it before them all, saying, "I do not know what you are saying." And when he had gone out to the gateway, another girl saw him and said to those who were there, "This fellow also was with Jesus of Nazareth." But again he denied with an oath, "I do not know the Man!" And a little later those who stood by came up and said to Peter, "Surely you also are one of them, for your speech betrays you." Then he began to curse and swear, saying, "I do not know the Man!" Immediately a rooster crowed. And Peter remembered the word of Jesus who had said to him, "Before the rooster crows, you will deny Me three times." So he went out and wept bitterly. (NKJV)*

Peter wrapped his whole life around Jesus. His confidence seemed to be an asset. But his confidence failed, and when he denied Christ, his world fell apart. "Wept bitterly" in Greek actually means "a piercing, violent cry." For the next three days after Jesus hung on the cross and died, Peter lived in agony. He most likely repeatedly rehearsed his denial. He may have asked himself a thousand times, "Why did I respond like that? I love Jesus!" But he had no peace.

what others say

F. B. Meyer

Then, forgetting his own grief, he turned and looked at Peter, not with anger or reproach, but remembering and reminding. Many waters cannot drown his love! We too may fail him, deny, and crucify him afresh. But when our heart turns back in an agony of grief and remorse, he will renew us again unto repentance.[4]

Such a grievous failure would have driven most men into depression. Some men might have even committed <u>suicide</u> like Judas Iscariot did after he betrayed Jesus. But Peter somehow had the

go to

support
1 Thessalonians
2:11–12

courage to persevere. He was even meeting with the disciples, which was a wise thing to do.

When we are feeling discouraged or depressed because we have failed, the best thing we can do is meet with other Christians. Most of the time, that's the thing we least want to do, but to let us know there is hope we need the <u>support</u> of others who have also failed.

I'll Pick Jesus Over a Huge Catch

> JOHN 21:3–7 *Simon Peter said to them, "I am going fishing." They said to him, "We are going with you also." They went out and immediately got into the boat, and that night they caught nothing. But when the morning had now come, Jesus stood on the shore; yet the disciples did not know that it was Jesus. Then Jesus said to them, "Children, have you any food?" They answered Him, "No." And He said to them, "Cast the net on the right side of the boat, and you will find some." So they cast, and now they were not able to draw it in because of the multitude of fish. Therefore that disciple whom Jesus loved said to Peter, "It is the Lord!" Now when Simon Peter heard that it was the Lord, he put on his outer garment (for he had removed it), and plunged into the sea. (NKJV)*

As a fisherman, this was Peter's big score. He had struck it rich. However, when he learned that Jesus was on the shore, he compared the wealth in his net to the relationship he had with Jesus. No more denials, no more water-walking attempts, and no more fish! Peter threw himself into the water and swam to Jesus.

what others say

Warren W. Wiersbe

It was time for Jesus to take over the situation, just as he did when he called Peter into discipleship. He told them where to cast the net; they obeyed, and they caught 153 fish! We are never far from success when we permit Jesus to give the orders, and we are usually closer to success than we realize.[5]

Even though the disciples had given up on their former discipleship life, Jesus's compassionate calling to them shows his understanding and desire to woo them back to the mission he started to train them for.

annulled
repealed

At times we may become discouraged and leave the calling or mission God has given us. But if we'll hear him call us "children" and "lads" in a compassionate voice, we may be inspired again to serve him in the way he wants us to.

Career Move: From Fisherman to Shepherd

JOHN 21:15–19 *So when they had eaten breakfast, Jesus said to Simon Peter, "Simon, son of Jonah, do you love Me more than these?" He said to Him, "Yes, Lord; You know that I love You." He said to him, "Feed My lambs." He said to him again a second time, "Simon, son of Jonah, do you love Me?" He said to Him, "Yes, Lord; You know that I love You." He said to him, "Tend My sheep." He said to him the third time, "Simon, son of Jonah, do you love Me?" Peter was grieved because He said to him the third time, "Do you love Me?" And he said to Him, "Lord, You know all things; You know that I love You." Jesus said to him, "Feed My sheep. Most assuredly, I say to you, when you were younger, you girded yourself and walked where you wished; but when you are old, you will stretch out your hands, and another will gird you and carry you where you do not wish." This He spoke, signifying by what death he would glorify God. And when He had spoken this, He said to him, "Follow Me." (NKJV)*

Jesus had a meal of fish all ready to be eaten when Peter and the disciples arrived from their huge catch. After eating, Jesus concentrated on Peter and gave him a chance to redeem himself. Jesus asked Peter if he loved his Savior more than the disciples sitting there. Peter was able to put aside his great guilt and tell Jesus that he did indeed love him. How healing that must have been to be able to express it to Jesus's face after denying him.

Jesus was giving Peter his marching orders for the future, indicating he would be the shepherd of the flock of new Christians. He was also predicting that Peter would die in a stretched-out position—which is exactly what happened—through crucifixion. Peter may not have been able to comprehend Jesus's meaning at that time.

what others say

Max Lucado

What did he do? He met them at their point of pain. Though death has been destroyed and sin **annulled**, he has not retired. The resurrected Lord has once again wrapped himself in flesh, put on human clothes, and searched out hurting hearts.[6]

What must the disciples have said to Jesus as he sat beside them in his resurrected body? Did they want to know what the future held for them? Did they believe he would now be around forever in his new body? Did Peter feel the most uncomfortable? Did Peter want to say something about the denial but couldn't? Or maybe he did say something and that's why Jesus started to give him new hope.

The Church Has Begun

ACTS 2:14 *But Peter, standing up with the eleven, raised his voice and said to them, "Men of Judea and all who dwell in Jerusalem, let this be known to you, and heed my words." (NKJV)*

After Jesus <u>rose</u> into heaven, the disciples waited to be filled with the Holy Spirit as Jesus had <u>instructed</u> them. After they were filled with the Spirit, Peter truly became a new person filled with more of God's power and less of himself.

what others say

Lloyd John Ogilvie

There is no need I have ever heard articulated by individuals or the Church that could not be met by the Holy Spirit. Our need for wisdom, knowledge, faith, healing, discernment, and freedom are his gifts.[7]

Peter revealed his changed nature in the ways shown in the following chart:

Peter's Leadership Activities

Scripture	Peter's Activities	What His Activities Say About Him
Acts 2:14–36	Peter was the first one to give a sermon and explained Pentecost.	He was quickly established as a primary leader of the new church.
Acts 3:1–26	Peter healed a lame man at the temple gates and then gave a sermon to those watching. He also healed Aeneas (9:32–35) and Dorcas (9:36–43).	He had great power and looked for every opportunity to share.
Acts 4:1–31	Peter and others were imprisoned for preaching but refused to stop.	He was more interested in pleasing God than man.

rose
Acts 1:9

instructed
Acts 1:8

Peter's Leadership Activities (cont'd)

Scripture	Peter's Activities	What His Activities Say About Him
Acts 5:1–11	Peter confronted Ananias and Sapphira about their lie.	He was able to confront with love and strength.
Acts 12:3–19	Peter was asleep in prison and an angel miraculously set him free.	Peter didn't worry much. He could sleep in prison when his life was in danger.
1 Peter	Peter wrote this letter to Christians in Asia Minor encouraging them to see their sufferings as opportunities to represent Jesus.	He himself suffered persecution and persevered.
2 Peter	Peter wrote this letter to the same Christians, most likely just before his death as a martyr. He addressed the problems of false doctrine and teachers.	He was concerned about the condition of the church and made every effort to help other Christians.

what others say

F. B. Meyer

It seemed as though a very special illumination had been given him by the Holy Spirit of Inspiration, that he might understand the Scriptures and perceive the relevance to Jesus of all things written in the Law of Moses, the Prophets, and the Psalms.[8]

Peter's Death

Peter died most likely between AD 64 and AD 66. He died as a martyr through crucifixion. Some commentators believe, based on some first-century writers, that he was forced to watch the crucifixion of his wife before his death. He then requested he be put on the cross upside down because he felt he wasn't worthy of dying the same way Jesus did.

Jesus told Peter he would die for his faith. That makes some of the last words he ever wrote even more significant. He was a bold man who came full circle from mountaintop to deepest valley, yet finished his life strong and dedicated to the Lord. We can learn from his words and live with real purpose in our lives.

key point

Chapter Wrap-Up

- Peter was one of the first disciples of Jesus and impulsively offered to walk on the water toward Jesus. When he grew fearful, he began to sink. He called to Jesus and Jesus rescued him. This incident serves as a picture of how we can overcome life's storms if we stay focused on Jesus. (Matthew 14:22–32)

- When Jesus asked the disciples who they thought he was, Peter quickly answered for them saying Jesus was the Christ, the Son of God. (Matthew 16:13–20)

- Peter was accused of being with Jesus while Jesus was being tried as a traitor. Peter denied ever knowing him. When he realized he had fulfilled Jesus's prediction of his denials, he wailed with grief. (Matthew 26:69–75)

- After Jesus was resurrected and appeared to many, he had a meal with Peter and the disciples. Jesus asked Peter three times whether he loved him. Peter said he did and Jesus gave him the mission of shepherding his followers. (John 21:15–19)

- After the Holy Spirit was given to the disciples on Pentecost, Peter established himself as a primary leader by giving the first sermon, and with powerful results. (Acts 2:14)

Study Questions

1. When Peter was walking on the water toward Jesus, what distracted him and caused him to sink?

2. Who did Jesus say had inspired Peter's answer as he identified Jesus as the Messiah?

3. What did Peter do when he realized he had denied Jesus?

4. After Peter denied knowing Jesus, how did Jesus make Peter feel better and know he was forgiven?

5. Who was the first person to give a sermon after the disciples experienced the infilling of the Holy Spirit?

Chapter 16: Men in Ministry— Lessons in Following Christ

Chapter Highlights:
• Mark Finds
  Redemption
• Barnabas Encourages
• Andrew Influences
• Thomas Sees
• James Leads

Let's Get Started

Whether during Jesus's walk here on earth or after, powerful men spread the news that Jesus offered God's unconditional love. John the Baptist was his forerunner and prepared the way. Then others wrote about him, like Luke, Mark, Matthew, John, and James. Others, such as Philip and Andrew, were part of Jesus's hearty band of disciples. And then there were the ones in the early church, like Stephen. We'll have a better chance of succeeding by understanding those who did a good job before us.

go to

cousins
Luke 1:36

wilderness
Luke 1:80

John the Baptist—Cousin of the Messiah

MATTHEW 3:13–17 *Then Jesus came from Galilee to John at the Jordan to be baptized by him. And John tried to prevent Him, saying, "I need to be baptized by You, and are You coming to me?" But Jesus answered and said to him, "Permit it to be so now, for thus it is fitting for us to fulfill all righteousness." Then he allowed Him. When He had been baptized, Jesus came up immediately from the water; and behold, the heavens were opened to Him, and He saw the Spirit of God descending like a dove and alighting upon Him. And suddenly a voice came from heaven, saying, "This is My beloved Son, in whom I am well pleased." (NKJV)*

John the Baptist and Jesus were cousins born six months apart. They may not have had much contact because they lived far from each other and John began living in the wilderness as a young man.

In a prophetic utterance his father foretold John's ministry when he was born. He predicted, "And you, child, will be called the prophet of the Highest; for you will go before the face of the Lord to prepare His ways, to give knowledge of salvation to His people by the remission of their sins, through the tender mercy of our God, with which the Dayspring from on high has visited us; to give light to those who sit in darkness and the shadow of death, to guide our feet into the way of peace" (Luke 1:76–79 NKJV).

beheaded
Matthew 14:10

doubts
Matthew 11:1–6

baptism
1 Peter 3:21

John the Baptist was <u>beheaded</u> because of his strong witness to the evil King Herod's court.

Isaiah had prophesied about John the Baptist's ministry many years previously when he wrote, "The voice of one crying in the

what others say

John A. Martin

When a king traveled the desert, workmen preceded him to clear debris and smooth out the roads to make his trip easier. In Luke the leveling of the land was a figurative expression denoting that the way of the Messiah would be made smooth because through John a large number of people were ready to receive Jesus' message.[1]

wilderness: 'Prepare the way of the LORD; make straight in the desert a highway for our God. Every valley shall be exalted and every mountain and hill brought low; the crooked places shall be made straight and the rough places smooth; the glory of the LORD shall be revealed, and all flesh shall see it together; for the mouth of the LORD has spoken'" (Isaiah 40:3–5 NKJV). Yet, even after John the Baptist baptized Jesus and heard of his continuing ministry, John had <u>doubts</u> about Jesus's authority. He sent a message from prison and asked Jesus if he was indeed the one who was predicted to come. Jesus sent a message back saying that his works proved he was the Messiah.

John the Baptist was named that because his ministry was to call people to repentance and then baptize them. The <u>baptism</u> itself did not save them from their sins, but their repentance did.

key point

Baptism is a formal and public declaration of the cleansing work that God does in your heart when you ask Jesus to come into your life and forgive you. Baptism represents a burial into water that symbolizes your death to sin. And just as you rise up out of the water, some day, you will be resurrected from the grave to reside in heaven.

Luke—Chronicler of Jesus and the Early Church

go to

doctor
Colossians 4:14

birth
Luke 1:26–2:20

youth
Luke 2:41–52

Gentiles
Acts 15:7

LUKE 1:1–4 *Inasmuch as many have taken in hand to set in order a narrative of those things which have been fulfilled among us, just as those who from the beginning were eyewitnesses and ministers of the word delivered them to us, it seemed good to me also, having had perfect understanding of all things from the very first, to write to you an orderly account, most excellent Theophilus, that you may know the certainty of those things in which you were instructed. (NKJV)*

If your doctor told you he'd written a book, would you imagine that it would be detailed and specific? Most of us imagine a <u>doctor</u> as one who is interested in details and is careful in evaluations. Luke must have been that kind of doctor. He was very meticulous as he interviewed people and researched the material for his two-volume book.

There's a good possibility that Luke interviewed Mary, the mother of Jesus, in order to gain the information that only he included in his book. Plus, Luke's goal in writing his Gospel account was to present Jesus as the Son of Man. He showed Jesus's human side through the details of his <u>birth</u> and <u>youth</u>. Luke is the only Gospel writer who mentioned any part of Jesus's growing up years.

Luke wanted to communicate in both volumes of his book (vol. 1: Luke; vol. 2: Acts) that Jesus wanted both Jews and Gentiles to know of his salvation. Thus, Acts also chronicles the decision of the early church fathers to support giving Jesus's message to the <u>Gentiles</u>.

what others say

Robert H. Schuller

Acts presents the origin of our faith with extreme accuracy. Archaeologists confirm that Luke was among the most reliable historians of antiquity. A master of the Greek language, Luke gives the most detailed account of the early church of all the Gospels and Epistles.[2]

New Testament
Colossians 4:14;
2 Timothy 4:11;
Philemon 24

fled
Mark 14:51–52

We can tell when Luke joined Paul's traveling missionary group in the book of Acts. It was while Paul was in Troas. Luke didn't name himself but he wrote, "Now after [Paul] had seen the vision, immediately we sought to go to Macedonia, concluding that the Lord had called us to preach the gospel to them" (Acts 16:10 NKJV). Previously in the account, there was no mention of "us" or "we." It was "he" or "they." Luke must have written the first part of the book based on his interviews of others. Then he included his own first-hand account of Paul's missionary activities and did so throughout the end of the book.

The writings of Luke make up a little over a fourth of the Greek <u>New Testament</u>. Although he's not mentioned specifically as the author of Luke and Acts, he is mentioned in other parts of the New Testament.

Humility is a worthy goal that Luke seemed to have made a part of his life. He doesn't try to take credit for what he did. He was content to give the great news about Jesus's gift of salvation. If we can have the same perspective, we'll be able to respond with more humility in our actions and thinking. God wants us to be unconcerned with who gets credit for his work within us.

Mark—Original Comeback Kid

> ACTS 15:37–41 *Now Barnabas was determined to take with them John called Mark. But Paul insisted that they should not take with them the one who had departed from them in Pamphylia, and had not gone with them to the work. Then the contention became so sharp that they parted from one another. And so Barnabas took Mark and sailed to Cyprus; but Paul chose Silas and departed, being commended by the brethren to the grace of God. And he went through Syria and Cilicia, strengthening the churches.* (NKJV)

Mark and his mother used their home as a meeting place for the Christians. He was exposed to Christ's claim on his life and was a believer. He later wrote the book of Mark and many scholars believe Mark was writing about himself when he mentioned a young man who <u>fled</u> during Jesus's arrest.

Mark's weakness of leaving when the going got tough would pop
up again when he left Paul and Barnabas on their first missionary
journey. Paul rejected any suggestion that Mark would accompany
him on the next trip. As a result, Barnabas took Mark under his wing
and went to Cyprus. Barnabas made an investment in Mark that paid
off in dividends. Mark later became the author of one of the Gospels
of the Bible.

Later, Paul became a close friend of the young disciple when Mark
redeemed himself through faithful service. Mark also became a missionary partner of Paul, Peter, and Barnabas. Paul changed his mind
about Mark and in the end considered him an important asset. He
wrote, "Only Luke is with me. Get Mark and bring him with you,
for he is useful to me for ministry" (2 Timothy 4:11 NKJV).

We don't know why Mark left, but missionaries had it really hard
in those days. We need to consider when we sign up for something
in the Lord's work whether we will carry through to the end no matter what. Count the cost before agreeing to serve the Lord so that
you'll persist until the end.

If you have gotten off on the wrong foot with your manager at
work, or a leader at church, or a coworker, you can trust God to
change their mind about you if you will serve faithfully and cheerfully over the long haul. If God can change the strong-willed Paul's
mind about Mark, then he can change anyone's mind.

Barnabas—The Encourager

ACTS 4:36–37; 9:26–27 *And Joses, who was also named
Barnabas by the apostles (which is translated Son of
Encouragement), a Levite of the country of Cyprus, having
land, sold it, and brought the money and laid it at the apostles'
feet. . . . And when [Paul] had come to Jerusalem, he tried to*

alongside
Acts 11:24–26

pariah
a person rejected by
others, an outcast

join the disciples; but they were all afraid of him, and did not believe that he was a disciple. But Barnabas took him and brought him to the apostles. And he declared to them how he had seen the Lord on the road, and that He had spoken to him, and how he had preached boldly at Damascus in the name of Jesus. (NKJV)

Trouble Shooter

Barnabas was born a Levite. He was a generous and wealthy man who sold land and gave the proceeds to the disciples to be shared with others. Barnabas's commitment to Christ was apparent, for he sacrificed a comfortable life to walk the countryside for Jesus.

News of this reached the ears of the church at Jerusalem, and they sent Barnabas to Antioch. "When [Barnabas] came and had seen the grace of God, he was glad, and encouraged them all that with purpose of heart they should continue with the Lord. For he was a good man, full of the Holy Spirit and of faith. And a great many people were added to the Lord" (Acts 11:23–24 NKJV).

what others say

Lloyd John Ogilvie

While the church in Jerusalem resisted, Barnabas was a reconciler. His response to Jesus always spelled responsibility for someone who was misunderstood or resisted. Barnabas threw opinion and caution aside and interceded for Paul with the Jerusalem church. The Greek actually implies that he took him by the hand and led him in among the Apostles to assert his belief in the authenticity of Paul's conversion, convictions, and new character.[4]

Will Rogers once said he never met a man he didn't like. Good ol' Barnabas was a lot like that because he could see the potential in others. He never let a tough exterior persona or a shy, insecure personality keep him at arm's length. He knew each person's worth and invested his time and energy in their lives. That's how Barnabas saw Saul, even before he was known as Paul. "Then Barnabas departed for Tarsus to seek Saul. And when he had found him, he brought him to Antioch" (Acts 11:25–26 NKJV). Saul was feared and a **pariah** in the Christian community. It was Barnabas who came alongside and eased him into Christian history.

Barnabas possessed exceptional people skills. It was no surprise he was sent to provide leadership for the new church in Antioch. It was also no surprise he picked up Paul along the way. Barnabas was content to support others with his inspiring influence. He would never shy away from the spotlight, but his real skill was putting others on stage.

The responsibility to develop those we lead lands near the top of every priority list. However, it is one of the most neglected leadership skills. It takes work. The excuses are endless: it takes too much time to delegate, I'll do it myself, I can do it better. . . . Each may be true, but those who look to our leadership should expect us to support them and provide opportunities for growth. Not all of us can be an inspirational Barnabas, but if we commit in our hearts to care for those we lead, we will find the energy and time to develop others.

Matthew—Despised Tax-Collector Turned Disciple

MATTHEW 9:9–10 *As Jesus passed on from there, He saw a man named Matthew sitting at the tax office. And He said to him, "Follow Me." So he arose and followed Him. Now it happened, as Jesus sat at the table in the house, that behold, many tax collectors and sinners came and sat down with Him and His disciples. (NKJV)*

Since tax collectors normally skimmed money from the collections they made, they were despised throughout the land. Jesus challenged Matthew to leave behind a cushy job, high pay, and special benefits. If anyone had to really count the cost, it was Matthew. Yet, he left it all to live an **itinerant** disciple's life following Jesus around.

Matthew, also called Levi, brought two things into his service as an apostle. First, his immediate and active faith. He abandoned wealth for a relationship with Jesus. He felt so strongly about Jesus that he invited his fellow tax collectors and other sinners to a dinner date with Jesus. Second, his pen and keen sense for collecting information. Matthew was probably the type of guy who had a bunch of pens filling a pocket protector on his shirt. No detail was too small to escape his notice when he wrote the first book of the New Testament, carefully linking the Old Testament prophecies to Jesus's fulfillment of them.

itinerant
nomadic

feast
Luke 5:29

R. C. Sproul

Jesus, as was the case with other rabbis in the ancient world, was what we call a peripatetic teacher. That is a fancy way of saying he was a teacher who walked around as he taught. As Jesus walked around the land of Palestine his disciples would literally walk behind him, committing to memory the words he would utter to them on their travels.[5]

Matthew referred to himself as a "tax collector." This referred to his former distasteful—in fact, hated—occupation and his humility about being chosen as a disciple of Jesus. Another aspect of his low-key persona was revealed when he referred to the dinner he hosted for Jesus. In Luke's account, Luke referred to it as a "great <u>feast</u>." Apparently, Matthew didn't want to brag about the big shindig he had put on for Jesus.

Matthew's Gospel account has more references to coins than anywhere else in the other three Gospels. Of course, this goes along with his former occupation as a tax collector. He had been very interested in money!

apply it

Finances can be a source of great strain in a Christian's life. Although Jesus doesn't call everyone to sacrifice everything, like he did Matthew, he does want us to have the correct perspective about any money that we do have. "Command those who are rich in this present age not to be haughty, nor to trust in uncertain riches but in the living God, who gives us richly all things to enjoy" (1 Timothy 6:17 NKJV). How willing are you to surrender control of your money to God? That serves as an indicator of your commitment to Christ.

Andrew—Passed Along the Good News

> JOHN 1:40–42 *One of the two who heard John speak, and followed Him, was Andrew, Simon Peter's brother. He first found his own brother Simon, and said to him, "We have found the Messiah" (which is translated, the Christ). And he brought him to Jesus. Now when Jesus looked at him, He said, "You are Simon the son of Jonah. You shall be called Cephas" (which is translated, A Stone).* (NKJV)

Only the book of John gives us three brief glimpses of Andrew. Each time he was found bringing others to Jesus. First, he brought his brother, Peter. That was like bringing Mark McGwire to play baseball in your friends' sandlot game. Within seconds the star of the game changed and all the attention focused away from Andrew. But Andrew didn't care. He loved his brother and he loved Jesus. Next, Andrew knew Jesus needed to feed a large crowd, so he found a small <u>boy</u> with some fishes and bread. He saw a need and his faith was acted upon by Jesus. Finally, some men wanted to <u>see</u> Jesus, and he took them to Jesus.

go to

boy
John 6:8–9

see
John 12:20–22

what others say

John MacArthur Jr.

Andrew is the picture of all those who labor quietly in humble places; not with eye service as men pleasers, but as servants of Christ doing the will of God from the heart. Andrew is not a pillar like Peter, James, and John—he is a humbler stone.[6]

His brother, Peter, was filled with a passion that spilled onto everyone. Andrew was filled with a passion that seeped into others' hearts. His passion for Christ and others was never played with power but with grace and gentleness.

Every leader worth his salt will include a man like Andrew on his team; a salt-of-the-earth guy that just gets the job done with dignity and class. Fanfare doesn't motivate him, appreciation does. Ambition is not his power source, commitment is. When you find men like this, hire them. If you hire them, keep them.

Thomas—Doubter but No Coward

JOHN 11:16; 20:24–29 *Then Thomas, who is called the Twin, said to his fellow disciples, "Let us also go, that we may die with Him." . . . Now Thomas, called the Twin, one of the twelve, was not with them when Jesus came. The other disciples therefore said to him, "We have seen the Lord." So he said to them, "Unless I see in His hands the print of the nails, and put my finger into the print of the nails, and put my hand into His side, I will not believe." And after eight days His disciples were again inside, and Thomas with them. Jesus came, the doors being shut, and stood in the midst, and said, "Peace to you!" Then He said to Thomas, "Reach your finger here, and look at My hands; and reach your hand here, and put it into My side. Do not be unbelieving, but believing." And Thomas answered and said to Him, "My Lord and my God!" Jesus said to him, "Thomas, because you have seen Me, you have believed. Blessed are those who have not seen and yet have believed." (NKJV)*

Jesus had just announced he was going back to Bethany, which is only two miles west of Jerusalem. All the disciples tried to talk him out of the trip because they believed he—and they—would be killed. It was Thomas who first affirmed his love and commitment for Christ when he in essence said, "If we go with him, we'll die, but let's go anyway." So, when Jesus insisted on leaving, Thomas tried to rally his peers, in his own pessimistic way. It took courage and initiative to make that statement. Thomas may have been a doubter, but he was no coward.

Like the other disciples, Thomas fled after Jesus was arrested. He was depressed and confused. This confusion was rooted in his pessimism. Earlier, Jesus told the disciples he would leave and prepare a place for them. Thomas had asked, "Lord, we do not know where You are going, and how can we know the way?" (John 14:5 NKJV). His mind was spinning with confusion. He had found the Messiah and now he discovered Jesus would leave them behind.

what others say

Warren W. Wiersbe

We call him "Doubting Thomas," but Jesus didn't rebuke him for unbelief: "Be not faithless, but believing." Doubt is often an intellectual problem: we want to believe, but the faith is overwhelmed by problems and questions. Unbelief is a moral problem; we simply will not believe.[7]

Thomas appears to be a pessimist. His glass was always half empty. Faced with Jesus's death, the glass was no longer half empty, but shattered on the ground. Ten men told Thomas that Jesus was alive. But Thomas would not listen to unsubstantiated claims, even from trustworthy men. He had to see for himself. The good news is that he got the proof he sought, but Jesus proclaimed a special blessing to those who believe more readily than Thomas.

John—The One Jesus Loved

JOHN 13:21–23 *When Jesus had said these things, He was troubled in spirit, and testified and said, "Most assuredly, I say to you, one of you will betray Me." Then the disciples looked at one another, perplexed about whom He spoke. Now there was leaning on Jesus' bosom one of His disciples, whom Jesus loved.* (NKJV)

go to

Gaius
Acts 19:29

Originally, John (see Illustration #28) wanted to call down fire from heaven upon some Samaritan villagers who didn't welcome Jesus. After that incident, Jesus named John and his brother, James, the "sons of thunder." But after a long walk with Jesus, John changed, and he became known as the author of love. The theme of 1 John, which he penned, is love.

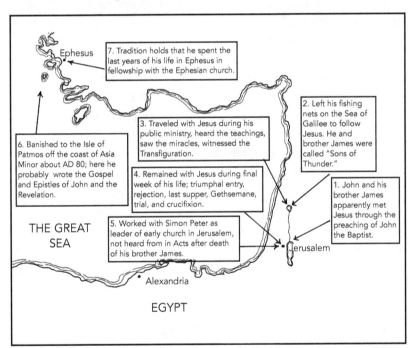

Ephesus

7. Tradition holds that he spent the last years of his life in Ephesus in fellowship with the Ephesian church.

2. Left his fishing nets on the Sea of Galilee to follow Jesus. He and brother James were called "Sons of Thunder."

3. Traveled with Jesus during his public ministry, heard the teachings, saw the miracles, witnessed the Transfiguration.

6. Banished to the Isle of Patmos off the coast of Asia Minor about AD 80; here he probably wrote the Gospel and Epistles of John and the Revelation.

4. Remained with Jesus during final week of his life; triumphal entry, rejection, last supper, Gethsemane, trial, and crucifixion.

1. John and his brother James apparently met Jesus through the preaching of John the Baptist.

THE GREAT SEA

5. Worked with Simon Peter as leader of early church in Jerusalem, not heard from in Acts after death of his brother James.

Jerusalem

• Alexandria

EGYPT

Illustration #28
The Life of John—This map shows where major events occurred in John's life. The events are numbered chronologically.

The Books of the Bible Written by John

Books John Wrote	Purpose
Gospel of John	Represent Christ's deity so that others will believe.
1 John	Encourage believers to enjoy fellowship with God because of his great love for them.
2 John	Love others with discernment.
3 John	Letter to Gaius encouraging faithful service and generosity.
Revelation	A recounting of the revelatory messages John received from the resurrected Christ about the end of the world.

place of honor
Mark 10:35–40

Patmos
Revelation 1:9

transformation
Romans 12:2

John had been transformed. The jealous, fiery follower of Christ wrote the Gospel of John and never used his own name. The fact that Jesus could love a man who had wanted to kill the Samaritans and had connived for a <u>place of honor</u> in heaven filled John's heart with gratitude. Referring to himself as the disciple "whom Jesus loved" was recognition of his sinful past and God's forgiveness.

John ended his days in exile on the island of <u>Patmos</u>. While there, he received the revelation of the last days of the world.

John, and his brother James, of course, had assertively asked Jesus for the privilege of sitting at Jesus's right hand in heaven. They prefaced it this way: "Teacher," they said, "we want You to do for us whatever we ask" (Mark 10:35 NKJV). Better add presumption and pride to John's résumé. His desire to be closer to Jesus demonstrated some spiritual growth, but can you imagine the audacity of making a request like this behind the backs of the other disciples? This was an important moment for John. Jesus replied, "Whoever desires to become great among you shall be your servant. And whoever of you desires to be first shall be slave of all. For even the Son of Man did not come to be served, but to serve, and to give His life a ransom for many" (Mark 10:43–45 NKJV). John seemed to gain control of his zeal and strong convictions as he put Jesus's words into action. Love and service turned his heart around.

John had some issues of anger and narrow-mindedness to deal with before he matured. Look how he responded when he found other believers raining on his parade: "Teacher," said John, "we saw someone who does not follow us casting out demons in Your name, and we forbade him because he does not follow us" (Mark 9:38 NKJV). He was very assertive and rigid in his thinking. But God changed even that.

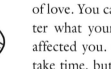

Anyone can change. John changed from a man of anger to a man of love. You can too. No matter what people say about you. No matter what your reputation is. No matter how your childhood has affected you. God can do an inside <u>transformation</u> of you. It may take time, but he has the power and desire to do it. All you have to do is obey.

James—Brother of the Messiah

go to

brother
Matthew 13:55

believe
John 7:5

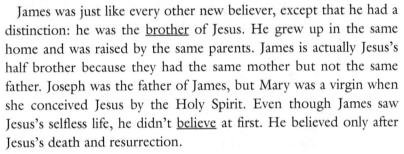

the big picture

Acts 15:13-21

In the early church family, a disagreement arose among the leadership about whether the good news about Jesus should be presented to Gentiles and if so, whether they should be circumcised. Several people shared their opinions and experiences and then James, the brother of Jesus, spoke up and offered a solution. The Gentiles should be welcomed into the church. They didn't need to become circumcised, but they should abstain from food polluted by idols, from sexual immorality, from the meat of strangled animals and from blood. Everyone agreed.

James was just like every other new believer, except that he had a distinction: he was the <u>brother</u> of Jesus. He grew up in the same home and was raised by the same parents. James is actually Jesus's half brother because they had the same mother but not the same father. Joseph was the father of James, but Mary was a virgin when she conceived Jesus by the Holy Spirit. Even though James saw Jesus's selfless life, he didn't <u>believe</u> at first. He believed only after Jesus's death and resurrection.

In the early church, James was president of the first council. He was martyred by being thrown off the pinnacle of the temple. When that didn't kill him, he was stoned to death.

James's name was often listed first when church leaders were named. The apostle Paul wrote, "When James, Cephas, and John, who seemed to be pillars, perceived the grace that had been given to me, they gave me and Barnabas the right hand of fellowship, that we should go to the Gentiles and they to the circumcised" (Galatians 2:9 NKJV). In the writings of the Bible, the most prominent person was often listed first. It showed respect for his position.

James wrote the letter to Christians that became the book of James. James wanted his readers to focus on staying joyful in the midst of great difficulties or persecution. He also stressed the definition of real faith versus faith based on works. Since he was known as "the Man with Camel's Knees" because of the extensive time he spent on his knees praying, we aren't surprised that his letter also emphasizes prayer.

go to

combining
Acts 4:35

Prayer is one of the main ways to build our spiritual life. In fact, without prayer it is impossible to grow as a Christian. James wrote, "Confess your trespasses to one another, and pray for one another, that you may be healed. The effective, fervent prayer of a righteous man avails much" (James 5:16 NKJV). We can pray for others, confess our own sins in prayer, refuse to worry through prayer, and ask for God's direction in prayer.

Stephen—First Martyr

ACTS 7:54–60 *When they heard these things they were cut to the heart, and they gnashed at him with their teeth. But he, being full of the Holy Spirit, gazed into heaven and saw the glory of God, and Jesus standing at the right hand of God, and said, "Look! I see the heavens opened and the Son of Man standing at the right hand of God!" Then they cried out with a loud voice, stopped their ears, and ran at him with one accord; and they cast him out of the city and stoned him. And the witnesses laid down their clothes at the feet of a young man named Saul. And they stoned Stephen as he was calling on God and saying, "Lord Jesus, receive my spirit." Then he knelt down and cried out with a loud voice, "Lord, do not charge them with this sin." And when he had said this, he fell asleep. (NKJV)*

Stephen was first mentioned in the New Testament as "full of faith and the Holy Spirit" (Acts 6:5 NKJV). He was chosen, along with six other men, to take care of a particular problem in the early church. Some Grecian believers complained that their widows weren't getting enough in the distribution of the food. At this point, all the believers were <u>combining</u> their assets and providing for everyone equally, but some thought their friends weren't getting equal treatment. To solve the problem, the seven men were chosen.

Although we don't know anything about Stephen's background, we know he "did great wonders and signs among the people" (Acts 6:8 NKJV). He was doing so many great things that he stood out from many other Christians, and some who didn't believe in Jesus as the Messiah argued with him. But they couldn't refute what he said. They became so frustrated in their feeble attempts to stop his preaching that they accused him of speaking blasphemy against

Moses and God. As a result, he was <u>called</u> before the Sanhedrin and defended himself by reviewing the history of the Jews.

But when he said they were stiff-necked people, the judges didn't like it. This created a riot, and he was stoned to death. In that crowd of angry people was a man named Saul, who later would become the apostle Paul. Stephen was the first martyr for the Christian church.

called
Acts 6:11–15

Lloyd John Ogilvie

Stephen had been healed by Christ's unlimited, unmerited, unearnable love. He was a released man. Defensiveness, self-justification, and competitiveness were gone. Graciousness became the discernible trait of his personality. He had the disposition of Christ.[8]

Stephen was the first but not the last martyr of the Christian church. Many of the original apostles were murdered because of their faith: Peter, Paul, and James. In the following two thousand years, many Christians were killed for their faith and, unfortunately, it still happens today.

The Sanhedrin

Who	Comprised of 71 Jewish spiritual leaders
What	Religious and civil institution that acted like the highest court in the land that judged Stephen, Jesus, and paid off Judas for turning on Jesus
Where	In the area by the north wall of the temple mount
When	63 BC—AD 70
Why	Exercised powers lower courts didn't have; could judge the king

Few of us will have to face the possibility of losing our lives in order to tell others about Christ, and yet somehow we still find it hard to tell others about Jesus and his love. When we aren't bold to share, we can remember that other people's approval or view of us is insignificant in comparison to the joy of knowing that God approves of us.

Philip—Powerful Witness

JOHN 6:5–7 *Then Jesus lifted up His eyes, and seeing a great multitude coming toward Him, He said to Philip, "Where shall we buy bread, that these may eat?" But this He said to test him, for He Himself knew what He would do. Philip answered Him, "Two hundred denarii worth of bread is not sufficient for them, that every one of them may have a little."* (NKJV)

Philip was present when Jesus turned water into wine. He had seen Jesus's many miracles, and when Jesus asked Philip to provide bread for the multitude, you would expect his answer to be, "Master, you speak it into existence, and I'll pass it around!" Not Philip. He heard the specific question, looked at the crowd, and crunched some numbers in his head. His precise answer allows us to see the real Philip. The details of the challenge blinded Philip to a miraculous solution, and Jesus knew it.

Some people wanted to see Jesus, but Philip had to first ask Andrew about it. What would have happened if those same people had approached Peter, the bold one? Just how quickly would Peter have grabbed those men and ushered them to the Savior? No delay, no questions, only action. In contrast, Philip had to check to see if it was okay. His cautious behavior limited his view of the gospel.

what others say

John MacArthur Jr.

Philip was a materialist—a man of practical, common-sense measurements. He was methodical and mechanical, with very little understanding of the supernatural. He was a facts-and-figures guy, always going by what appeared on the human level.[9]

apply it

We all have worked with someone like Philip or have a friend like him. Ask one question from your coworker or friend and get a detailed answer, including graphs and charts. Philip was the consummate analytical personality. Details were important, and thinking outside traditional boundaries was scary to him. He could easily be called a perfectionist.

The rallying cry of the analytical person is, "We have never done it this way!" If you identify with Philip, realize that your reluctance to move quickly can often lead to analysis paralysis. This is a subtle form of perfectionism. Details, facts, and understanding are important, but living in powerful faith moves us away from our personal tendencies and into action that brings honor to God. Let your actions expand to your vision. It doesn't always have to be perfect. Instead seek <u>excellence</u>, which is doing the best you can in God's <u>power</u>.

excellence
1 Thessalonians 4:1

power
Philippians 4:13

Timothy—Youthful and Timid Pastor

ACTS 16:1–5 *Then he came to Derbe and Lystra. And behold, a certain disciple was there, named Timothy, the son of a certain Jewish woman who believed, but his father was Greek. He was well spoken of by the brethren who were at Lystra and Iconium. Paul wanted to have him go on with him. And he took him and circumcised him because of the Jews who were in that region, for they all knew that his father was Greek. And as they went through the cities, they delivered to them the decrees to keep, which were determined by the apostles and elders at Jerusalem. So the churches were strengthened in the faith, and increased in number daily. (NKJV)*

Timothy was raised in an area which is now the country of Turkey. His mother was Jewish, and he started studying the Scriptures as a youth. Paul described him this way: "From childhood you have known the Holy Scriptures, which are able to make you wise for salvation through faith which is in Christ Jesus" (2 Timothy 3:15 NKJV).

Many people believe that Timothy and his mother became believers on Paul's first missionary journey. As he grew stronger in his faith, he became involved with a group of believers. His faith in Christ was apparent, and other believers had commended this young man to Paul. Timothy joined Paul on his second missionary journey, but to avoid any possible hindrance during evangelism with the Jews, Timothy voluntarily submitted to circumcision. Talk about an act of commitment!

Timothy had many wonderful qualities, and he had some real struggles. Yet he was appointed by Paul to be a pastor in a church that had some challenges. Paul had confidence in him and wrote two letters to him to encourage him. Those letters became our biblical books of 1 Timothy and 2 Timothy. The following chart shows Paul's perspective of his spiritual son.

Timothy's Qualities and Struggles

Quality	Struggle	Scripture
Loved	"For this reason I have sent Timothy to you, who is my beloved and faithful son in the Lord, who will remind you of my ways in Christ, as I teach everywhere in every church" (NKJV).	1 Corinthians 4:17
Fearful	"And if Timothy comes, see that he may be with you without fear; for he does the work of the Lord, as I also do" (NKJV).	1 Corinthians 16:10
Dependable	"But you know his proven character, that as a son with his father he served with me in the gospel" (NKJV).	Philippians 2:22
Insecure	"Let no one despise your youth, but be an example to the believers in word, in conduct, in love, in spirit, in faith, in purity" (NKJV).	1 Timothy 4:12
Discouraged	"This charge I commit to you, son Timothy, according to the prophecies previously made concerning you, that by them you may wage the good warfare, having faith and a good conscience, which some having rejected, concerning the faith have suffered shipwreck" (NKJV).	1 Timothy 1:18–19
Encouraging	"[We] sent Timothy, our brother and minister of God, and our fellow laborer in the gospel of Christ, to establish you and encourage you concerning your faith" (NKJV).	1 Thessalonians 3:2
Selfless	"But I trust in the Lord Jesus to send Timothy to you shortly, that I also may be encouraged when I know your state. For I have no one like-minded, who will sincerely care for your state" (NKJV).	Philippians 2:19–20

Timothy faced the challenge of dealing with Christians in his church who believed that being godly guaranteed they would have earthly gain. That's why Paul wrote to him, "Now godliness with contentment is great gain" (1 Timothy 6:6 NKJV). He stressed contentment because earthly gain wasn't supposed to be the motive for acting in a godly fashion. And Timothy knew that. He had seen that Paul's life as a missionary wasn't an easy life, nor was it one that gained him earthly wealth. Timothy needed some encouragement because he frequently felt intimidated by people.

what others say

Bruce H. Wilkinson and Larry Libby

Timothy himself seemed to be locked in a deep struggle with this question of inner contentment. A number of Bible expositors have drawn this assumption from the tone and content of Paul's two letters to his young associate.[10]

Paul wrote to Timothy, "But you, O man of God, flee these things and pursue righteousness, godliness, faith, love, patience, gentleness" (1 Timothy 6:11 NKJV). Paul was encouraging Timothy to lead and build his church. When we face the challenges of building our families or marriages, this challenge holds true for us. As men we can have two reactions to this challenge. First, we could feel convicted that the title "man of God" doesn't seem to fit and that we rarely pursue godly things. Or second, our hearts could soar and receive the affirmation that we are indeed men of God.

Either reaction can awaken (if we let it) an adventure deep in our souls that we are "more than conquerors through Him who loved us" (Romans 8:37 NKJV). God loves us and wants the best for us. That means strong marriages and healthy families. Knowing that he gives us this kind of love and that he also provides the power we need gives us the motivation to run from temptation and pursue godly living. It's a choice; it's a step of action.

Titus—Paul's Trusted Servant

TITUS 1:5 *For this reason I left you in Crete, that you should set in order the things that are lacking, and appoint elders in every city as I commanded you—(NKJV)*

Just imagine. You have just started a company, movement, or important cause. You have persuasively generated a core of leaders and followers. All are enthusiastic about the mission, and you are encouraged by what has happened. Now you leave and must find just one man to take over the operation. That is the exact situation Paul faced. Who would you choose? What qualities would you look for?

Paul led Titus to faith in Christ and mentored him by taking him on mission trips. In Paul's letters to the Corinthians, Paul described Titus with adjectives like <u>caring</u>, <u>diligent</u>, <u>comforting</u>, and <u>joyful</u>.

Approximately AD 63–64, Paul and Titus left Timothy behind in Ephesus and traveled to Crete. After developing and building a new church there, Paul left Titus behind to help provide leadership for the Cretan churches. Paul's letter to Titus instructed him how to lead and teach the Cretan churches. He challenged Titus to invest in others with his leadership and wisdom, regardless of how difficult some people can be.

caring
2 Corinthians 8:16

diligent
2 Corinthians 8:17

comforting
2 Corinthians 7:6

joyful
2 Corinthians 7:13

As a young and fairly inexperienced pastor, Titus had a challenge in trying to bring order to the church at Crete. He had to appoint elders and teach doctrine that would help the Cretans to see their unrighteous and immoral behavior as wrong. Just like the pastors in many of the other churches, Titus also had to deal with false teachers who tried to make people think they needed to be circumcised in order to be saved. Titus must have been very brave to take on this challenging assignment.

what others say

Rick Warren

Paul told Titus, "God's people should be bighearted and courteous" (Titus 3:2, The Message). In every church and in every small group, there is always at least one "difficult" person, usually more than one. These people may have special emotional needs, deep insecurities, irritating mannerisms, or poor social skills. You might call them *EGR* people—"Extra Grace Required."[11]

Titus's Distinguishing Qualities

Quality	Passage	Scripture
Titus was a messenger of money and was trusted	"For I bear witness that according to their ability, yes, and beyond their ability, they were freely willing, imploring us with much urgency that we would receive the gift and the fellowship of the ministering to the saints. And not only as we had hoped, but they first gave themselves to the Lord, and then to us by the will of God. So we urged Titus, that as he had begun, so he would also complete this grace in you as well" (NKJV).	2 Corinthians 8:3–6
Enthusiastic in his service	"But thanks be to God who puts the same earnest care for you into the heart of Titus. For he not only accepted the exhortation, but being more diligent, he went to you of his own accord. And we have sent with him the brother whose praise is in the gospel throughout all the churches" (NKJV).	2 Corinthians 8:16–18
Paul's fellow worker	"If anyone inquires about Titus, he is my partner and fellow worker concerning you. Or if our brethren are inquired about, they are messengers of the churches, the glory of Christ" (NKJV).	2 Corinthians 8:23
A Greek	"Yet not even Titus who was with me, being a Greek, was compelled to be circumcised" (NKJV).	Galatians 2:3

Whether or not you have a position of leadership in a church or ministry, you are manager over people in business, or you are leading your family, Titus's example of trusting God to empower him for a challenging task should strengthen you. If God has called you to do something, he will <u>equip</u> you. He wants you to do everything, whether in ministry, business, or home, as if you were doing it <u>specifically</u> for him. Because you are doing it for his glory.

go to

equip
2 Timothy 3:17

specifically
Colossians 3:17

Onesiphorus—Unashamed Follower

2 TIMOTHY 1:16–18 *The Lord grant mercy to the household of Onesiphorus, for he often refreshed me, and was not ashamed of my chain; but when he arrived in Rome, he sought me out very zealously and found me. The Lord grant to him that he may find mercy from the Lord in that Day—and you know very well how many ways he ministered to me at Ephesus. (NKJV)*

Paul was writing to Timothy about Onesiphorus. He pointed out how Onesiphorus would visit and encourage him in jail while other friends would avoid his prison scene. His tenacity to hunt down a friend in need set Onesiphorus apart from others who didn't go out of their way to help Paul.

what others say

Alexander Whyte

From one barrack-prison therefore to another Onesiphorus went about seeking for Paul day after day, week after week, often insulted, often threatened, often ill-used, often arrested and detained. . . . Till, at last, his arms were round Paul's neck, and the two old men were kissing one another and weeping to the amazement of all. . . . Noble-hearted Onesiphorus! We bow down before thee.[12]

Right after Paul referred to Onesiphorus in his letter to Timothy, Paul wrote, "You therefore, my son, be strong in the grace that is in Christ Jesus" (2 Timothy 2:1 NKJV). He was trying to encourage Timothy to have the same strength and the same compassion as Onesiphorus.

apply it

If someone were to write to a friend of yours commending your character, would it say you could be depended upon to seek out a need and then fill it? Would it say the strength of your character was always helpful?

strengthen your family

Nicodemus—Radical Change of Heart

JOHN 3:1–10 *There was a man of the Pharisees named Nicodemus, a ruler of the Jews. This man came to Jesus by night and said to Him, "Rabbi, we know that You are a teacher come from God; for no one can do these signs that You do unless God is with him." Jesus answered and said to him, "Most assuredly, I say to you, unless one is born again, he cannot see the kingdom of God." Nicodemus said to Him, "How can a man be born when he is old? Can he enter a second time into his mother's womb and be born?" Jesus answered, "Most assuredly, I say to you, unless one is born of water and the Spirit, he cannot enter the kingdom of God. That which is born of the flesh is flesh, and that which is born of the Spirit is spirit. Do not marvel that I said to you, 'You must be born again.' The wind blows where it wishes, and you hear the sound of it, but cannot tell where it comes from and where it goes. So is everyone who is born of the Spirit." Nicodemus answered and said to Him, "How can these things be?" Jesus answered and said to him, "Are you the teacher of Israel, and do not know these things?" (NKJV)*

As a Pharisee, Nicodemus was trained as a scholar and was a member of the Sanhedrin, a council of Jews ruling over Jews. Jesus had been critical of the Pharisees who were a part of the Sanhedrin, and he then challenged them face-to-face. But one of them, Nicodemus, sensed something happening in his heart as he watched and heard Jesus. He knew there was something missing from his life, and Jesus somehow had made a connection.

Obviously fear must have rushed through his heart, because aligning himself to Jesus could put everything he valued in jeopardy. But like a moth to a flame, although he was afraid he might get burned, he made an evening rendezvous with Jesus. Nicodemus had power, position, and fame, but he recognized the darkness within his soul. He must seek out the light of the world. He wasn't brave enough to talk with Jesus during the day, so he waited until the night.

When they met, Jesus challenged Nicodemus to consider believing a new concept: that he could be born again. In fact, Jesus speaks the most famous verse in the Bible to explain salvation to Nicodemus: "For God so loved the world that He gave His only begotten Son, that whoever believes in Him should not perish but have everlasting life" (John 3:16 NKJV).

This timid man apparently believed Jesus, because sometime later, he raised a procedural point in Jesus's favor before the Sanhedrin. And they noticed. "Nicodemus (he who came to Jesus by night, being one of them) said to them, 'Does our law judge a man before it hears him and knows what he is doing?' They answered and said to him, 'Are you also from Galilee? Search and look, for no prophet has arisen out of Galilee'" (John 7:50–52 NKJV).

Nicodemus had to change his heart a lot to believe what Jesus said. He had to abandon his well-thought-through and set ideas. Later, Joseph of Arimathea asked Pilate for the body of Jesus, and Nicodemus helped him prepare Jesus's <u>body</u> for burial. He wouldn't have done that unless he had believed in Jesus as Messiah because that action made him liable to be kicked out of the Sanhedrin.

go to

body
John 19:38–42

heart
Revelation 3:20

person
2 Corinthians 5:17

what others say

Charles F. Stanley

There likely was a rustle in the trees that night. The wind was blowing where it wished, and Nicodemus was piqued and puzzled. He had heard the words and seen the miracles of Jesus of Nazareth, and now he had come to meet the Man. The fact that the ornate robe of this Pharisee fluttered in the wind held more than a little symbolism; Nicodemus was about to discover his beliefs as fragile as the clothing that touted them.

The conversion of Nicodemus is one of the Bible's most touching accounts. It is evidence of the transforming power of Jesus Christ and what He can do to the heart that seeks truth and longs for more than this world can deliver. The English translation of the name Nicodemus in its original language means "innocent blood." The nineteenth chapter of John reveals why it is a perfect fit.[13]

Jesus tells everyone in their hearts who is willing to listen: You must be born again. That can happen to anyone as they ask him to come into their <u>heart</u>, admit they have sinned, and ask for his cleansing. Then he makes them a new <u>person</u>.

apply it

We can also take great comfort in recognizing that Jesus didn't reprimand or reject Nicodemus because he came to Jesus in the night. Jesus didn't say, "Well, unless you're willing to risk coming during the day, I won't talk with you." Instead, Jesus accepted what Nicodemus could give, limited though it was, and then knew there would be a transformation within Nicodemus that eventually would empower him to reveal to everyone his alignment with Jesus.

Zaccheus—The Taxman Cometh

LUKE 19:1–10 *Then Jesus entered and passed through Jericho. Now behold, there was a man named Zaccheus who was a chief tax collector, and he was rich. And he sought to see who Jesus was, but could not because of the crowd, for he was of short stature. So he ran ahead and climbed up into a sycamore tree to see Him, for He was going to pass that way. And when Jesus came to the place, He looked up and saw him, and said to him, "Zaccheus, make haste and come down, for today I must stay at your house." So he made haste and came down, and received Him joyfully. But when they saw it, they all complained, saying, "He has gone to be a guest with a man who is a sinner." Then Zaccheus stood and said to the Lord, "Look, Lord, I give half of my goods to the poor; and if I have taken anything from anyone by false accusation, I restore fourfold." And Jesus said to him, "Today salvation has come to this house, because he also is a son of Abraham; for the Son of Man has come to seek and to save that which was lost." (NKJV)*

Tax collectors were known for their dishonesty in collecting more taxes than required. And this rich, tax-collecting, little government man was hated by everyone. Yet Zaccheus wanted to see Jesus at all costs. Perhaps he'd heard of the great things Jesus had done. Or maybe he had actually heard Jesus speak but because of his small stature he hadn't been able to reach him. But on that day, he climbed a tree. Imagine his shock when Jesus called his name. How did Jesus know *his* name? The crowd reacted strongly. Why would Jesus have anything to do with this odious little man? Zaccheus reacted with glee, thinking, *Jesus? Dinner? My house?* A lonely rich man was going to have dinner guests. Perhaps Jesus would be his first guest since he started his government job.

Zaccheus was a man who had spent his whole life stealing from others, and after a little dinner conversation with Jesus, he committed to restoring all those losses fourfold! That is huge. He went into dinner with a life marked by privilege and wealth, and finished his meal time marked by surrender and restitution. That is salvation in action.

what others say

Edward F. Markquart

Zaccheus was changed, from being greedy to generous, from selfish to selfless, from a thieving heart to thankful heart.

> How did this happen? What did Jesus say to him when they were alone? I mean, Zacchaeus only had to pay back what he stole plus 20%; but he *wanted* to. 400%!!! And then he volunteered to give 50% of his goods away to the poor!!! 50%!!! He didn't *have* to; he *wanted* to. There is a huge change in the level of financial generosity within his heart.[14]

One measure of a man is his willingness to make right what he had made wrong. Zacchaeus voluntarily said he would recompense those he cheated. Zacchaeus had been changed from a greedy man into a righteous man because of Jesus's presence.

Chapter Wrap-Up

- John the Baptist was Jesus's cousin and prepared the hearts of men to receive the teaching of Jesus. (Matthew 3:13–17)

- Luke was a physician who was a part of Paul's missionary journeys. He investigated Jesus's life and the early Christian church and wrote about them. (Luke 1:1–4)

- John Mark (later called Mark) grew stronger after Barnabas believed in him and took him on their own missionary trip. (Acts 15:37–41)

- Barnabas was quickly established in the early church as an encouraging kind of person who saw the best in everyone. (Acts 4:36–37; 9:26–27)

- Matthew, the tax collector, left behind his dishonest work in order to become a full-time follower of Jesus. He also ended up writing the Gospel account named for him. (Matthew 9:9–10)

- Andrew, one of the original disciples, quietly and subtly influenced people to believe in Jesus. (John 1:40–42)

- Thomas was a wholehearted follower of Jesus, even willing to die with him. But when he'd been told Jesus had risen from the dead, he didn't believe it until he saw Jesus personally. (John 11:16; 20:24–29)

- John was changed from an angry man to one whom Jesus loved. He was later given the privilege of writing the last book of the Bible: Revelation. (John 13:21–23)

- James was Jesus's half brother who, after believing Jesus's death and resurrection, became an early church father. (Acts 15:13–21)
- Stephen became the first Christian martyr when his words about Jesus convicted his hearers, who, as a result, stoned Stephen to death. (Acts 7:54–60)
- Philip's faith wasn't strong enough to trust that Jesus could create the bread that the multitude needed. (John 6:5–7)
- Timothy was already a Christian when Paul met him and saw his potential as a missionary and pastor. (Acts 16:1–5)
- Titus was a young Christian man given the responsibility by Paul to be pastor of the churches in Crete. (Titus 1:5)
- Onesiphorus determinedly looked for Paul and finally found him imprisoned. (2 Timothy 1:16–18)
- Nicodemus was a Pharisee who talked to Jesus at night and was told by Jesus he needed to be born again. (John 3:1–10)
- Zacchaeus became a believer in Jesus and showed his faith by restoring things he had stolen as a tax gatherer. (Luke 19:1–9)

Study Questions

1. Why didn't John the Baptist want to baptize Jesus?

2. Why did Luke feel qualified to write a history of Jesus's life on earth?

3. Why didn't Paul want to take John Mark with him and Barnabas on their next missionary trip?

4. How did Barnabas first establish himself as an encouraging kind of person in the early church?

5. What kind of life did Matthew leave in order to become a disciple of Jesus?

6. How did Andrew share his faith with others?

7. Why didn't Thomas believe that Jesus had risen from the dead?

8. What special quality was John known for and why?

9. Who was a brother of Jesus who didn't believe in him at first but then became a leader of the Christian church?

10. Who was the first martyr in the Christian church, and why was he stoned to death?

11. Jesus gave a challenge to Philip. What was it, and how did Philip respond?

12. What was Timothy's background?

13. What did Paul want Titus to do?

14. How did Onesiphorus endear himself to Paul?

15. What spiritual concept did Nicodemus have trouble believing that Jesus told him about?

16. How did Zacchaeus show that Jesus had made a difference in his life?

Appendix A - Time Line

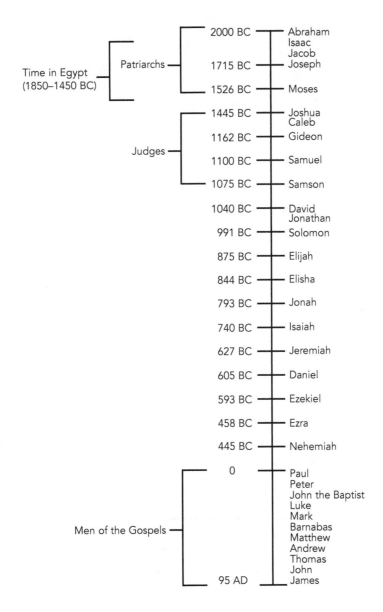

		2000 BC	—	Abraham Isaac Jacob
Time in Egypt (1850–1450 BC)	Patriarchs	1715 BC	—	Joseph
		1526 BC	—	Moses
		1445 BC	—	Joshua Caleb
	Judges	1162 BC	—	Gideon
		1100 BC	—	Samuel
		1075 BC	—	Samson
		1040 BC	—	David Jonathan
		991 BC	—	Solomon
		875 BC	—	Elijah
		844 BC	—	Elisha
		793 BC	—	Jonah
		740 BC	—	Isaiah
		627 BC	—	Jeremiah
		605 BC	—	Daniel
		593 BC	—	Ezekiel
		458 BC	—	Ezra
		445 BC	—	Nehemiah
	Men of the Gospels	0	—	Paul Peter John the Baptist Luke Mark Barnabas Matthew Andrew Thomas John
		95 AD	—	James

Appendix B - Paul's Missionary Journeys

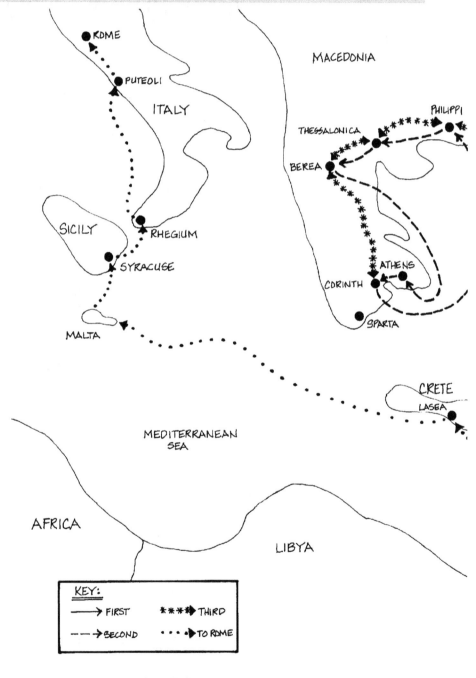

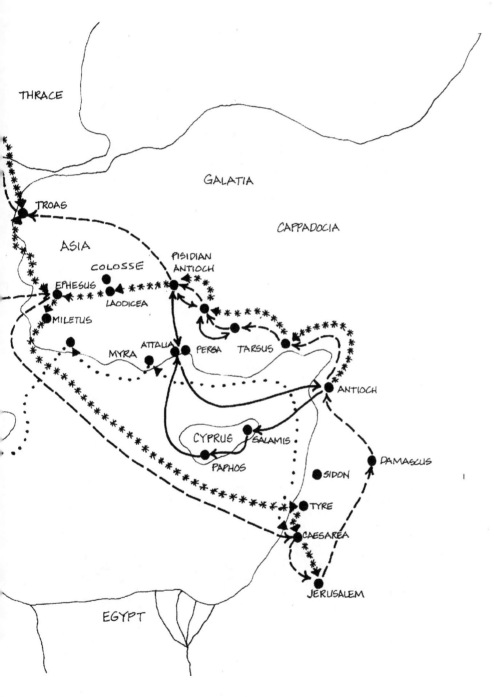

THRACE

GALATIA

CAPPADOCIA

TROAS

ASIA

COLOSSE

PISIDIAN
ANTIOCH

EPHESUS

LAODICEA

MILETUS

MYRA

ATTALIA

PERGA

TARSUS

ANTIOCH

CYPRUS

SALAMIS

DAMASCUS

PAPHOS

SIDON

TYRE

CAESAREA

JERUSALEM

EGYPT

Appendix C - The Answers

Chapter 1: Adam—Man of Dust and Destiny

1. God told Adam he could eat from any tree in the garden except from the Tree of the Knowledge of Good and Evil. If he did eat from the forbidden tree, he would die (Genesis 2:16–17).
2. God called all of creation "very good" except the fact that Adam was alone (Genesis 2:18).
3. None of the animals were sufficient as Adam's "helper" (Genesis 2:19–20).
4. Adam's job of taking care of the earth began to be painful toil and he would have to work hard. Eve's pain in childbearing was greatly increased, and her husband would rule over her. The serpent would crawl on his belly from then forward, and the woman's offspring was destined to "bruise" the head of the serpent (Genesis 3:14–19).
5. Adam named Eve. Eve means "living" because Adam was recognizing her ability to create a new life (Genesis 20).

Chapter 2: Abraham—Father of Promise

1. God promised to make Abram a great nation, receive blessings, have a great name, be a blessing to others, and cause those who cursed him to be cursed themselves (Genesis 12:2–3).
2. Abram initially thought his heir would be his servant, Eliezer (Genesis 15:2).
3. Sarai offered her maid, Hagar, to be a substitute wife. Abraham's son, Ishmael, was born from this union (Genesis 16:1–16).
4. God changed Abram's and Sarai's names to Abraham and Sarah (Genesis 17:5, 15).
5. Abimelech saw the miracle of Isaac's birth and the great blessings God gave Abraham (Genesis 21:22).
6. God told Abram to sacrifice Isaac on an altar on Mount Moriah (Genesis 22:2).

Chapter 3: Isaac—Man of Patience and Submission

1. "Isaac" means "laughter," so named because of the improbability of a woman birthing a son at age ninety and because of the joy his birth brought (Genesis 17:19).

2. Isaac was praying and meditating when Rebekah arrived (Genesis 24:63).
3. Isaac favored Esau because Esau was a skillful hunter and man of the field (Genesis 25:27).
4. Isaac lied because Rebekah was very beautiful and he thought the king would want to kill him in order to take her as his wife (Genesis 26:9).
5. Isaac was easily deceived because he was blind and was spiritually blinded by his appetites (Genesis 27:1, 9).

Chapter 4: Jacob—Deceiver Who Learned Dependence on God

1. Rebekah favored Jacob because he was peaceful and a man of the tents. Isaac favored Esau because he hunted game and Isaac loved meat (Genesis 25:27–28).
2. By putting Esau's clothing and an animal's skin on Jacob to simulate Esau's smell and hairy arms, Rebekah and Jacob fooled Isaac. Rebekah also cooked a goat into tasting like venison (Genesis 27:14–23).
3. Laban justified marrying the "wrong" daughter to Jacob because customarily the younger sister could not be married before the older one (Genesis 29:26).
4. Israel means "he who struggles with God" (Genesis 32:28).
5. Jacob thought Joseph had died because his sons produced Joseph's coat with blood on it, and allowed Jacob to conclude wild animals had killed his son (Genesis 37:33).

Chapter 5: Joseph—Obedient Servant

1. Jacob preferred Joseph over his other sons because Joseph was born to him in his old age (Genesis 37:3).
2. When the other brothers wanted to kill Joseph, Reuben suggested they put him into a pit. He planned to rescue Joseph later (Genesis 37:22).
3. God first provided the dreams of the cupbearer and baker for Joseph to interpret correctly and then the cupbearer told Pharaoh about Joseph when Pharaoh had a dream that no one could interpret (Genesis 40–41).

4. Joseph caused his brothers' grain money to be replaced in their sacks when they returned to their homeland on the first trip and he put one of his silver cups in Benjamin's bag on their second trip (Genesis 42:25; 44:12).

5. Joseph's brothers were afraid that he would punish them for the cruel ways they had treated him thirteen years before (Genesis 50:18).

Chapter 6: Moses—Man of Humility and Strength

1. Moses fled his princely existence when people found out that he had killed an Egyptian and Pharaoh wanted to kill him (Exodus 2:15).

2. Moses said he would not be able to deliver Israel because he didn't think he was anyone special (Exodus 3:11), the Israelites wouldn't believe him (Exodus 4:1), and he couldn't speak well (Exodus 4:10).

3. Miracles leading up to Israel's release from Egypt included: the Nile River turned to blood, frogs, lice, flies, animal diseases, boils, hail, locusts, darkness, and death of firstborn (Exodus 7–11).

4. Moses didn't feel as weary once he delegated his work and God provided meat for the people to eat (Numbers 11:16–23).

5. Moses prayed for Miriam's healing and didn't hold a grudge (Numbers 12:1–13).

Chapter 7: David—Man After God's Own Heart

1. Saul ridiculed David's offer to battle Goliath by saying David was an inexperienced youth while Goliath was a seasoned warrior (1 Samuel 17:33).

2. Saul's son, Jonathan, became David's best friend (1 Samuel 18:1).

3. David took care of Jonathan's son, Mephibosheth (2 Samuel 9:1–13).

4. David should have been fighting with his men on the battlefield (2 Samuel 11:1).

5. Though David fled the kingdom, he had one advantage because his adviser, Hushai, became an adviser to Absalom and gave him wrong advice (2 Samuel 17:7–14).

Chapter 8: Men of Strong Faith—Lessons in Perseverence

1. The ark was 450 feet long, 75 feet wide, and 45 feet high (Genesis 6:15).

2. The rainbow was a sign of God's promise to never destroy everything on the earth through a flood again (Genesis 9:15).

3. God permitted Satan to hurt Job only with God's limitations (Job 1:12; 2:6).

4. Job reasoned that if he accepted good from God, he should accept adversity too (Job 2:10).

5. Aaron, the brother of Moses, was secondary in leadership in leading the Israelites' out of Egypt (Exodus 4:27–31).

6. Enoch walked with God, and God took him (Genesis 5:18–24).

7. High places refer to the hills where Canaanites worshiped at their altars (2 Chronicles 16:13–17:1–19).

Chapter 9: Men of Power—Lessons in Might and Missteps

1. Samson nagged his parents into getting him a wife from the Philistines (Judges 14:1–4).

2. Delilah nagged Samson until he was sick of resisting her (Judges 16:1–22).

3. Elijah called down fire from heaven to burn up a sacrifice that was covered with water, while the prophets of Baal could not (1 Kings 18:1–39).

4. God provided physical nourishment, a time for Elijah to vent his feelings, and a new purpose in life (1 Kings 19:9–21).

5. Elisha asked Elijah for a double portion of God's power (2 Kings 2:7–10).

6. Elisha showed his "double portion" by doing many more miracles for God than Elijah did (2 Kings 2:19–22; 4–6; 13).

7. Joab's primary hard-hearted action was murdering other people (2 Samuel 3:26–29).

Chapter 10: Men of Wisdom—Lessons in Obeying God's Word

1. Samuel was a true prophet of God because everything he predicted came true (1 Samuel 3:19).

2. Solomon showed wisdom by his unique solution to the problem of two women claiming the same baby (1 Kings 3:27).

3. Scribes were highly trained men who were well educated in the Scriptures (Ezra 7:10).

4. The people praised God, lifted their hands in praise, bowed down and worshiped God with their faces to the ground (Nehemiah 8:6).

Chapter 11: Men of Courage—Lessons in Strength and Bravery

1. Caleb tried to overcome the Israelites' fear by insisting the land was good and that God would give it to them because God was with them (Numbers 14:7–9).

2. Joshua was commanded to obey the Law and meditate on it day and night (Joshua 1:7–9).

3. Gideon said he was too young and from a weak family (Judges 6:14–16).

4. Jonathan snuck into the Philistine camp and told his armor bearer that if the Philistines invited them to come ahead, that meant the Israelites would have victory. The Philistines did call to Jonathan, and Jonathan and his armor bearer started a victory right then (1 Samuel 14:10–15).

5. Jonathan made a covenant with David and put his robe and armor on David so that he would be protected (1 Samuel 18:1–4).

6. Jonathan encouraged David by affirming that David would indeed live to become king (1 Samuel 23:15–18).

Chapter 12: The Prophets—Lessons in Speaking the Words of God
1. An angel touched a burning coal to Isaiah's lips and pronounced him clean (Isaiah 6:6–7).
2. Jeremiah expressed grief and sadness over his nation's sins by crying all the time (Jeremiah 9:1–2).
3. One of Ezekiel's toughest challenges was the death of his wife (Ezekiel 24:16–18).
4. Daniel did not want to eat unclean food (food not prepared God's way) (Daniel 1:8–9, 17b).
5. Jonah was called to preach to the people in Nineveh (Jonah 1:1–3).

Chapter 13: Jesus—Very God and Very Man
1. They were amazed and asked, "Who can this be?" (Matthew 8:23–27).
2. John wrote that Jesus was in the beginning with God making the world and John called him the "Word" (John 1:1–4).
3. Jesus was born of a virgin (Isaiah 7:14).
4. A bondservant as he became a man (Philippians 2:5–8).
5. So that he could live as a model for every Christian (2 Corinthians 3:18).

Chapter 14: Paul—Passionate Writer for God
1. Jesus appeared to Paul in a bright light, spoke to Paul, and blinded him. This Damascus road encounter convinced Paul that Jesus was the Messiah (Acts 9:1–8).
2. The Christians in Antioch heard the Holy Spirit's direction through prayer and fasting (Acts 13:1–3).
3. Paul was beaten, stoned, shipwrecked, attacked, falsely accused, and went without sleep, food, and drink (2 Corinthians 11:24–28).
4. Paul and Barnabas shared with the early church leaders their exciting results from preaching to the Gentiles (Acts 15:12).
5. Paul did not want John Mark to join their missionary trip since Mark had left prematurely on the previous trip (Acts 15:36–41).

Chapter 15: Peter—Growing in Faith
1. Peter could no longer walk on water when he focused on the wind and grew afraid (Matthew 14:22–32).
2. Jesus said God had revealed to Peter that Jesus was the Christ (Matthew 16:13–20).
3. Peter left and wept bitterly, even wailed, upon realizing he had denied Jesus (Matthew 26:75).
4. Jesus showed his forgiveness to Peter by giving Peter three opportunities to express his love for Jesus, and by asking Peter, "Feed My sheep" (John 21:15–19).
5. Peter gave the world's first Holy Ghost–filled Christian sermon (Acts 2:14).

Chapter 16: Men in Ministry—Lessons in Following Christ
1. John the Baptist believed he wasn't worthy to baptize the Son of God (Matthew 3:13–17).
2. Luke made a careful investigation into Jesus's life and death (Luke 1:1–4).
3. Paul did not trust John Mark because John Mark had left them while they were in Pamphylia before their work was done (Acts 15:37–41).
4. Barnabas took Saul (later called Paul) and introduced him around to the early Church fathers when other believers feared Saul (Acts 4:36–37; 9:26–27).
5. Matthew was formerly a tax collector (Matthew 9:9–10).
6. Andrew took his brother, Peter, to go see Jesus, telling him Jesus was the Messiah (John 1:40–42).
7. Thomas doubted because he wasn't there when Jesus first appeared in physical form to the other disciples (John 20:24–29).
8. John was called the one whom Jesus loved (John 13:21–23).
9. James was Jesus's half brother (Acts 15:13–21).
10. Stephen was the first martyr, and because he preached Jesus and made unbelievers angry with him, he was stoned (Acts 7:54–60).
11. Jesus asked Philip to feed the multitude, but Philip didn't have enough faith and said they didn't have enough money or food (John 6:5–7).
12. Timothy had been a believer in Jesus for a short time when Paul arrived. After that, Paul took Timothy with him on many missionary journeys and then assigned him to become a pastor (Acts 16:1–5)
13. Paul wanted Titus to oversee the church in Crete and appoint elders (Titus 1:5).
14. Onesiphorus looked high and low for Paul and finally found him chained up (2 Timothy 1:16–18).
15. Nicodemus had a hard time understanding how he could be born again because he only thought of it in a physical way and not a spiritual way the way Jesus intended (John 3:1–10).
16. Zacchaeus gave half of his goods to the poor, and whatever he took incorrectly, he promised to restore fourfold (Luke 19:1–10).

Appendix D - The Experts

Arthur, Kay—Author of many books and well-known speaker.

Baxter, J. Sidlow—Preacher and author, born in Australia and grew up in England.

Bridges, Jerry—Best-selling author and Bible teacher is on the collegiate ministry staff of the Navigators.

Briscoe, D. Stuart—Pastor of Elmbrook Church in Waukesha, Wisconsin. Speaker and author of many books, including *Tough Truths for Today's Living*.

Buckingham, Jamie—Ordained minister who wrote more than forty books. Former spiritual overseer of the Tabernacle Church in Melbourne, Florida.

Carlyle, Thomas—Scottish historian, critic, and sociological writer.

Chambers, Oswald—Itinerant evangelist and Bible college teacher. Most of his works were compiled posthumously by his wife in 1917.

Cole, Edwin Louis—Founder and president of Christian Men's Network. Speaks to men across the world.

Colson, Charles R.—Former presidential adviser who went to prison during the Watergate era. Came to Christ and is the founder of Prison Fellowship, a worldwide ministry.

Constable, Thomas L.—Director of D. Min. studies and associate professor of Bible Exposition at Dallas Theological Seminary.

Duncan, Ligon—President of the Alliance of Confessing Evangelicals and senior minister in Mississippi. He is currently the moderator of the General Assembly of the Presbyterian Church in America.

Evans, Dr. Tony—Senior pastor of Oak Cliff Bible Fellowship in Dallas and author of many books.

Farrar, Steve—President of Point Man Leadership Ministries in Dallas, Texas. Active speaker and author of a number of books.

Fensham, F. Charles—Professor of Semitic Languages at University of Stellenbosch in South Africa.

Flynn, Leslie—Former pastor of Grace Conservative Baptist Church in Nanuet, New York. Author of several books, including *Me Be Like Jesus?*

Getz, Gene A.—Former pastor of Fellowship Bible Church of Dallas, Texas. Associate professor of Practical Theology at Dallas Theological Seminary.

Graham, Billy—Widely known around the world as an evangelist and author.

Hayden, Dan—After many years of serving as a pastor and seminary professor, Dan began producing the daily radio feature, *A Word from the Word*. He has authored several books.

Hendricks, Howard—Professor at Dallas Theological Seminary. Author and speaker at Promise Keepers events.

Hendriksen, William—Author of *New Testament Commentary: Ephesians*.

Henry, Matthew—Pastor and biblical expositor who wrote a seven-volume *Commentary on the Bible* for which he is still remembered 250 years later.

Hercus, John—Writer and Australian eye-specialist.

Hobbs, Herschel H.—Well-known pastor of the international *Baptist Hour* broadcast. Former president of the Southern Baptist Convention.

Hybels, Bill—Senior pastor of Willow Creek Community Church and the author of many books, including *Honest to God*.

Ironside, H. A.—Internationally known Bible teacher and preacher with more than sixty volumes of writings.

Jensen, Irving L.—Author, professor, and chairman of the department of Bible at Bryan College.

Jewell, John—Bishop of Salisbury and exiled by Queen Mary. He was active in the British Reformation movement.

Johnson, Phillip E.—Retired UC Berkeley American law professor and author. He is considered the father of the intelligent design movement, which criticizes the theory of evolution.

Keller, W. Phillip—Writer known for insightful devotional commentaries.

Kidner, Derek—Author of several biblical works and former warden of Tyndale House, Cambridge, U.K.

Lawrence, John W.—Professor of Bible and Theology at Multnomah bible College in Portland, Oregon.

Lewis, C. S.—Author, scholar of English literature, and famous Christian apologist. He wrote fictional works, the most popular of which are *The Chronicles of Narnia*. He also wrote many books defending traditional Christianity.

Libby, Larry—Editor at Multnomah Press, Portland, Oregon. Coauthored a book with Bruce Wilkinson.

Lucado, Max—Pastor, writer, and speaker. He is the voice of *UpWords*, a daily fifteen-minute radio program.

MacArthur, John, Jr.—Senior pastor of Grace Community Church in Southern California and author of many books.

Marquart, Edward L.—Author of several books and pastor of Grace Lutheran church in Seattle since 1973.

Martin, John A.—Assistant professor of Bible Exposition and assistant academic dean and director of summer school of Dallas Theological Seminary, Dallas, Texas.

McDowell, Josh—Author of numerous books and vocal apologist for the Christian faith.

McGee, J. Vernon—Well-known radio preacher who created a five-year Bible study program, *Thru the Bible*. This program is still widely popular today.

Meyer, F. B.—Pastor, speaker, supporter of missions, and prolific writer.

Morley, Patrick M.—Founder and chairman of Morley Properties. Also writes and speaks to men and women across the country.

Ockenga, Harold—Religious leader and educator, co-founder of Fuller Theological Seminary, Pasadena, California. First president and one of the founders of the National Association of Evangelicals.

Ogilvie, Lloyd John—Chaplain to the United States Senate. Frequent speaker on radio and television and the author of many books.

Ortlund, Raymond C., Jr.—Assistant professor of Old Testament at Trinity Evangelical Divinity School and ordained minister.

Packer, James I.—Teaches systematic and historical theology at Regent College in Vancouver, British Columbia. Author of numerous books.

Palau, Luis—International evangelist who was born in Argentina. His daily radio programs in Latin America and Spain reach millions of people. Author of many books.

Penn-Lewis, Jessie—Christian author during the late 1800s.

Pollock, John—Ordained Anglican priest who has authored several books on history and biography, including an authorized biography of Billy Graham.

Pritchard, Ray—Pastor and guest lecturer who has written more than twenty books.

Redpath, Alan—Late pastor of Charlotte Chapel in Edinburgh, Scotland, Scotland's largest Baptist congregation. Writer and speaker.

Richards, Larry—Award-winning editor of several study Bibles and author of over one hundred books that cover subjects such as theological and biblical studies, church leadership, and devotional writings. Larry (aka Lawrence O.) Richards is a general editor of the Smart Guide to the Bible™ series.

Ross, Allen P.—Chairman and professor of Semitics and Old Testament Studies, Dallas Theological Seminary.

Schuller, Robert H.—Pastor of the Crystal Cathedral in Southern California. Author of numerous books, Schuller is well known for his weekly television broadcast, *Hour of Power*.

Scott, Stuart W.—Graduate with a D. Min. from Covenant Theological Seminary. Associate professor of Biblical Counseling at The Master's College, Santa Clarita, California.

Sproul, R. C.—Theologian, minister, teacher, and chairman of the board for Ligonier Ministries. Author of many books.

Stanley, Charles—Best-selling author and pastor of the nearly 16,000-member First Baptist Church in Atlanta, Georgia.

Stedman, Ray—Longtime pastor of Peninsula Bible Church in Palo Alto, California, and author of *Body Life* and twenty-seven other books.

Swindoll, Charles—Former president of Dallas Theological Seminary. Author and pastor in the Dallas, Texas, area.

Unger, Merrill F.—Former pastor and professor of Old Testament studies at Dallas Theological Seminary. Author of many books and reference works.

Warren, Rick—Best-selling author and founding pastor of Saddleback Church in Lake Forest, California.

Webb, Barry G.—Head of the Old Testament department at Moore Theological College in Sydney, Australia.

Whyte, Alkexander—Scottish divine. During his life (1817-1921) was minister of the Free Church of Scotland and principal and professor at New College, Edinburgh.

Wiersbe, Warren W.—Author of more than eighty books. Speaker, writer, and radio minister.

Wigglesworth, Smith—English preacher and author of a number of books.

Wilcock, Michael—Vicar of St. Nicholas's Church, Durham, England, and former director of pas toral studies at Trinity College, Bristol. Author of *The Message of Chronicles* and other books.

Wilkinson, Bruce—Founder and former president of Walk Thru the Bible Ministries in Atlanta, Georgia.

Yancey, Philip—Editor-at-large for *Christianity Today* magazine. Author of six Gold Medallion Award-winning books, including *Where Is God When It Hurts?*

Endnotes

Chapter 1

1. Allen P. Ross, *The Bible Knowledge Commentary*, ed. John F. Walvoord and Roy B. Zuck (Wheaton, IL: Victor Books, 1985), 30.
2. Charles Swindoll, *Laugh Again* (Dallas, TX: Word Publishing, 1991), 193–94.
3. Raymond C. Ortlund Jr., *Recovering Biblical Manhood and Womanhood* (Wheaton, IL: Crossway Books, 1991), 101.
4. Herschel H. Hobbs, *The Origin of All Things* (Waco, TX: Word, 1975), 48.
5. Alan Redpath, *The Making of a Man of God* (Old Tappan, NJ: Revell, 1979), 67.
6. Hobbs, *The Origin of All Things*, 52.

Chapter 2

1. Charles R. Swindoll, *The Living Insights Study Bible* (Grand Rapids, MI: Zondervan Publishing House, 1996), 21.
2. Harold Ockenga, *Women Who Made Bible History* (Grand Rapids, MI: Zondervan, 1979), 22.
3. Gene Getz, *Abraham: Trials & Triumphs* (Glendale, CA: Gospel Light Publications, 1976), 30.
4. Jamie Buckingham, *The Promise of Power*, comp. Judith Couchman (Ann Arbor, MI: Servant Publications, 1998), 62.
5. Swindoll, *The Living Insights Study Bible*, 24.
6. Smith Wigglesworth, *Dare to Believe*, comp. Judith Couchman (Ann Arbor, MI: Servant Publications, 1997), 40.
7. Getz, *Abraham: Trials & Triumphs*, 81.
8. *Life Application Bible Notes* (Wheaton, IL: Tyndale House Publishers and Grand Rapids, MI: Zondervan Publishing House, 1991), 34.
9. Hobbs, *The Origin of All Things*, 108.
10. Oswald Chambers, *My Utmost for His Highest* (Uhrichsville, OH: Barbour and Company, 1963), 79.
11. Swindoll, *The Living Insights Study Bible*, 29.

Chapter 3

1. Swindoll, *The Living Insights Study Bible*, 26.
2. Hobbs, *The Origin of All Things*, 118.
3. J. Vernon McGee, *Genesis: Volume II* (Pasadena, CA: Thru the Bible Books, 1975), 281.
4. William Hendriksen, *New Testament Commentary: Ephesians* (Grand Rapids, MI: Baker, 1967), 261.
5. Swindoll, *The Living Insights Study Bible*, 34.

Chapter 4

1. Hobbs, *The Origin of All Things*, 126.
2. Bruce H. Wilkinson and Larry Libby, *Talk Through Bible Personalities* (Atlanta, GA: Walk Thru the Bible Ministries, Inc., 1983), 12–13.
3. Hobbs, *The Origin of All Things*, 131.
4. Wigglesworth, *Dare to Believe*, 127–28.
5. Wilkinson and Libby, *Talk Through Bible Personalities*, 16–17.
6. Gene A. Getz, *Joseph: From Prison to Palace* (Ventura, CA: Regal Books, 1983), 33–34.
7. Swindoll, *Living Insights Study Bible*, 43.
8. Getz, *Joseph: From Prison to Palace*, 35.
9. Kay Arthur, *Lord, I Want to Know You* (Sisters, OR: Multnomah, 1992), 64.

Chapter 5

1. Leslie Flynn, *Joseph: God's Man in Egypt* (Wheaton, IL: Victor Books, 1979), 25.
2. Ross, *The Bible Knowledge Commentary*, 87.
3. Billy Graham, *Freedom from the Seven Deadly Sins* (Grand Rapids, MI: Zondervan, 1955), 41.
4. Getz, *Joseph: From Prison to Palace*, 49.
5. Swindoll, *Living Insights Study Bible*, 48.
6. Patrick M. Morley, *The Man in the Mirror* (Brentwood, TN: Wolgemuth & Hyatt, 1989), 47.
7. Matthew Henry, *Unabridged Commentary Matthew Henry's Commentary on the Whole Bible: New Modern Edition Database*

(Hendrickson Publishers, 1991, 1994, electronic markup copyright 1995 by Epiphany Software), Genesis 41:14.

8. Merrill Unger, *Unger's Bible Dictionary* (Chicago, IL: Moody Press, 1985), 989.
9. Flynn, *Joseph: God's Man in Egypt*, 117.
10. Morley, *The Man in the Mirror*, 237.
11. Getz, *Joseph: From Prison to Palace*, 136.
12. Max Lucado, *He Still Moves Stones* (Dallas, TX: Word Publishing, 1993), 110.
13. Philip Yancey, quoted in *Men's Devotional Bible* (Grand Rapids, MI: Zondervan Publishing, 1993), 42.
14. Ed Cole, *Manhood 101* (Tulsa, OK: Honor Books, n.d.), 9.

Chapter 6
1. Wilkinson and Libby, *Talk Through Bible Personalities*, 29–30.
2. Jamie Buckingham, *The Promise of Power*, comp. Judith Couchman (Ann Arbor: MI: Servant, 1998), 98.
3. Wilkinson and Libby, *Talk Through Bible Personalities*, 32.
4. Buckingham, *The Promise of Power*, 99.
5. Max Lucado,
6. John Hercus, *Pages from God's Casebook* (Downers Grove, IL: InterVarsity Press, 1962), 30.
7. John F. Walvoord, *The Bible Knowledge Commentary: Old Testament* (Wheaton, IL: Victor, 1985), 120.
8. Charles R. Swindoll, *Moses: A Man of Selfless Dedication* (Anaheim, CA: Insight for Living, n.d.), 81.
9. Lucado, *He Still Moves Stones*, 60–61.
10. Chambers, *Growing Deeper with God*, 16.
11. Gene A. Getz, *Moses: Moments of Glory, Feet of Clay* (Ventura, CA: Gospel Light, 1976), 138.
12. Ibid., 156.

Chapter 7
1. F. B. Meyer, *Samuel the Prophet* (Fort Washington, PA: Christian Literature Crusade, 1978), 200.
2. Alan Redpath, *The Making of a Man of God* (Old Tappan, NJ: Revell, 1962), 107.
3. Thomas Carlyle, *John Bartlett's Familiar Quotations* (Boston, MA: Little, Brown and Company, 1980), 474.
4. Charles R. Swindoll, *David: A Man of Passion & Destiny* (Nashville, TN: Word, 1997), 172.
5. John W. Lawrence, *Life's Choices* (Portland, OR: Multnomah Press,1975), 39.
6. Greg Laurie, *The Great Compromise*.
7. Swindoll, *David: A Man of Passion & Destiny*, 248.

8. Steve Farrar, *Point Man* (Sisters, OR: Multnomah, 1990), 75.

Chapter 8
1. Hobbs, *The Origin of All Things*, 74.
2. Chambers, *Growing Deeper*, 34.
3. Charles Colson, as quoted in *Men's Devotional Bible* (Grand Rapids, MI: Zondervan Publishing House, 1993), 517.
4. Jessie Penn-Lewis, *The Story of Job* (Overcomer Literature Trust, 1902), 99.
5. Larry Richards, *The Bible: The Smart Guide to the Bible* (Nashville, TN: Thomas Nelson Publishers, 2007).
6. Rick Warren, *Purpose Driven Life* (Grand Rapids, MI: Zondervan, 2002), adapted from pages 30–33.
7. Getz, *Abraham: Trials & Triumphs*, 98–99.
8. Summarized from *The Bible Knowledge Commentary*, Old Testament, 189.
9. Getz, *Abraham: Trials & Triumphs*, 138.
10. Jerry Bridges, *The Practice of Godliness* (Colorado Springs, CO: Navpress, 1996), 17.
11. Max Lucado, *Come Thirsty* (Nashville, TN: W Publishing Group, 2004), 68.

Chapter 9
1. Michael Wilcock, *The Message of Judges* (Downers Grove, IL: InterVarsity Press, 1992), 130.
2. Tony Evans, *Returning to Your First Love* (Chicago, IL: Moody Press, 1995), 198.
3. Swindoll, *Living Insights Study Bible*, 252.
4. Wilcock, *The Message of Judges*, 143.
5. John Jewell, *Near to the Heart of God*, comp. Bernard Bangley (Wheaton, IL: Harold Shaw, 1998), quoted in *Of the Holy Scriptures*, April 8.
6. Chambers, *Growing Deeper*, 47–48.
7. J. Sidlow Baxter, *Mark These Men* (Grand Rapids, MI: Zondervan, 1960), 12.
8. W. Phillip Keller, *Elijah: Prophet of Power* (Waco, TX: Word Books, 1980), 89.
9. Chambers, *My Utmost for His Highest*, 215.
10. Hendricks, *Standing Together*, 105.
11. Wilkinson and Libby, *Talk Through Bible Personalities*, 117.
12. Farrar, as quoted in *Men's Devotional Bible*, 360.
13. Wilkinson and Libby, *Talk Through Bible Personalities*, 122
14. Evans, *Returning to Your First Love*, 80.
15. Merrill, *The Bible Knowledge Commentary*, 467
16. Redpath, *The Making of a Man of God*, 199.
17. Merrill, *The Bible Knowledge Commentary*, 473.
18. Evans, *Returning to Your First Love*, 80.
19. Constable, *The Bible Knowledge Commentary*, 491.

Chapter 10

1. Wilkinson and Libby, *Talk Through Bible Personalities*, 50.
2. F. B. Meyer, *Samuel the Prophet* (Fort Washington, PA: Christian Literature Crusade, PA), 72.
3. Farrar, *Point Man*, 218.
4. Meyer, *Samuel the Prophet*, 135.
5. Constable, *The Bible Knowledge Commentary*, 494.
6. James I. Packer, *Knowing God* (Downers Grove, IL: InterVarsity Press, 1981), 30.
7. Wilkinson and Libby, *Talk Through Bible Personalities*, 104.
8. Ray Stedman, *Is This All There Is to Life?* (Sisters, OR: Multnomah Press, 1985), 35.
9. Morley, *The Man in the Mirror*, 85.
10. F. Charles Fensham, *The Books of Ezra and Nehemiah* (Grand Rapids, MI: William B. Eerdmans, 1982), 105.
11. Derek Kidner, *Ezra & Nehemiah* (Downers Grove, IL: InterVarsity Press, 1979), 68–69.
12. Lucado, *He Still Moves Stones*, 99.
13. Bill Hybels, *Too Busy Not to Pray* (Downers Grove, IL: InterVarsity Press, 1988), 81.
14. Charles Swindoll, *Hand Me Another Brick* (Nashville, TN: Thomas Nelson, 1978), 137.

Chapter 11

1. W. Phillip Keller, *Joshua: Man of Fearless Faith* (Dallas, TX: Word Books, 1983), 36.
2. Chambers, *Growing Deeper*, 67.
3. Charles Swindoll, *Second Wind: A Fresh Run at Life* (Sisters, OR: Multnomah Press, 1977), 67.
4. Keller, *Joshua: Man of Fearless Faith*, 18.
5. Redpath, *The Making of a Man of God*, 238.
6. Wilcock, *The Message of Judges*, 79.
7. Buckingham, *The Promise of Power*, 76.
8. Arthur, *Lord, I Want to Know You*, 129.
9. Hybels, *Men's Devotional Bible*, 243.
10. Wilcock, *The Message of Judges*, 82.
11. Buckingham, *The Promise of Power*, 77.
12. W. Phillip Keller, *Mighty Man of Valor* (Old Tappan, NJ: Revell, 1979), 115.
13. Wilkinson and Libby, *Talk Through Bible Personalities*, 61.
14. Hercus, *Pages from God's Casebook*, 91.
15. Luis Palau, *Heart After God* (Sisters, OR: Multnomah, 1978), 40.
16. Gene A. Getz, *David: God's Man in Faith and Failure* (Ventura, CA: Gospel Light, 1978), 63–64.
17. Redpath, *The Making of a Man of God*, 61.

Chapter 12

1. Barry G. Webb, *The Message of Isaiah* (Downers Grove, IL: InterVarsity Press, 1996), 58.
2. Irving L. Jensen, *Isaiah Jeremiah: A Self Study Guide* (Chicago, IL: Moody Bible Institute, 1968), 66.
3. H. A. Ironside, *Ezekiel* (New York, NY: Loizeaux Brothers, 1949), 164.
4. Farrar, *Point Man*, 137.
5. Swindoll, *Second Wind: A Fresh Run at Life*, 8.
6. D. Stuart Briscoe, *Taking God Seriously* (Dallas, TX: Word, 1986), 73.

Chapter 13

1. Josh McDowell, *Evidence That Demands a Verdict* (San Bernardino, CA: Here's Life Publishers, 1972), 135.
2. Phillip E. Johnson, *The Right Questions* (Downers Grove, IL: InterVarsity Press, 2002), 63–64.
3. http://www.pbc.org/dp/stedman/john/3831.html (accessed April 15, 2006).
4. Josh McDowell and Bob Hostetler, *Beyond Belief to Convictions* (Carol Stream, IL: Tyndale House Publishers, 2002), 62.
5. Dan Hayden, *The Name Above All Names* (Wheaton, IL: Crossway Books, 2004), 18.
6. Ray Pritchard, *Credo* (Wheaton, IL: Crossway Books, 2005), 63–64.
7. Ligon Duncan, quoted at Together for the Gospel Conference, April 28, 2006, at www.adrian.warnock (accessed April 28, 2006).
8. C. S. Lewis, *Mere Christianity*, rev. ed. (New York, NY: Macmilian Publishing Co., Collier Books, 1952), 155.
9. Stuart W. Scott, *Think Biblically* by John McArthur, ed. Richard L. Mayhue, John A. Hughes (Wheaton, IL: Crossway Books, 2003), 162.
10. Charles Swindoll, *Questions Christians Ask Bible Study Guide* (Fullerton, CA: Insight for Living, 1989), 12.

Chapter 14

1. Chamber, *Growing Deeper*, 71.
2. Warren W. Wiersbe, *The Bible Exposition Commentary* (Victor Books, 1983), 456.
3. Morley, *The Man in the Mirror*, 67.
4. Wiersbe, *The Bible Exposition Commentary*, 462.
5. John Pollock, *The Apostle: A Life of Paul* (Colorado Springs, CO: Chariot Victor Publishing, 1994), 54–55.
6. Lucado, *He Still Moves Stones*, 128.
7. Pollock, *The Apostle: A Life of Paul*, 237.

Chapter 15

1. Hobbs, *The Origin of All Things*, 109.
2. Philip Yancey, *The Jesus I Thought I Knew* (Grand Rapids, MI: Zondervan, 1995), 21.
3. John MacArthur Jr., *The Master's Men* (Van Nuys, CA: Word of Grace Communications, 1982), 15.
4. F. B. Meyer, *Peter the Man* (Wheaton, IL: Good News Publishers, 1959), 43.
5. Wiersbe, *The Bible Exposition Commentary*, 397.
6. Lucado, *He Still Moves Stones*, 88.
7. Lloyd John Ogilvie, *Drumbeat of Love* (Waco, TX: Word, 1976), 34.
8. Meyer, *Peter the Man*, 56.

Chapter 16

1. Martin, *The Bible Knowledge Commentary New Testament*, 211.
2. Robert H. Schuller, *The New Possibility Thinkers Bible* (Nashville, TN: Thomas Nelson, 1996), 1281.
3. Wiersbe, *The Bible Exposition Commentary*, 465–66.
4. Ogilvie, *Drumbeat of Love*, 135.
5. R. C. Sproul, *Before the Face of God* (Grand Rapids, MI: Baker, 1993), 134–35.
6. John MacArthur Jr., *The Master's Men* (Van Nuys, CA: Word of Grace Communications, 1982), 29.
7. Wiersbe, *The Bible Exposition Commentary*, 393.
8. Ogilvie, *Drumbeat of Love*, 88.
9. MacArthur, *The Master's Men*, 46.
10. Wilkinson and Libby, *Talk Through Bible Personalities*, 203.
11. Warren, *The Purpose Driven Life*, 149.
12. Alexander Whyte, *Bible Characters* (Grand Rapids, MI: Zondervan, 1952), 44.
13. Charles F. Stanley, "Illuminated by Love" http://www.intouch.org/myintouch/mighty/nicodemus_78037.html (accessed March 31, 2006).
14. Edward F. Markquart, "Stewardship," http://www.sermonsfromseattle.com/stwerardship_zacchaeus.htm (accessed March 31, 2006).

Index

A

Aaron, 27, 88, 95, 96, 131–42
Abiathar, 197–98
Abimelech, 36, 106
Abishai, 181, 184
Abner, 179–80
abomination, 25, 37
  definition, 25
Abraham
  covenant with God, 17, 21, 22, 24
  faith of, 16, 25–29
  God's promises to, 15, 22, 23, 26, 27
  name change, 24
  patriarch, 15
  testing of, 18
Abraham's travels
  illustration, 17
Abram
  become a great nation, 23
  faith of, 15, 19, 21
  first time God appears, 16
  God's appearances and challenges to, 17–21, 24
  half-truth told by, 18
  name change, 24
  theophany, 17
Absalom, 112–14, 182–85
Achan, 37

Adam
  Eve as complement to, 7
  as namer of animals, 6
  rib of, 6, 17
  without a companion, 3
Adam and Eve
  fellowship with God, 3
Adonijah, 115, 187, 197–99
affirmed, 27, 57, 250, 318
Ahab
  chased Elijah, 165
  marriage to Jezebel, 162
  set up an altar for Baal, 162
Ahaziah, 149, 171
Amasa, 185–87
ambivalence
  definition, 70
Ammon, 181
Amnon, 112, 183
Ananias, 37, 307
ancient Jerusalem, 216
ancient world, 216, 316
Andrew, 309, 316–17, 324
Angel of the Lord, 235–37
angels
  disguised as men, 24
  guardians, 106
  provide for the people of God, 106
anger
  dealing with, 220
  Lord's, 95

never adds constructively to God's purposes, 220
annulled
  definition, 305
Antioch, 289, 314, 315
apostles, 313, 314, 323, 325
Arab, 23, 218
Ark of the Covenant, 121, 123
  illustration, 121
armor, 101, 133, 160–61, 245
Artaxerxes, 209–11, 223, 224
Arthur, Kay
  on Jehovah-shalom, 238
  on our unchanging Jehovah, 57
Asahel, 179–80
ashamed, 8, 213, 259
Asher, 43, 51
Asherah, 238
Ashtoreths, 192, 193
ask for God's help, 23, 224
ask for God's miracles, 35
Assyria, 262
Astarte
  illustration, 16
authority, 23, 38, 45, 133, 148, 163, 176, 199, 280
  definition, 163

B

Baal, 155, 162, 165–66, 178, 193, 238
  illustration, 165
baptism, 310
Barak, 51
Barnabas, 289, 291–92, 295–96, 312–15
barren
  definition, 50
  Hannah as, 191
  Rachel as, 50
  Rebekah as, 35
  Sarah as, 26, 35
Bathsheba, 110, 111, 115, 117, 181, 197–99
Baxter, J. Sidlow, 162
Belial
  definition, 156
benefits of honesty, 47
Bethel, 54, 55, 173, 244
Bildad, 127, 128
Bilhah, 43
birthright, 35, 43, 46, 58
  definition, 43
bitterness, 63, 198, 220, 264, 277
blaming, 10, 94, 125, 126, 151
blasphemy, 322
blessing, 17, 20, 31, 38, 40, 46, 47, 53, 58, 59, 97, 116, 174, 175, 204, 318
boat, 120, 121, 269, 298–99, 304
born again, 32, 330, 331
breach
  definition, 22
Bridges, Jerry, 144
Briscoe, D. Stuart, 263
Buddha in India, 210
Buckingham, Jamie
  on Gideon, 237, 240
  on Jethro and Moses, 81

on Moses's learning the principles of leadership, 83
on obeying God, 19

C

Cain, 142, 143
Caleb, 227–31, 250, 251
Canaanites, 17, 33, 36, 74, 145
  definition, 33
Carlyle, Thomas, 108
celebration, 90, 197, 204
census, 114, 186, 222
Chaldeans, 15, 17
Chambers, Oswald
  on faith, 28
  on God's direct provisions, 93
  on God's perspective, 229
  on Job's faith, 124
  on Paul's humility, 288
  on the spirit of obedience, 161
  on the view of the Christian Life, 168
chastised
  definition, 18
Chedorlaomer, 20
Christianity, 16, 167, 262, 271, 272
circumcised, 24, 29, 84, 85, 291, 295
circumcision, 24, 234, 325
cistern, 255, 256, 257
  definition, 256
  illustration, 255
Cole, Edwin Louis, 75
Colson, Charles, 127
commitment, 6, 98, 107, 121, 143, 172, 199, 257, 261, 302, 314, 316–18

to God, 107, 121, 143, 316
compassion, 127, 128, 131, 170, 256, 265, 304, 305, 329
compensate
  definition, 50
complacency, 9
confession, 112, 213, 216, 222, 300
Confucius in China, 210
consequences
  of choices, 115
  of disobedience, 6, 50
  of lying, 47
  of sin, 9, 13, 111, 113, 276
Constable, Thomas L.
  on Joab's pending death, 188
  on Solomon's revenge, 198
consumed, 82, 168, 201, 237
  definition, 82
contentment, 15, 45, 195, 198, 207, 208, 326
contrite, 22, 111
  definition, 111
coup
  definition, 197
covenant
  Abraham's, with God, 17, 21, 24
  David and Jonathan's, 247
  definition, 21, 122
  Noah's, with God, 122, 123
  solemn transaction, 22
creation, 3, 4, 5, 32, 122, 123, 151, 271, 274, 277
Creator, 5, 6, 7, 9, 123, 263, 276

cross, 73, 90, 157, 255, 277
Cyrus, King, 209, 210, 211

D

Iraq, 4
Ironside, H. A., 258
Isaac
  "laughter," 26, 31
Ishmael, 23, 26, 27, 29, 50
island, 64, 294, 320
Israelite, 67, 79, 93, 97, 98, 102, 103, 104, 195, 206, 249, 251, 257
Israelite Territory
  illustration, 102
Issachar, 43, 51
itinerant
  definition, 315
Ittai, 184

J

Jared, 142
Jehoshaphat, 145–49, 151
Jehovah, 15, 16, 28, 31, 33, 124, 160, 167, 210, 238, 253
Jehovah God, 15, 16, 31, 124, 126, 160, 165, 167, 210, 213
Jehovah-shalom, 238
Jensen, Irving L., 256
Jericho, 37, 173, 176, 177, 178, 234, 332
Jeroboam, 162, 262
Jethro, 81, 84
Jewell, John, 160
Jewish, 18, 43, 44, 75, 146, 213, 222, 269, 287
Jewish High Council, 75
Jewish Law, 146, 260, 287
Jezebel, 162, 168, 169, 188
  threatened Elijah, 168
Jezreel, 169
Joab, 108, 111–16, 179–89

strength in battle, 179
Joash, 235
Jochebed, 79, 80, 98
John the Baptist, 51, 273, 309, 310, 333, 334
  beheading of, 310
  birth of, 309
  cousin to the Messiah, 309
  had doubts about Jesus's authority, 310
Johnson, Phillip E., 270
Jonah, 262–65
  preaching, 263
  whale, 263
Jonathan
  covenant with David, 21
Jordan, 92, 164, 171, 174, 175, 234, 309
Joshua, 22, 51, 163, 227–35, 250–51
Judas Iscariot, 303

K

Keller, W. Phillip
  on the condition of our souls and spirits, 167
  on Gideon, 244
  on Joshua, 231
  on the sounds of the spirit, 227
Kidner, Derek, 213

L

Laban, 49, 50, 51, 52, 57, 59
  Jacob will be tricked and cheated by, 49
lack of faith, 19, 24, 96, 169
Lamb, 90, 284
language, 17, 311
laughter, 26, 31, 121
  Isaac, 26, 31

mocking, 26
Law of Moses, 237, 307
Lawrence, John W., 112
Lazarus, 125, 284
  death of, 125, 284
Levi, 43, 51, 211
Lewis, C. S., 277
Larry Libby
  on Elisha, 172, 177
  on Jacob, 53
  on Jacob and the ladder analogy, 48
  on Moses, 80, 82
  on Samuel, 192, 206
lifestyle, 62, 81, 270
  immoral, 62
lions, den of, 261, 262, 265
  Daniel in, 260
  illustration, 260
literature, 259
living God, 274, 300, 316
living soul, a, 3
longsuffering, 176, 292
  Lord is peace, the (Jehovah-shalom), 238
Lord's tent, 204
loyalty, 20, 72, 113, 182, 188, 189, 249
Lucado, Max
  on faith, 84
  on Joseph, 73
  on prayer, 145, 215
  on the resurrected Lord, 305–6
  on the sufferings of Christ, 92
  on world religions, 293
Luke, 280, 292, 309, 311, 312, 316, 333
  chronicler of the early church, 311
  chronicler of Jesus's life, 311
  physician, 311

Luther, Martin, 162
lying, 18, 37, 46, 47, 223

M

MacArthur, John, Jr.,
  on Andrew, 317
  on Peter, 302
  on Philip, 324
Macedonia, 290, 294, 312
macho men, 238
"man of the field," 44
marauding
  definition, 20
Markquart, Edward F.,
  332
Martin, John A.
  on the book of Luke,
  310
  on Elijah, 162
McDowell, Josh
  on Jesus, 269, 274
McGee, J. Vernon, 34
meditate, 144, 163, 233,
  239
meditating, 34, 40
Melchizedek, 17, 20
men of faith, 37, 119
men who failed, 274
mentor, 62, 162, 170,
  171, 192
Mephibosheth, 109, 110,
  116, 250
mercy, 25, 26, 72, 147,
  188, 191, 197–98,
  213, 309, 329
Merrill, Eugene H.
  on David, 181, 184
Messiah, 90, 109, 253,
  254, 295, 300, 308,
  309, 310, 316, 318,
  321, 322, 331
messianic chapters, 281
Methuselah, 142
Meyer, F. B.
  on Samuel's prayers, 193

Michal, 104, 107
Midianites, 63, 64, 235,
  236, 239, 243, 250
mind of Christ, 158
minister, 133, 326
mission, 54, 254, 292,
  304, 327
Moab, 92
money, 63, 70, 207, 219,
  224, 315, 316
moral, 46, 86, 159, 170,
  225
Morley, Patrick M.
  on current culture, 208
  on following Christ, 290
  on satisfying our need
    to be significant, 66
  on suffering, 71
mortal, 275
Moses
  faithful servant of God,
  97
  friend of God, 97
motives, 98, 124, 149,
  200, 222, 235
Mount Avarat, 123
Mount Carmel, 165, 169
Mount Horeb, 82, 169
Mount Moriah, 27
Mount Sinai, 92
musician, 102

N

Nabal, 105, 106
Nadab, 133, 136, 137
Nahor, 27
naked, 7, 10, 125
nakedness, 8, 9, 290
naming the animals, 6
Naphtali, 43, 51
Nathan, 108, 110, 111,
  115, 203
Nazareth, 269, 271, 278,
  279, 303, 331
Nazirite, 153, 154, 155,

156, 188
Nazirite vow, 154
negative feelings, 217
negative mind-set, 93
negative words, 224
Negev Desert, 168
new church, 292, 306, 315
new creation, 4, 32
new name, 24, 30, 52, 59,
  238, 297
Nicodemus, 330, 331,
  334, 335
  member of the
    Sanhedrin, 330
  radical change of heart,
  330
Nineveh, 262, 263
Ninevites, 263
noble, 222, 224
noble-hearted, 329
non-Jew, 212
northern kingdom, 262
northern tribes, 162

O

obedience, 24, 29, 63,
  86, 121, 161, 225,
  265, 279
  to God, 120, 225
occupation, 316
Ockenga, Harold, 17
Ogilvie, Lloyd John
  on Barnabas, 314
  on the Holy Spirit, 306
  on Stephen, 323
Onesiphorus, 294,
  329, 334, 335
  unashamed follower,
  329
  visited Paul in jail, 329
one-third, 45
Ortlund, Raymond C.,
  Jr., 7

142, 143, 161, 322
spiritual strength, 75, 231, 235
spiritual tenor, 11
spiritual things, 35, 175
spiritual weakness, 209
Sproul, R. C., 316
Stanley, Charles, 331
Stedman, Ray
  on enjoyment, 207
  on Jesus, 271
Stephen, 75, 287, 309, 322, 323, 334
  first martyr, 322
  stoning, 96, 287
strength, 37, 67, 75, 88, 103, 161
stress, 109, 205
studying the Word, 37
Succoth, 242
supernatural peace, 56
Swindoll, Charles R.
  on Abraham, 16, 20
  on Absalom's death, 113
  on Caleb, 230
  on the Christian home, 132
  on freedom, 5–6
  on God's rescue
  on grace, 110
  on having authority, 38
  on idolotary, 55, 89
  on the importance of the Resurrection, 284
  on Jonah, 263
  on lust, 65
  on Samson's revenge
  on walking by faith, 29
sympathize, 73, 181

T

tabernacle, 94, 134, 137, 192, 222, 232
  definition, 137
temple

God's, 134
Solomon's, 203, 209
temptation, 5, 38, 65, 66, 73, 107, 114
test at the altar, 15
testimonies, 19, 143
thanksgiving, 114
theophany, 17
  definition, 17
things of this world, 9
Timnah, 154, 156
Timothy
  voluntarily submitted to circumcision, 325
  youthful and timid pastor, 325
Titus, 294, 327, 328, 329
tradition, 237, 275, 319, 324
  definition, 294
treason, 198, 294
Tree of the Knowledge of Good and Evil, 3, 5, 8, 13
  definition, 5
Tree of Life, 3
twelve stones, 166, 234
Twelve Tribes of Israel, 50, 58, 166
twins, 35, 44, 45
two "nations" were born, 44
two-thirds, 45

U

unbelievers, 33, 147, 157
uncircumcised, 154, 245
unconditional love and grace, 22, 39, 309
Unger, Merrill F., 69
Uriah, 110, 111, 117, 181–82, 185
usury, 219
  definition, 219

V

vilified
  definition, 290
vindicated, 150
vision, 53, 103, 253, 312
  of the future, 132
  of God, 93, 253

W

waiting, 15, 21, 25, 31, 123
  for Isaac, 15
  for Moses, 135
  for a son, 21
walls of Jerusalem, 215, 216, 217, 225
  illustration, 216
war against Jehoshaphat, 148
Warren, Rick
  on the benefits of knowing your purpose, 133
  on God's people, 328
wealth, 47, 64, 201, 205, 304, 315
Webb, Barry G., 254
whirlwind, 129, 161, 173, 176
whirlwind and fire, 175
Whyte, Alexander, 329
wickedness, 26, 262
Wiersbe, Warren W.
  on doubt, 318
  on Jesus, 304
  on spreading the gospel, 289
  on troubles in the church, 313
Wigglesworth, Smith
  on faith, 22
  on Jacob, 52
Wilcock, Michael
  on Gideon, 236, 239

Printed in the USA
CPSIA information can be obtained
at www.ICGtesting.com
JSHW061129030924
69164JS00005B/28